ART, MESSIANISM AND CRIME

ART, MESSIANISM AND CRIME

*A Study of Antinomianism in Modern
Literature and Lives*

Stoddard Martin

St. Martin's Press   New York

All rights reserved. For information, write:
St. Martin's Press, Inc., 175 Fifth Avenue, New York, NY 10010
Printed in Hong Kong
Published in the United Kingdom by The Macmillan Press Ltd.
First published in the United States of America in 1986

ISBN 0–312–05271–5

Library of Congress Cataloging in Publication Data
Martin, Stoddard, 1948–
Art, messianism, and crime.
Bibliography: p.
Includes index.
1. Psychology and literature.   2. Literature, Modern–
History and criticism.   3. Creative ability.   4. Failure
(Psychology)   5. Antinomian personality.   6. Criminal
psychology.   I. Title.
PN56.P93M4   1985   801'.92   85–14189
ISBN 0–312–05271–5

Contents

Acknowledgements

Thanks to Geoffrey Layton, who partly inspired this book and discussed many points during its gestation; also to Cathleen Burnham and Jim Jameson for inspiration, to Daphne Jameson, Christine Salmon, and my mother for encouragement, and to Julia Steward, Frances Arnold, Valery Rose and Graham Eyre for editorial care and attention. Special thanks to William Wilkins, in whose house most of the book was written and whose *pointilliste* painting of *Musiciens ambulans* led me on (see cover illustration), and to Anna Haycraft, a fine writer whose Catholic faith does not inhibit the widest moral speculation.

The author and publishers should also like to thank A. P. Watt Ltd, on behalf of Michael and Anne Yeats, and Macmillan Publishing Co. Inc., New York, for permission to quote extracts from W. B. Yeats's 'The Second Coming'.

1 Introductory: The Artist-*Manqué*

The idea for this book has been disturbing me ever since I began my first critical study, *Wagner to the Waste Land*, which ended with the suggestion that the trajectory of several European artists of the late Romantic and early Modernist period was towards a kind of breakdown.[1] The idea was provoked further when I discovered in my second book, *California Writers*, that in some respects the literary–artistic tradition of the state I had come from led to the mini-apocalypse of the Manson murders.[2] It seemed that in focusing on a type of literature I was being driven towards consideration of a type of personality: that the significance of what I was doing led beyond literary towards psychological – or more exactly moral – questions. What is the romantic artist? What is the value of his work? What is the relationship between that work and culture, or civilization, as a whole? To what extent can he go 'beyond good and evil'? To what extent, further, is the social philosophy which allows his existence demonstrating its own latent urge to self-destruction – or, if you will, 'deconstruction'?[3]

The appropriate initial question here would seem to be: 'What is an artist?' A more universalizing approach might be to ask, 'What is the artist-*manqué*?' Baudelaire is, perhaps, the obvious figure in whom the two come together. He existed, barely, as a critic. His *succès de scandale* of *Les Fleurs du mal* hardly brought him tranquillity in which to recollect – quite the reverse – and that body of poems reflects the enormous portion of 'spleen' produced in an artist who 'realized his genius' at an early age, yet was not able to expose it satisfactorily until years later, if ever. One does not mean to suggest that Baudelaire's infernal view of the world was solely or even primarily the result of artistic rejection. However,

1

such events as the trial for obscenity and exclusion from the Académie no doubt deepened and strengthened a *malaise* already brought on by financial and psychological hardships related to family, epoch, and environment;[4] and it is apparent that his vision grew more horrific as the comfort and hopes of youth receded (compare 'À celle qui est trop gaie', for instance, to 'La Vie antérieure').

Baudelaire to himself was, at least for a time, a successful artist – successful in the sense, as said above, of having 'realized his genius'. From this point of view, it might be argued that he was not truly an artist-*manqué*; and, of course, posterity has removed him from that category. Still, in his lifetime – and not only in the respect that he failed commercially and with the most exalted critics (Sainte-Beuve, for instance) – Baudelaire was unsuccessful. The necessity of reforming *Les Fleurs du mal* three times attests to difficulties not only between author and censor, but also between artist and muse. 'Between the conception and the creation falls the shadow.' Baudelaire is an example of the truth that even the most successful artist will contain the artist-*manqué*. He contains him and will continue to contain him in what Keith Walker has called 'the transcendental sense'[5] – that is, for so long as it is impossible to find the perfect expression of some idea he is burning to formulate.

Shakespeare was an artist-*manqué* in this respect throughout the period when he was unsuccessfully trying to formulate the perfect romantic comedy; only, perhaps, at the moment he completed *The Tempest* was he released from the state.[6] Wagner too falls into the category. From 1848, when he conceived *Siegfried's Death*, until 1876, when he produced the *Ring*, he was, against the standard of the perfect artwork he had explicitly laid out, unsuccessful; and, even when the *Ring* was finally produced, with all the imperfections and ludicrousness of that original staging, he must have felt – in fact did feel – that there was an element of failure in it. The point here is that the artist-*manqué* is not only within the successful artist; he is, inevitably, throughout most of the successful artist's career, the artist himself. From this it would follow that the most intimately felt problem of the artist should be that of the artist-*manqué*; and the job of the critic might be defined as determining when and how and to what extent the accomplished artist falls back into his natural state of artist-*manqué*-ism.

Wilde's Lord Henry Wotton takes it a step further: 'bad' art, he avers, is where personality reveals itself most fascinatingly.[7]

Shakespeare revelled in the blackness of the *Henry VI–Richard III* sequence at the beginning of his career, preceding success, and returned to a similar mood, albeit in more refined forms, in the tragedies and 'problem plays' which preceded his perfected 'farewell' work. Wagner conceived his first great black persona, the Dutchman, during an early phase of disappointment; his next, Ortrud, during a period of discontent with his status as *Kappelmeister* at Dresden; and his great black tableaux of the *Ring* during long years of exile and rejection. Arthur Symons wrote his most decadent plays – *Cesare Borgia, Nero, Agrippina*, and so on – after his attempts at producing poetic drama had failed and he had suffered a breakdown; Wilde's glorification of 'the criminal nature', *Salomé*, came at the end of a period of disquiet at not being able to 'realize his genius' in a form acceptable to the public. There is danger in making a sweeping statement here; nevertheless, one can argue that in these cases as well as many others the phenomenon of artistic frustration is likely to exacerbate tendencies to shock (*épater le bourgeois*), challenge conventional morality, explore areas of decay, parade the ego, cast one's personae as messiahs, and sensationalize crime.

If this is the case with successful artists in times of eclipse, then what of those obvious artists-*manqué* who have neither the talent nor the discipline to ride out long periods of apprenticeship, experimentation, and sheer waiting for mind to mate with muse? Aren't their more actual failures likely to lead to more ominous aberrations? This is a governing problem of this book; nor is its significance limited to the aesthetic/academic. In the first place, two figures towards whom the study proceeds – Hitler and Manson – turned their backs on their 'art' to become 'men of action'. In the second, the artist-*manqué* is only one incarnation of Romantic man, who – like Goethe's Faust – is ever striving, over-reaching, not-quite-achieving. We might equally be talking about big businessmen always trying to put together spectacular deals (John DeLorean) or millions of petty hustlers in modern cities who reel from one dubious 'scam' to another until drawn down into pathetic crimes. There are as many variants of the type as there are visions of success or gradations of failure.

Romantic man belongs to the era of capitalism, which institutionalizes mobility, rather than to feudalism or socialism, which attempt kinds of fixity. Napoleon, who rose with the burgeoning of capitalist France, embodies him and fits into this pattern to a degree. He jettisoned scholarship and novel-writing as soon as action swept him up, yet continued to identify himself with heroes of romance as he pursued his self-interested rise. Napoleon, however, passed through the zone of crime to construct, in apparent good faith, systems of justice for posterity. Nor, with the petulance of the would-be messiah, did he respond to his fall by trying to destroy himself, his creations, or even those who had brought him down. The type we are concerned with is, by either natural or environmental factors, prevented from achieving such balance. Neither the truly great-man-*manqué* in the transcendental sense nor the Walter Mitty incapable of turning dream into deed, he is distinguished – in both his imperfect art and his reactive action – by a lack of a redeeming sense of social *goodness*.

In selecting subjects, I have been guided by this consideration as well as several others. Since the problem presented itself as one of the Romantic period, I did not turn to the remoter past to assess classical instances (Nero and others). Moreover, wanting to confine myself to Western tradition, I resisted intrusion of the mid-Eastern or Oriental, except inasmuch as ideas were imported. Geographical variety in the West was a consideration, as were differentiation in social background, artistic predilection, and type of 'crime'. Thus among lives focused on we have a French aristocratic man of letters from a decadent period of the eighteenth century, a German bourgeois would-be painter–architect from the 'twilight' of the nineteenth century, and an American lumpen-proletarian singer–songwriter from a volatile period of the twentieth century. The first was a sex criminal, the second a political tyrant, the third a mass murderer. Each fancied himself an artist yet was not satisfactorily accepted as such; each developed in prison philosophies to justify crime; and each committed crimes, though none to the degree threatened – and at least in the case of Sade there is significant distance between crimes fantasized and those actually achieved.

Two overall themes deserve mention here. The first we have already touched on: crime as a response, or partial response, to rejection as an artist. The second is related: how much art itself may operate as a motivation to crime in the frustrated artist-*manqué*. Here I am thinking of the service to which Hitler put Wagner and Manson the Beatles of the 'white' album, a problem which is essentially religious. Holy art (Wagner and rock music) is taken by devotees who have been thrown out of the temple, as it were, and perverted into self-serving dogma. In relation to the 'grail orders' of acceptable culture – the art establishment of turn-of-the-century Vienna or entertainment business of sixties' Hollywood – these demoralized devotees operate as Klingsors: self-mutilated 'evil' magicians bent on destroying said orders and supplanting them with their own dogmatized cults. The connection of Sade with the pattern becomes clear when we consider that his most notorious scenario, *Les 120 Journées de Sodom*, takes place in an isolated and classically 'evil' château run by absolute rulers on an absolute system, reinforced by terror and designed specifically to produce sexual violation and murder.

Originally I had thought to discuss Baudelaire, not Sade. But to read even Baudelaire's most sadistic utterances against the spectacle of maim and murder in Sade's opus, or the facts of maim and murder in Hitler's and Manson's careers, is to be in the cool, attractive territory – the ultimately 'safe' territory – of the true artist concerned with spiritual good as well as evil. To a large extent, Baudelaire only studied 'sin' in order to suffer from and rail against it (the theme of artistic 'curiosity' which we shall return to in considering Wilde). He might be useful for showing how the vision of a legitimate artist can influence the artist-*manqué* towards aberration (Hitler's mentor Houston Stewart Chamberlain was an aesthete in Baudelairean Paris as a young man). But the main object here is to assess the attraction of what is conventionally regarded as 'evil' in life, not theory. Thus the case of Baudelaire is confined to some remarks *en passant*, as is that of

Nietzsche, whose philosophy might otherwise be considered the best overall introduction to the subject.

While setting sights on aberrant lives, I have also included substantial discussion of these concepts 'art', 'messianism' and 'crime' in the light of relevant psychology, politics and metaphysics – that is, the chapters on Marcuse, anarchism and the occult. The chapter on Wilde constitutes a pivot between the 'literature' and 'life' halves of the study and so, from a critical point of view, provides a unifying statement for the whole. As Keith Walker has observed,[8] Wilde more than any other Romantic – Nietzsche and Baudelaire included – previewed the great issues which would affect the twentieth century (and may have suggested the best response to them). Moreover, it is from Wilde – with thanks too to Colin Haycraft[9] – that I have taken the 'label' which furnishes the subtitle of the book and binds it together: antinomianism. About this should be said a few words.

I had thought, in a fanciful take-off on Nietzsche, to describe the book as 'A Genealogy of Immorality in Modern Literature and Lives'. This might have had a certain commercial ring and access of easy understanding. But 'immoral' is a cheaply used generalization which fails to convey the sense of a left-hand' tradition at work behind the subject. Nor is the study comprehensive enough to be called a 'genealogy'. 'Antinomy' comes from the Greek meaning 'against' and 'law' and is defined as 'the mutual incompatibility, real or apparent, of two laws'.[10] 'Antinomian' is a term Luther coined to describe Protestants who saw such an antithesis between Gospel and Pentateuch, 'Love' and 'Law', that they believed themselves 'released from conformity to Old Testament polity as a whole'. This implies an age-old elitist aspiration to rise above and beyond Earthly sanctions and suggested to Luther those heretics who had 'mistaken or perverted St Paul's doctrine of justification by faith in the interests of immoral licence' – specifically the medieval Manichaeans, who, 'holding their spiritual being to be unaffected by the action of matter, regarded carnal sins as being, at worst, forms of bodily disease'. After Luther, the term continued to have currency, especially in England, where it was applied to various fanatical sects appearing during the Civil War (also the time, according to George Woodcock, of the birth of anarchism[11]) which 'denied that an elect person sinned, even when committing acts in themselves gross and evil'.

Glancing at the table of contents, the reader will note that three later chapters of the book are devoted to what I refer to as 'Sixties' *Zeitgeist*. These are meant as a lead-in to Manson's would-be reign of terror and discuss factors contributing towards it: pop Buddhism, the cult of the American *Wandervögel*, Kerouac, Hermann Hesse, drugs, Timothy Leary, Artaudian 'cruelty', rock music, and the 'successful' version of what Manson-as-artist aspired to be: Jim Morrison. At the same time, they suggest the 1960s as our ultimate destination: an era in which antinomian undercurrents rose to the surface in such powerful waves that they seemed for a moment about to sweep away the old *mores* of Western civilization for ever.

2 Marcuse's 'Erotic Reality'

Herbert Marcuse became a figure of notoriety in the 1960s. Some time after migrating from Hitler's Europe he had written a book, *Eros and Civilization*,[1] which radicals on both sides of the Atlantic liked to invoke as an explanation for the forces they wanted to set loose against a 'repressive establishment'. Marcuse himself became a symbol of the dangerous, alien, 'pinko' professor when he lectured at the University of California; and Governor Ronald Reagan was in sympathy with those reactionaries who wanted to run him out of the state. In fact, Marcuse's book and philosophy look rather academic in a world daily more threatened by nuclear holocaust. What seemed revolutionary about them at the time was the attack not merely on Freud – which is laced with admiration in any case – but on his successors: Jung, Reich and Fromm, among others. These great psychologists were unable, as Marcuse saw it, to understand the new balance which had to be forged between 'performance' and 'pleasure' principles.

Freud formed his system on belief in the need for primacy of the former. Civilization for him was dependent on 'inhibition' of two primary forces, sexuality and the destructive urge (see *Eros and Civilization*, p. 95) – that is, on repression of Eros and Thanatos. Because of the 'fatal enemy' of *time*, Freud did not believe that the pleasure principle could ever attain its goal: to 'be happy'. This in Freud's terms meant 'a subsequent fulfilment of a prehistoric wish' – specifically (in men) resolution of the Oedipus complex (p. 165). It did not constitute, as some revisionists would propose, a mere infantile craving for security with mother, but the first instance of an eternal yearning for combination with the (female) principle of gratification (p. 211). The life-force itself is born in this erotic instinct, but it must be checked – broken in cases even –

8

if the individual is to achieve maturity, meaning satisfactory performance in work and interpersonal relations. Frustration of Eros in turn gives birth to the death-instinct, which in the disturbed personality can lead to 'colossal brutality' (mass murder), giving way to the Nirvana principle (quiescent suicide), or various pathologies in between.

Freud's view of man's fate is tragic, as Marcuse presents it; and Marcuse praises the father of psychoanalysis for not denying the material basis of this fate in an effort to 'spiritualize want'. Jung embodies the latter impulse. Marcuse mocks him for trying to 'expurgate the instinctual dynamic' and 'purify the psyche' (p. 191). Jung attempts to obscure reality with 'pseudo-mythology', 'idealistic ethics and religion', and 'a philosophy of the soul'. This approach can lead, in Marcuse's view, to totalitarianism. The opposite approach – the idea of Wilhelm Reich that sexual liberation *per se* can be 'a panacea for individual and social ills' – can lead, equally disastrously, to a 'sweeping primitivism'. Erich Fromm's 'art of loving' is in some respects more attractive; but Marcuse takes issue with an 'ideology of internalization', in which an 'adjusted' person is 'blamed' for having 'betrayed the "higher self", the "human values" ', and is depicted as 'haunted by "inner emptiness and insecurity" in spite of his triumph in the "battle for success" ' (p. 206). Fromm's implication that a man need hardly concern himself with material well-being if he has achieved 'inner strength and integrity' raises Marcuse's suspicions. As he remarks:

> The style suggests the Power of Positive Thinking to which the revisionist critique succumbs. It is not the values that are spurious, but the context in which they are defined and proclaimed: 'inner strength' has the connotation of that unconditional freedom which can be practised even in chains and which Fromm himself [elsewhere] denounce[s].

It is not enough to be 'free' and in poverty or prison anymore than to be 'unfree' because of Freudian or Jungian repression, or Reichian excess. Freedom, if to be obtained at all, demands a more all-embracing, transcendental effort; and Marcuse sets out to show the various ways in which such an effort might be mounted.

Western philosophy, he argues, has not shown the way. True freedom for Hegel, for instance, involved 'risk of life', because 'the very content of human freedom is defined by mutual "negative relation" to the other' (p. 99). Possible freedom only exists in 'the idea'. 'Liberation' thus requires 'a spiritual event'. Such an event, Marcuse points out, is dependent on 'remembrance'; but this is inadequate; for, in reality, remembrance no more than 'absolute knowledge' can 'redeem that which was and is'. Only Nietzsche among Western philosophers has drawn near to overcoming this 'ontological' impasse; but even his idea of the 'will-to-power' falls short:

> Man comes to himself only when the transcendence has been conquered – when eternity has become present in the here and now. Nietzsche's conception terminates in the vision of the closed circle – not progress, but the 'eternal return'   (p. 104)

Beyond the limits of Western philosophy's 'system of reason', based on the ameliorative idea of 'becoming', lies an ever-revolving inner realm of 'being', towards which Nietzsche's 'eternal return' beckons. This Marcuse identifies as the homeland of Eros, where all activity is directed towards the pleasure principle. But man – at least Western man 'from Plato to the "*Schund und Schmutz*" laws of the modern world' (p. 132) – has driven this realm underground, as well as 'the insights contained in the metaphysical notion' surrounding it. 'They have survived', Marcuse concludes, 'in eschatological distortion, in many heretic movements, in the hedonistic philosophy.' Portentously he adds, 'Their history has still to be written.'

Fantasy is the first way by which man might proceed towards an 'erotic reality', where 'the life instincts would come to rest in fulfilment without repression' (p. 123). The type best suited to lead to this destination is not the 'predominant culture-hero of the West', Prometheus, with his eternal rebellion against the gods (itself a version of the performance principle), but his opposite, Orpheus or Narcissus,[2] a more passive version of Nietzsche's Dionysus, eternal antagonist of the Apollonian deity who 'sanctions the logic of domination, the realm of reason'. This Orphic-Narcissistic type has, in performance-principle terms, an ' "impossible" attitude and existence' (p. 135). He is a 'drop-out', at best poetic, offering 'something for the soul and heart'. He does not 'teach any message', however – 'except perhaps the negative one that one cannot defeat death'.

Marcuse quotes Baudelaire here, specifically the refrain from 'L'Invitation du voyage' –

> La, tout n'est qu'ordre et beauté,
> Luxe, calme et volupté*

– also, a passage from 'Mon coeur mis à nu': 'La vraie civilization . . . n'est pas dans le gaz, ni dans la vapeur, ni dans les tables tournantes. Elle est dans la diminution des traces du pêché originel.'† He goes on to suggest that Orphic–Narcissistic images are 'those of the Great Refusal', a term borrowed from the Surrealists. He defines that refusal as resistance to 'separation from the libidinous object'. In Freudian terms this object must be, ultimately, the 'mother' of 'prehistoric' Oedipal dreaming. From non-divorce from this original 'wife', the Orphic–Narcissistic type gains an 'oceanic feeling', which comprises not only his Narcissistic 'withdrawal from reality' but also a fundamental 'oneness with the universe'. 'Beyond all immature autoeroticism, [the Orphic–Narcissistic type] has a fundamental relatedness to reality which may generate a comprehensive existential order.' As if consciously devising an apology for flower-child disciples of Jack Kerouac, Marcuse comments, 'If [the Orphic–Narcissistic type's] attitude is akin to death and brings death, then rest and sleep and death are not painfully separated and distinguished: the Nirvana principle rules throughout. . . . And when he dies he continues to live as the flower that bears his name' (p. 137).

If fantasy is a first, unordered step towards 'erotic reality', art, born of fantasy is a second, ordered one. 'Since the awakening of the consciousness of freedom, there is no genuine work of

---

* *Translation*: 'There is nothing but order and beauty, luxurious, calm and voluptuous.'

† *Translation*: 'True civilization is not found in petrol, nor in steam, nor in turn-tables. It is in the reduction of original sin.'

art that does not reveal the archetypal content: the negation of unfreedom' (p. 121). Marcuse's definition is romantic and radical ('Art allies itself with the revolution'), based in large part on his affinity for the *avant-garde* European artists of his youth, whose objective, as he sees it, was to achieve a condition of life 'without anxiety'. But their kind of art, like fantasy, can only earn convention's opposition in the end. Its visions of brave new orders will be relegated to 'safe' no man's lands of 'utopia', its agitations for aesthetic new 'lifestyles' condemned before courts of 'theoretical and practical reason'. Clownish, dandaical eccentricity may be tolerated in acknowledged geniuses or 'decadent Bohemians'; others, however, take such ways up at their peril. Pervasive, anarchic *commedia del'arte* cannot, in short, be granted by the performance principle so long as the latter intends to continue its dominance (p. 125).

This dominance, of course, is exactly what Marcuse would like to end. He believes the aesthetic self-realization should be life's 'governing principle'; and, like Wilde of 'The Critic as Artist', he turns to ideas of the German *Aufklärung*, specifically of Kant, from whose 'Critique of Judgment' he extrapolates:

A third 'faculty' must mediate between theoretical and practical reason – a faculty that brings about a 'transition' from the realm of nature to the realm of freedom and links together the lower and higher faculties, those of desire and those of knowledge. . . . This third faculty is that of judgment. Judgment is aesthetic, and its field of application is art. (p. 144)

The primary dialectic to be synthesized by this 'third force' is between 'sensuousness', which the performance principle has suppressed, and rational morality. Because the performance principle has balanced morality against sensuousness, 'aesthetic reconciliation' involves strengthening the latter – perhaps, ultimately, 'liberating' it from the 'repressive domination of reason' altogether (p. 148). As a principle of balance, aesthetics must be compensatory and partisan (Marcuse adds a philological note to reinforce this alliance between 'aesthetics' and 'the senses'). Aesthetic reality transcends morality. It can be described as 'purposiveness without purpose' or 'lawfulness without law'.

Marcuse finds further support for his argument in Schiller,[3] who defines this third mediating-force as the *play impulse*, whose objective is 'beauty' and goal is 'freedom' (p. 152). We are in the realm here of the fairies of *A Midsummer Night's Dream*, ornamental tricksters who stand outside of and between the rational but sensuously baffled society of Theseus's court and the instinctual but dumb herd of Bottom and his mates. The play of such spirits aims at 'abolition of the repressive controls that civilization has imposed on sensuousness', ergo Oberon's drugging of Titania and Puck's deceptions of the two pairs of lovers. The *play impulse* alarmed Freud, and Jung predicted that it could 'bring about a "release of repression" which would entail "a catastrophe of culture" '. Schiller, however, is 'willing to accept the risk' of such a catastrophe and a 'debasement' of the extant culture's values 'if this would lead to a higher culture'. Marcuse agrees with him. Ideal art, he summarizes, would (1) transform work into play; (2) raise sensuousness *vis-à-vis* reason; and (3) attempt to conquer *time*, which – as already stated in relation to Freud – is 'destructive of lasting gratification'.

So far so good. The individual proceeds towards a new 'erotic' reality through fantasy, which liberates his Orphic–Narcissistic sensuousness, and art, which elevates it in a new balance with reason. Individuals readied, society must now be prepared for harmonization of their various 'erotic realities' into a non-repressive new order. With the classic faith of the soft socialist, Marcuse believes that the material basis of *abundance* for this exists and can be sustained (p. 156). With an equally romantic faith, he suggests that erotic instincts, once liberated from 'surplus repression', can develop a 'libidinal rationality'. Here, however, the first strong qualification enters; for Marcuse is as adamant that the removal of surplus repression must be *total* as Marx was that the socialist revolution must be worldwide:

> Free development of transformed libido *beyond* the institutions of the performance principle differs essentially from the release of constrained sexuality *within* [them]. . . . The latter process *suppresse*[s] sexuality; the libido continues to bear the mark of suppression and manifests

itself in the hideous forms . . . sadistic and masochistic orgies of desperate masses, of 'society elites', of starved bands of mercenaries, of prison and concentration camp guards. Such release of sexuality provides a periodic necessary outlet for unbearable frustration; it strengthens rather than weakens the roots of instinctual constraining; consequently, it has been used time and again as a prop for suppressive regimes. (p. 164)

Here is one example of the difficulty Marcuse foresees when trying to advance liberation from individual to group. A more hopeful picture proceeds from the 'ideal of libidinal work relations' set out by the most eccentric of social utopians, Fourier. His vision, as Marcuse describes it, is based on the idea of an *attraction industrielle*, which in its turn derives from an *attraction passionnée* inherent in man. The latter *attraction* can be channelled to produce three positive results: (1) 'the creation of "luxury, or the pleasure of the five senses"'; (2) 'the formation of libidinal groups (of friendship and love)'; (3) 'the establishment of a harmonious order, organizing these groups for work in accordance with the development of individual "passions" (internal and external "play" of faculties)'. Fourier in this way 'comes closer than any other utopian socialist to elucidating the dependence of freedom on non-repressive sublimation'. On the other hand, his 'detailed blueprint' for putting vision into practice grants organization to a 'giant' bureaucracy and thus opens the door for new repression. 'The working communities of the *phalanstère*,' Marcuse is forced to conclude, 'anticipate "strength through joy" rather than freedom, the beautification of mass-culture rather than its abolition' (p. 174).

In general, when we arrive at group-man, Marcuse's thought begins to betray a traditional romantic scepticism. The academic is suspicious of utopias and senses against his will (against his argument even) that society's history of reversion to the performance principle is not to be broken. Latent is the conclusion that only scattered individual rebellions can succeed. Nevertheless, Marcuse attacks American post-Freudians for disparaging individuals who pursue self-realization by joining radical groups – in particular Harry Stack Sullivan, who had this to say of members of the 'new left':

The person who believes that he *voluntarily* cut loose from his earlier moorings and *by choice* accepted new dogmata, in which he has diligently indoctrinated himself, is quite certain to be a person who has suffered great insecurity. He is often a person whose self-organization is derogatory and hateful. The new movement has given him group support for the expression of ancient personal hostilities that are now directed against the group from which he has come. The new ideology is especially palliative of conflict in its promise of a better world that is to rise from the debris to which the present order must first be reduced. In this utopia, he and his fellows will be good and kind – for them will be no more injustice, and so forth. If his is one of the more radical groups, the activity of more remote memory in the synthesis of decisions and choice may be suppressed almost completely, and the activity of prospective revery channelled rigidly in the dogmatic pattern. In this case, except for his dealings with his fellow radicals, the man may act as if he had acquired [a] psychopathic type of personality. . . . He shows no durable grasp of his own reality or that of others, and his actions are controlled by the most immediate opportunism, without consideration of the probable future.[4]

To this, Marcuse responds with the fierceness of someone under personal attack and sounds notes anticipating R. D. Laing's idea that society is as likely to be 'psychologically imbalanced' as the 'disturbed' individual. It may be others' 'self-organization' which is 'hateful', he points out; not his own. Apparent destructiveness in the 'new dogmata' may be constructive inasmuch as it may aim at 'a higher stage of realization'. Radical departures may, in short, be preferable to the 'prevailing' standards of health, maturity and achievement, which, in contemporary middle-class culture, as Sullivan elsewhere points out, are 'often no particular reflection of anything more than one's socio-economic status'. In sum, Marcuse is outraged that Sullivan and his kind could identify the pursuit of 'a better world' with 'revery'. 'Mankind's sacred dream of justice for all' cannot be reduced to 'the personal resentment of maladjusted types' (p. 202).

Marcuse is not eager to admit frustration. Conceived before the
'sexual revolution' of the 1960s and 1970s and without consideration of the failure of attempts at 'erotic reality' in the past,
this book remains a polemic in hopes that mankind might
be able to forge a new order. Throughout, however, threads
the sense that all such idealistic dreaming is doomed, by the
very phenomenon that made Freud disbelieve in sustainable
happiness – the intransigence of *time*:

> From the myth of Orpheus to the novel of Proust, happiness
> and freedom have been linked with the idea of the recapture
> of time. . . . Eros penetrating into consciousness, uses
> memory in his effort to defeat time in a world dominated by
> time . . . Remembrance alone provides the joy without the
> anxiety over its passing and thus gives it an otherwise
> impossible duration. . . . Still, this defeat of time is artistic and
> spurious; remembrance is no real weapon unless it is translated
> into historical action.   (p. 186)

Art provides hope; but, in the end, 'aesthetic reality' is
revealed as no more than an image of happiness. It can satisfy
Eros's inability to forget, but it cannot release him from his
fatal penchant for *not* forgetting. Nor can it defend him from
Reason's charge that that penchant is debilitating. By its
continual 'striving for eternity', Eros violates civilization's
fundamental charge that 'libidinal pleasure' exist only within
limitation. As Marcuse puts it: 'The striving for the preservation
of time in time, for the arrest of time for conquest of death, seems
unreasonable by any standard.'

In his Orphic–Narcissistic incarnation, Eros remains passive,
contemplative, ever-dreaming of the 'prehistoric' yearning, the
birth-love of mother and the womb. As this proves impossible
to regain, he becomes by his nature 'half in love with easeful
death', the Nirvana principle, which aspires to a condition
of 'constant gratification', where neither anxiety nor desire any
longer intrude. But this principle is unacceptable, either to a
society based on performance, or to the Promethean aspect of
the individual himself. Related subliminally to what Charles
Odier named the 'superid'[5] (a part of the superego
'representative of the primitive phase, during which morality
has not yet freed itself from the pleasure principle'),

it is regarded by the superego – both from outside and within the individual – as a 'neurotic factor', an expression of castration-wish rather than fear of castration-threat, and therefore a vestige of prenatal maternal–Narcissistic unity opposed to the life-force altogether. This manifestation the superego must destroy. In doing so, it reverses the Oedipal antagonism, and 'the hostile father is exonerated and reappears as the savior who, in punishing the incest wish, protects the ego from its annihilation in the mother' (p. 184).

The final road to 'freedom', thus – the last rebellion – is death. This is the most ambiguous, two-forked way of the three, the path through the psyche where man's ambivalence to his own liberation is most evident. On the one hand, death as the 'suicide' of Nirvana releases him from the pain of loss of the primal happiness; on the other, death as the superego killing that very Nirvana principle (and representatives of it who have not already 'killed' themselves) enables him to retain the life-force, which we have previously defined as Eros, but only in limited form. There is a checkmate here, proving, in conflict with Marcuse's wish, that 'erotic reality' is as destined to failure as any other system and setting the stage for Death to be invoked, either beautifully by the artist or fatalistically by the man-of-action, as a means to glorious transcendence.

3   Sade's Cult of Evil

Post-war fascination with Sade seems to have begun with
Albert Camus's essay 'La négation absolue' in *L'Homme révolté*.
It was furthered by Sartre's observations in *Saint Genet* and,
more significantly, by Simone de Beauvoir's 'Faut-il brûler
Sade'? These works benefited from the discovery early in the
century of the original manuscript of *Les 120 Journées de Sodom*,
the 'masterpiece' which Sade thought had been destroyed with
the Bastille on 14 July 1789 and spent the rest of his life
trying to revive in other literary forms. This notorious book,
which the author describes as 'the most impure tale ever told',
was published in America in the 1960s and has gone through
several editions since, including paperback. Though easily
obtainable, it is still officially banned in Britain, a fact which
has irritated biographers from the rhapsodically partisan
Norman Gear to the reluctant, ambivalent Ronald Hayman.
If, however, there were ever reason for book or author to be
banned, *Les 120 Journées* and Sade merit it. True, Sade may
have been 'more sinned against than sinning'; but the argument
is not conclusive. In large part, we must take him in the light
of a remark he puts in the mouth of one of the libertines of
Justine: 'He is like unto those perverse writers ... [whose]
single aim is ... to immortalize the sum of their crimes ...
and instigate the commission of crimes ... after their own
lives are at an end.'[1]

Modern interest in Sade, of course, goes back further than
the Existentialists. Sainte-Beuve regarded him, along with
Byron, as one of the prime movers of nineteenth-century
letters; so does Mario Praz, in *The Romantic Agony*. Swinburne
made an extensive study of him, marks of which are apparent
in his work, especially the 'novel' *Lesbia Brandon*. Baudelaire
says in *Journaux intimes*, 'To explain evil, we must always go
back to Sade – that is, to the natural man.'[2] Hayman uses this
quote as a kind of justification at the beginning of his

18

introduction; and in his final chapter – 'A Negative Strain' – he discusses the importance of Sade to the *poètes maudites*, especially Lautréamont and Rimbaud, also to the 'theatre of cruelty' of Artaud. From Hayman and others we hear too of the 'relationship' of Sade to a number of celebrated novelties of the *fin-de-siècle* – Dostoevsky, Huysmans, D'Annunzio, and Wilde, who would say of himself in *De Profundis*, 'In the lowest mire of Malebolge I sit between Gilles de Retz and the Marquis de Sade.'[3]

The most significant 'relationship', however, may be between this 'madman' of the end of the eighteenth century and another at the end of the nineteenth, Nietzsche. Both were moved to create a new language and philosophy – even, arguably, religion – out of a 'transvaluation of values'. Nietzsche, however, did not cut his philosophy with violent – often homicidal – pornographic; nor did he go to jail; nor did he ever commit even the most petty crime. Sade did. By any reasonable standard, many of his acts, from the whipping of Rose Keller to the forced ingestion of 'poisoned pastilles' by the four prostitutes of Marseilles, were criminal. Beauvoir and others have taken Sade at his word that he may have imagined the worst crimes but never committed them.[4] One commentator, however, voices doubts about this;[5] and the letter to his wife on which Sade's apologists base their argument must be viewed in light of the fact that everything he wrote was screened by the authorities – with the result that, in later years, he not only denied authorship of his most accomplished and successful work, *Justine*, but also falsified entries into his journal in order to present himself as less venal than he was.[6]

Commentators who gloss over Sade's transgressions are missing what was not lost on Baudelaire: that the value of Sade lies in his exploration of and attempted apologies for evil. Roland Barthes in his *Sade, Loyola, Fourier* compiles a list of 'semiological' details more impressive for their triviality than what they reveal about the essential Sade; and Barthes's conclusion that 'tact' may be a more significant Sadean legacy than violence tells more about author than subject.[7] Barthes is fetishistically fascinated by the fact that Sade was carrying a white muff when he accosted Rose Keller in the street on Easter Sunday 1768. Posterity, however, is more effected by the fact that he locked the poor woman into a darkened chamber, slashed her (reputedly) with a knife, and made her defecate on a cross. Amusing insights proceed from Barthes's comparison of Sade's 'system' and language to those of men from lives of religious devotion and political idealism. But one leaves his trendy 'structuralist' analysis hungry for the more basic facts of Sade's psychological identity, his intentions with others, his relation to his age and philosophical legacy. These are what concern us in this study. Sade may not fit precisely into an overarching pattern of the Orphic artist-*manqué* become criminal, but to a large degree he typifies the destination to which the pattern can lead.

What do we know about the man? He was born a hereditary aristocrat and brought up initially in the house of a royal prince. Always quite small, he may have suffered a kind of sibling violence in early childhood. His mother appears never to have taken an interest in him, nor his father either until he had become old enough to marry off profitably. At age four, he was sent to live with an uncle who was an *abbé* and libertine. If from his parents' indifference he took a blighted ability to love, from his uncle's example he learned of the hypocrisy of the church and the compulsion of physical urges. Childish petulance and bad temper did not surface until much later, however. As a student with the Jesuits and then in the army, he seems to have conformed to what was expected of him and behaved with politeness and charm. The Sadean 'energy' first evidenced itself in late teenage as an appetite for prostitutes. Still, as an oft-quoted letter to his father demonstrates,[8] Sade retained until well into his twenties a desire for approval as *good*.

The arranged marriage to a daughter of the *nouveaux riches* followed an affair with a young woman of his own class in which both parties contracted venereal disease; Sade was then thrown over for a rival. Anguish over this may have combined with memory of failure with his mother to trigger a sudden recklessness. Sade rebelled against the restriction of sexual relations with a wife who was neither his choice nor fulfilling to him. He took a series of actresses as mistresses and engaged prostitutes for sodomy, whipping and more bizarre practices. Watched by the police, he was also increasingly hounded by his mother-in-law, whom some have speculated was in love with him herself.[9] Whether this is fact or fancy, it is beyond doubt that Madame de Montreuil became obsessed with her son-in-law's activities; and, when he seduced and ran off with her second, favourite daughter, committing thereby a form of incest, she gave way to outrage and signed the notorious *lettre de cachet* by which he was incarcerated for most of the next fifteen years.

Much has been made out of the fact that Sade was held by this clearly unjust method and not for his 'crimes' (all charges against him were eventually dropped, though only through bribery and other similarly corrupt *ancien régime* practices); much too has been made out of the fact that, by the standards of the eighteenth century, Sade's morality was not entirely eccentric. Certainly Madame de Montreuil's vindictiveness did become extreme, but not until after Sade had repeatedly and wilfully abused her family and reputation, which were of overweening importance to her class in her day; nor was Sade's Don Giovanni-ism ever purely in pursuit of liberty, happiness, or other extolled virtues of the licentious Enlightenment. Even at this stage Sade's sexual antics were punitive, compensatory, vindictive themselves. Displaying an outsized capacity for imagination and energy, he also evinced an insatiable taste for degradation and inflicting pain. In spirit if not in fact, Sade's intent was criminal. Nor did many of her contemporaries view as unjust Madame de Montreuil's treatment of him.

Sade is an anti-Orpheus. He did not develop a 'criminal' urge because obsessed with some medallion of beauty he was forcibly torn away from. Loving emotion is absent from his work, as from most of what we know of his behaviour. To some extent, disparagement of sentiment was characteristic of the *Zeitgeist* – we can see it in Voltaire – but Sade's disparagement is not linked to witty detachment, or even hard-headed cynicism. Categorically, angrily, he wishes to drive from his world all vestiges of virtue – *good* – so that forcible self-gratification may have complete sway. The object may seem the same as Don Giovanni's. But, throughout Mozart's music and even the Don's utterances, there is admiration for innocence and beauty independent of its relation to the libertine's 'appetite'. Another work of the period,

Casanova's *Memoirs*, is, in contrast to Sade's opus, a testament (perhaps almost as surprising) to a man's ability to go through his career enjoying sex innumerable times with innumerable partners without ever – or almost ever – provoking a negative response.

Both in and out of prison Sade protested that incarceration could not possibly reform a man; and his works carry the repeated message that the only way to transcend feelings of guilt over one crime is to commit another and another, increasingly more vicious, until the taste for good has disappeared for ever.[10] This philosophy was a manifestation of Sade's defiance, a self-defence, a way of voicing titanic indignation at the injustice and hypocrisy of 'the system'. It was, too, deeply childish: a case of prolonged – indeed, nearly lifelong – tantrum-throwing; a cult of outrageous exhibitionism designed to draw attention to himself, taunt further punishment, and force the world thus to participate in *his* life. Sade ended in an asylum, the Napoleonic régime having decided it was most convenient to regard him as insane. At Charenton, Sade remained wild and provocative; but as a seventy-year-old he could hardly have done much actual harm. The ludicrousness of this final incarceration, especially following years of service to the First Republic, is a factor in modern sympathy for his 'cause'.

It is touching to consider the old man producing, directing, and acting in plays – his own and others' – for the lunatics; nor can one fail to be impressed by the humanity of his work as assessor of *assignats* and hospital commissioner during the Terror. Unfairly arrested at the end of that period, he only escaped the guillotine by accident; and, when the chance arose to denounce Madame de Montreuil, he took steps to ensure her and her family's safety. These points are raised by those who wish to humanize the man. The irony is that humanization is the precise opposite of what Sade seeks to do in his books. Out of the isolation of prison the natural *hauteur* of the hereditary aristocrat developed into an all-embracing misanthropy. Sade's fantasy became omnipotence and his desired point of view indifference. Writing alone could allow him to achieve these. With all the pent-up aggression in him, he could wreak his revenge on a hostile world: venalize the strong, tie up and dominate and destroy the weak, objectify everyone absolutely – himself in the process as well.

No evil magician who sought to charm innocents into occult doctrines or pied piper trying to lure them through illusions of love, Sade in his novels as in his early career simply wants to suborn, by money or deception, and lock his victims away in châteaux as gloomy and isolated as the medieval prisons he was inhabiting. Innocents become slaves, as prisoners do for the jailers; when their masters are done with them, they may be disposed of at will. To say that Sade was exposing in exaggerated form the viciousness of the *ancien régime* in such tableaux is of course true; but in fact, to the end, Sade was a member of that *ancien régime* himself (he clung for years to his country estates and demanded his 'rights' to rents); and his outrage is not so much at the fact that the system has allowed such excesses to go on as that it has prevented him from any longer participating in them. Sadistic glee continues to ooze from the pages of *Juliette*, written in advanced middle age. *Les 120 Journées* is a fantasy reminiscence on Sade's longest bout of libertinage when still a free man and feudal lord.

The book, as Barthes shows,[11] sets up a system as ordered as the *phalanstère* of Fourier or schools of St Ignatius – or, some would add, Nazi torture camps of contemporary legend. Sade's libertines collect forty-odd subjects to do their pleasure. Life in 'the Sadean city' is centred on *séances*: theatrical assemblies where obscene stories are told and then acted out, rather in the manner of Jesuit 'exercises'. Orgies develop, but there is no levity. Each evening turns into a perverted 'love feast', the Manichaean dogma pared in half as it were, so that only its evil – satanic – part remains. Grotesque acts are justified by endless philosophizing (the libertines are the only ones with unrestricted rights to free speech) in a monotonous language mixing higher metaphysics with pornographic vulgarism. Repetition reinforces a transvaluing dogma. Nature, we are told, is supreme. God does not exist – at least does not exist as *good* if at all. How could he, given that evil can so abound? Thus indoctrinated, we are prepared for descent from licence to crime.

In the weird, dark, ritualistic atmosphere, costumes are worn, sorcery is suggested, blasphemy is *de rigueur*, guilt and remorse excluded. Christian morality is denigrated, a cult of cruelty elevated in its place. Ropes and whips and knives are brandished, drugs employed to induce vomiting and shitting. Sodomy is exalted, vaginal sex spurned. Conception is regarded as an outrage; and any suggestion of disobedience is met with brutality. Fingers are broken off. Nipples are burned. Meanwhile, as their victims suffer, the libertines are bound by mutual admiration for each others' excesses. Like an adolescent bully gang, their 'brotherhood' is based less on friendship than on daring; and, as the ante is upped and upped, and crime leads to crime, and the erotic excitement of maim increases – as the Dionysian violence finally explodes – dead bodies and dismembered limbs are splattered about the once absolutely ordered theatrical space, until only a dozen of the original subjects remain – the strongest and most wicked – who, thus initiated, will now presumably go on to practice similar rites at other places in future.

Beauty, like emotion, is a major casualty. Hayman quotes a passage which goes on about the 'elegance', 'prettiness', and 'rosy pinkness' of a young woman's body, only to end, 'But, by God! These attractions did not last long. Four or five assaults from the Duke soon withered all their gracefulness.'[12] Delicacy is punished. Masturbatory images are conjured up only to be chased off by expressions of brute force, perhaps concomitant on the masturbatory act having been completed. Sade's descriptions of beauty are never so distinct as his descriptions of ugliness – the raddled old slut Fanchon, for instance – or oddity – the libertines' genitals, always rendered in minute detail and never normally sized. All this leads one back to what may be the most important qualification about Sade's writing: that almost all of it was conceived in dark, thick-walled cells where rats and mice roamed and sanitation hardly existed. *Cri de coeur* from the blackest pit, it is not surprising that it should comprise such hideous, apocalyptic excrescences. Nor is it easy to dispute the contention[13] that, had he not been confined for so long and under such conditions, Sade would not have become a writer at all.

De Beauvoir speculates that Sade was a coward.[14] She bases this on his description of the Duc de Blangis, whom he says –

given the right circumstances – could have been scared off by
a child. Beauvoir's speculation may be comforting – *humanizing* –
but there is little to corroborate it. Sade's career in the army
was marked by steady promotion, unlikely had he been a
coward. His escapes, from Miolans in 1773 and *en route* to
Vincennes in 1778, were bold, even fabulous. His refusal on
several occasions to be frightened out of Lacoste was brave to
the point of being foolhardy. It is true that Sade whimpered
and whined when the cards were stacked against him. But the
more consistent picture of him in his years of incarceration is
of a man defiantly standing up for his rights – indeed,
screaming for them, to the extent that every governor in
charge of him was driven to request his transfer. On 2 July
1789, he harangued the mob outside the Bastille through the
tin pipe which conveyed urine to the street. Hardly the act of a
coward, this earned Sade immediate removal to an asylum. It
may have even helped incite the event which opened the
Revolution.

The truth of Sade's character is probably that he became
like a caged animal. Snarling and snapping defiantly out of
habit, he would keep ever watchful for the weakness of his
masters and bound for freedom whenever chance allowed.
That he equivocated and truckled during the Terror is the
behaviour less of a hypocrite than of a survivor. Sade was
quite modern in this respect, rather like a character out of
Brecht. He played cat-and-mouse with the authorities, just as
his victims (Justine) learn to do with their captors; and, if
neither he nor his victims escaped as often as they liked, this
attests at most to a latent taste for the game, not surely to
cowardice. In later years, of course, Sade grew tired. Then,
too, as any prisoner must, he became reconciled in some way
to his condition, even accustomed to it. But the fact that he
learned to turn it to professional 'good' as a writer and later
actor–director–producer suggests merely compromise with the
inevitable, not constitutional cowardice.

This argument is important because, if Sade has a redeeming
quality, it is that same element in the aristocratic ethos which
lends a motif of redemption to Don Giovanni in the end:
courage. Sade would not – except under the most extreme

duress, and then only temporarily – 'repent'. He regarded himself as a law unto himself and the laws of man and 'God' imposed upon him as hideous, hypocritical presumptions. Like so many of the *philosophes* of his period, he substituted Nature for religion as a standard. But, unlike Rousseau and the general pastoral sentiment of most, he refused to accept Nature as benign. In allowing the existence of evil, Nature proclaimed herself to be indifferent at best, probably evil in essence. Any act could be justified on this basis, as 'in harmony' with Nature. At the same time, Nature was not in harmony with man but rather 'jealous' of him as a free-willed being she could never quite control. All-powerful yet impotent, eternally captive to her infinity, Nature in her restless motion and constant tension betrayed her secret wish: to destroy herself.[15]

A state of perfect apathy – of pure freedom from anything, even the requirement to exist – is ultimately wished for in the natural world as in the individual. To be saved from wanting – from emotion, which is based on that hideous impulse, desire – is the ultimate. Simply to be, feel, act without fear or even thought of consequence – that is the destination: what one might describe as a sort of active – even militant – Buddhism. From it – this nihilism – springs an absolute unconcern about death, one's own as well as anyone else's. Nor is there the slightest concern either about the destruction of civilization, or of the natural world. Nuclear holocaust, had Sade lived in our era, would perhaps have been pleasing – at least unalarming – to him. Like Shaw with his Darwinian theory of the 'life force',[16] Sade believed that in some form matter would go on. If the decay of a man's flesh provides compost from which acorns turn into oaks, so too his ashes might provide material for some other sort of new creation in the ineffable universality of space and time.

In this turn of mind Sade, like Nietzsche, betrays sphinx-like courage – lack of fear at least – and this is surely the strain which merited him a kind of hero status among certain Existentialists. Whatever else might be said about him, Sade is the perfect 'metaphysical rebel', accepting nothing, challenging everything. He stomps on the cross, mocks family, accuses the king and *ancien régime* with as much passion as any bloody-handed *sans-culotte*. Further, he is willing to desecrate his own dignity (the disgusting coprophagia of *Les 120 Journées* is the

pathological emblem of this). Nothing is sacred. Sade is in service
to no one – not even, in the end, to his own yearning for vengeful
mastery (his mercy to the Montreuils is the evidence here). He is,
however, as committed to the life-force as any healthy animal (a
suicide impulse seems to have been unknown to him): in his
willingness to undergo all kinds of nervous stimulation and
physical pain; in his continual wanderings out into uncharted
regions of the instincts; in his commitment to the total experience,
with all energies applied and constant experimentation.

That Sade was ever pressing out beyond the rim of the
possible so far as human morality is concerned distinguishes
him as a philosopher. His status as an artist, however, is
another matter. In his prose, we confront the rawness and
unreason of a man in a state of what he would call 'lubricity'.
Here is the tedium of what Hemingway would disparage as
'erectile writing'.[17] Nor is the dominant 'erectile' message –
that sexual excitement depends on a constantly increasing
ante of violence – convincing in the end. Love is too absent.
Sade's 'art' is a – perhaps *the* – great literary example of what
may be expressed by a bestial man when treated in a bestial
way: a cry from the 'other side', as it were – cry of a type that
a legitimate, contemplative artist might feel compelled to hear
and try to understand. But, for all the withering scorn he
applies to a world gone wrong, Sade as an artist must be
found *manqué*. Fatally unable to express alternatives of positive
value, he might be described as lacking a soul. If not missing
at birth, this was lost through either neglect or too much
confinement in warrants of passion and despair.

4 Wilde's Antinomian Aesthetic

In his manic pursuit of the bestial, Sade never denies the existence of wickedness, evil, sin. Hayman observes that Sade's whole *oeuvre* might be seen as 'a massive attempt to get rid of his evil';[1] and his libertines are continually describing a utopia (anti-utopia?) in which evil will no longer exist because it will be ubiquitous.[2] In this attachment to moral evil, Sade was 'unliberated', certainly as Marcuse means the term, also as Nietzsche might have had he used it. Nietzsche, a puritan whose life was free of pleasure, let alone vice, did not credit 'sin', laughed at the idea of 'wickedness', and was genuinely trying to move 'beyond good and evil' not just wallowing in the latter in perverted protest against the tyranny of a former gone hypocritical and corrupt. Sade belonged, unlike Nietzsche, to a Catholic tradition. His legacy can be seen in such figures as Baudelaire and Wilde, whose experiments in 'sin' are related to oppressive moral imperatives, both from society and within, and never untainted by guilt. Wilde in particular demonstrates this syndrome. Having a compulsion to live his life like a play, he was obliged in the end to react against his 'evil' – the killing of conscience attempted by Dorian Gray – with a dramatic revelation of what he had always known to be *good*: a falling of scales from the eyes, a losing of Lear-like hubris. This kind of development Sade appears to have wished for – 'May you be convinced [he writes in the finale of *Justine*] that true happiness is to be found nowhere but in Virtue's womb, and that if, in keeping with designs it is not for us to fathom, God permits that it be persecuted on Earth, it is so that Virtue may be compensated by Heaven's most dazzling rewards.' (p. 743) – but the energy and import of the vast bulk of Sade's opus is so heavily against faith in such an idea that it can only seem homilistic, fatuous, even parodistic: an

28

exaggerated instance of tacking, for form's sake, a 'moral' ending onto an immoral tale, like the finale of *Don Giovanni*.

By any reasonable standard of our age or most of history, Wilde was not criminal. However, like Sade, he nurtured a fascination for 'crime': it is there in almost everything he wrote, from the romanticization of terrorism in *Vera, or the Nihilists* to the sentimentalization of the condemned man in *The Ballad of Reading Gaol*.[3] Wilde's fascination, unlike Sade's combined sympathy with curiosity. However, its very abstract, 'wet' nature seems subliminally to have provoked him. Wilde's self-estimation as an 'individual' (in his *Weltanschauung* nearly synonymous with 'artist') required him always to dare something *more*; and, as he became increasingly influenced by the French of the 1880s (at the same time he was beginning in earnest his homosexual vagaries from wife and family), he pressed in his stories and statements of 'intention' towards more overt flirtation with criminal themes. 'Lord Arthur Savile's Crime' (1887) is a schematic, amusing fantasy on murder. 'The Portrait of Mr W. H.' (1889) deals in questions of artistic fakery and artistically induced self-destruction. 'Pen, Pencil and Poison' (1889) describes the career of a plagiarist and murderer. The great works of the *annus mirabilis* of 1890– 1 – *The Picture of Dorian Gray*, *Salomé* and *The Soul of Man under Socialism* – bring the idea of the noble element in criminality into full flower. And a fatal flower it proves to be. Through the moral turn of Wilde's nature and tradition, it could only be allowed to bloom for a moment. This has to do with the fact that, unlike Sade, Wilde is the essential Marcusan type: the 'genius or decadent Bohemian' who lives his life as a series of aesthetic sensations; a 'beautiful', yet ultimately 'sad'[4] embodiment of Orpheus–Narcissus.

And Christ; for this is the 'hero', that, in Wilde's dramatic presentation of personality, the doomed artist–individual merges into in the end. *Cri de coeur* of a man in prison, *De Profundis* draws its authority from the fact that its creator is at one now with the murderer, anarchist, lowest of the low – at least in society's terms. And society is now revealed as not only the Tartuffe of the plays but something blind, deeply cruel, tyrannical in its enforcement of a hypocritical *good*. Wilde in Reading Gaol is even more a victim of institutional injustice than Sade in his various prisons. But Wilde's response

is not to Prometheanly hurl curses of greater evil at evil; it
is to attempt to embrace the world – from his jailers to the
frozen branches of the tree out of his window[6] (*De Profundis*,
p. 115) – with cosmic sympathy. In a sense, Wilde is
attempting the same trick as Sade: to dominate his dominators,
through writing. But how different the effect is of one who
tries to do this through superior *good* rather than superior evil!
Few nowadays would suggest that posterity might be led
astray by reading Wilde's threnody to Lord Alfred Douglas.
Yet, in his linking of the criminal with the artist and both
with the divinely *good* outsider, Christ, Wilde may be
accomplishing something more subversive to civilization than
poor ranting Sade ever could. More seductive to the bourgeois
ear, Wilde's siren song is not less antinomian. Beckoning
towards Nirvana rather than universal destruction, it none the
less demonstrates a similar fall of Eros towards Thanatos and
yearning to wrap oneself in the cloak of moral self-righteousness,
in order to justify ever more self-oriented pursuit of 'expression'
in a world which can no longer be dealt with.

Justine is the work of Sade's most available in Wilde's time,
most notorious and regarded as having literary merit; and it is
the one work of Sade's which Wilde specifically mentions
(p. 63). Any similarity between its 'philosophy' and that of
Dorian Gray was probably not conscious. However, the
'insidious' book Lord Henry sends Dorian at the middle of his
progress, originally titled '*Le Secret de Raoul* par Catulle
Sarrazin',[5] suggests that strain of French letters harking back
to Sade and is identified with the force which lures the blond-
haired, blue-eyed, young innocent towards his doom. At the
end of his career, Dorian claims to Lord Henry, 'You poisoned
me with a book.' The older man responds innocently, 'You
and I are what we are, and will be what we will be. As for
being poisoned by a book, there is no such thing as that. Art
has no influence upon action. It annihilates the desire to act.
It is superbly sterile. The books that the world calls immoral are books that show the world its own shame. That
is all' (*Dorian Gray*, p. 218; hereafter abbreviated as '*DG*'). But
it is clear that Wilde is as alive to the possibility that a certain
kind of book/work-of-art may lead to corruption and crime –

indeed, that he may be writing such a book himself – as Sade was when he wrote those lines quoted at the beginning of the preceding chapter about a type of writer who takes his greatest pleasure in knowing that, whatever may happen to him, his words will live on to perpetrate evil throughout posterity. The ability to exert influence is the issue here. As Hayman says,[6] Sade's character and that of his libertines reflect the two joys of an earlier perverse work of the 'Age of Reason', Laclos's *Les Liaisons dangereuses*: (1) outmanoeuvring a skilful opponent, and (2) corrupting innocence. *Dorian Gray* deals in both themes, particularly the second. Lord Henry Wotton, whose personality most closely resembles Wilde's of the time, takes a conscious delight in manipulating his young Faust: 'There was something terribly enthralling in the exercise of influence . . . . To convey one's temperament into another as though it were a subtle fluid . . . . Dorian Gray . . . . He would seek to dominate him . . . . There was something fascinating in this son of Love and Death' (pp. 35–6).

The paradoxical philosophy Wilde's Mephisto employs is an elegant, house-broken version of the arguments Sade's libertines interminably spout at Justine. 'The aim of life is self-development,' Lord Henry says; 'to realize one's nature perfectly' (p. 17). Clement informs Justine, 'Egotism is Nature's fundamental commandment (*Justine*, p. 604; hereafter abbreviated as '*J*'). Lord Henry goes on about the 'New Hedonism' and remarks, 'The only way to get rid of temptation is to yield to it.' The libertine Roland proclaims, 'Enjoyment is the only law. Submit' (*J*, p. 681). Watching Dorian bury his face in some lilacs, Lord Henry murmurs, 'Nothing can cure the soul but the senses' (*DG*, p. 30). Justifying murder over morals, Dubois tells Justine, 'None but physical sensations are authentic' (*J*, p. 491). Meanwhile, Lord Henry also says, 'The great events of the world take place in the brain' (*DG*, p. 18); and Clement tells Justine, 'Imagination imparts to all objects their value' (*J*, p. 600). Neither statement is intended to curtail action. On the contrary, both are meant to encourage acting more antinomianly in order to stimulate the imagination further. 'Sin', Lord Henry tells Dorian, 'is the only real colour-element left in modern life' (*DG*, p. 29); Dubois instructs Justine, 'Crime's hand alone opens up unto us the door to life' (*J*, p. 482). Lord Henry mocks charity, bourgois liberalism, and common sense while extolling a 'philosophy of pleasure' (*DG*, p. 43); Sade's Clement says that 'the doctrine of brotherly love is a fiction', the poor would be victimizers had they only the power, happiness comes from contrast not equality, and men should 'seek their happiness howsoever they will' (*J*, p. 607). Aristocratic position and wealth are what enable Dorian to pursue his career of pure selfishness in the end, just as they are for Sade's libertines – compare 'His great wealth was a certain element of security' (*DG*, p. 112) and 'He has lots of money, and he's bad as bad' (p. 192) to Justine's 'The poorer I became, the more I was despised' (*J*, p. 468) and Coeur-de-Fer's brutal 'You must serve either our pleasures or our interests; your poverty imposes the yoke upon you' (p. 487). But it is the great god Nature who is invoked when there is need for justification: 'Pleasure is the only thing worth having a theory about', Lord Henry says; 'But I am afraid I cannot claim my theory as my own. It belongs to Nature, not to me. Pleasure is Nature's test, her sign of approval' (*DG*, p. 77). When Justine complains to Clement that a similar rationalization may lead to 'cruel tastes' the latter replies, 'What does it matter? Were Nature offended by [cruel] proclivities, she would not have inspired them in us' (*J*, p. 607).

Under this Sadean tutelage, Dorian develops in his soul (the picture) a 'touch of cruelty' (*DG*, p. 90). The 'poisonous theories' inspire 'a passion for impossible things'; 'suddenly there had fallen upon his brain that tiny scarlet speck that makes men mad'; and from the middle of the book, quite unlike *Justine* but rather in the spirit of its sequel *Juliette*, the victim becomes victimizer, the innocent the libertine. He becomes so in a more real sense than his tutor ever was; because, where Lord Henry was content to prattle shockingly, Dorian truly *feels* perverse impulses and is moved to act upon them. 'There were passions in him that would find their terrible outlet, dreams that would make the shadow of their evil real' (*DG*, p. 57). Fate takes control. Dorian lapses into that acceptance of inner impulse which is a *Leitmotiv* throughout Wilde's crime-meditating works. As Clement remarks to Justine, 'Ridiculous to ask a man to change his Nature – anyway, how could he do so?' (*J*, p. 599). He could attempt to do what Justine suggests: become virtuous, *good*. But Sade's libertines mock this with gushes of oratory; and Lord Henry dismisses the same idea at the end of Wilde's book just as he did at the beginning: 'Don't spoil [your life] by renunciations', he tells Dorian; 'At present you are quite a perfect type ... quite flawless' (*DG*, p. 216). Lord Henry, in fact, believes that conscious reformation is a fantasy: 'Life is not governed by will or intention. Life is a question of nerves, and fibres, and slowly built-up cells in which thought hides itself and passion has its dreams' (p. 217). This statement, surprising but perhaps essentially both Catholic and pagan in its scepticism about free will, echoes Sade's belief, derived from Holbach and La Metrie,[7] that men are compelled by 'electrical fluids' and physiological 'irritations': and it is precisely the rationalization Wilde himself has already used to explain the somnambulism of Dorian's depravity:

> There are moments, psychologists tell us, when the passion for sin, or for what the world calls sin, so dominates a nature, that every fibre of the body, as every cell of the brain, seems to be instinct with fearful impulses. Men and women at such times lose the freedom of their will. They move to their terrible ends as automatons move. Choice is taken from them, and conscience is either killed, or, if it lives at all, lives but to give rebellion its fascination, and disobedience its charm. For all sins, as theologians weary not of reminding us, are sins of disobedience. When that high spirit, that morning-star of evil, fell from heaven, it was as a rebel that he fell.
>
> Callous, concentrated on evil, with stained mind and soul hungry for rebellion, Dorian Gray hastened on. ... (p. 190)

If 'Beauty' was Wilde's ideal, in *Dorian Gray* more than any place except perhaps *Salomé* he pulls aside the veil to show the dark side of that moon-silvered phenomenon. 'There were moments when he looked on evil', Wilde writes of his young hero, 'simply as a mode through which he could realize his conception of the beautiful' (p. 147). This statement forms a coda to the chapter which chronicles Dorian's elegant, eccentric taste in philosophies (including 'mysticism, with its marvellous power of making common things seem strange to us, and the subtle antinomianism that always seems to accompany it' –

p. 133), perfumes, music, jewels, embroideries, costumes, and
figures in history, his spiritual precursors ('he had known
them all, these strange terrible figures that had passed across
the stage of the world and made sin so marvellous and evil so
full of subtlety' – p. 144): the Roman emperors Tiberius,
Caligula, Domitian, Nero; the Borgias and others of the
Renaissance adept at poisoning and Machiavellian plots; all
'the awful and beautiful forms of those whom Vice and Blood
and Weariness had made monstrous or mad'. These fascinate
him from on high, the Marlovian types. At the same time, he
is rumoured to have 'brawled' in 'distant parts of Whitechapel'
with 'foreign sailors' and 'thieves' and 'coiners' (p. 141); for,
with his easily jaded, entirely aesthetic measure of an
experience's worth, he finds the low intoxicating as well. The
extremes – all the extremes only, as for Sade, with his cult
of the disgusting body (Fanchon) side by side with the
unblemished virgin rose – attract. By its very novelty, the
repulsive gains the power the beautiful once had:

> Ugliness that had once been hateful to him because it made
> things real, became dear to him now for that very reason.
> Ugliness was the one reality. The coarse brawl, the
> loathesome den, the crude violence of disordered life, the
> very ugliness of thief and outcast was more vivid, in their
> intense actuality of impression, than all the gracious shapes
> of Art, the dreamy shadows of Song.   (p. 186)

Dorian, who started his progress being compared several times
to Narcissus,[8] is now moving beyond even Orpheus in the
underworld. Art, even, is behind him: as Marcuse told us, it
constitutes 'no real weapon' against the great demon *time*
unless 'translated into historical action'. In Dorian's story,
Orpheus–Narcissus's impulse to 'translate into historical action'
culminates in the knifing of the soul–picture, which symbolizes
more than mere suicide: an active, indeed savage, murder of
self. In Wilde's life the impulse is more Nirvana-seeking, as
the paeans to Sorrow and Mysticism in De Profundis suggest.[9]
In the real world, of which the novel is a representation and
to which Wilde's life stood – in his phrase – in 'symbolic
relation' (*De Profundis*, p. 77), the impulse, arguably, is
embodied in the successive Dionysian actions and reactions of

European culture in the first half of the twentieth century. Dorian's creed of will and contempt is in part crypto-Nazi. A refined British counterpart of Nietzsche's 'blond beast', he is even fitted out with disgust for the Jews – specifically for a 'hideous' creature who smokes a 'vile cigar', wears 'greasy ringlets', and runs a music-hall-cum-theatre (p. 48). Why does Dorian 'loathe' this 'monster'? Besides aesthetic distaste, he sees the Jew as representing the power of Money over Love, the latter being embodied by the actress Sybil Vane. Spiritual (and rich) as he is, Dorian ('Prince Charming') feels compelled 'to get [Sybil] out of the Jew's hands'. This he does, but only by luring the girl to suicide from a broken heart. Afterwards, Dorian does not even try to comfort Sybil's mother, let alone give her hard cash to free her from the usurer's grip. Here as elsewhere in his career of carelessness, Dorian displays the Sadean–Nietzschean–Nazi sense that 'guilt is ... naught but the idiotic murmuring of a soul too debilitated to dare annihilate it' and that 'remorse ... merely denotes an easily subjugated spirit' (*J*, p. 695).

Wilde is never entirely on Dorian's side in these passages of ruthless individualism. He takes pains to show the cancerous effect of cruelty on the man's inner life – the introduction of 'the worm' which Sade suggests (perhaps ironically) is inevitable:

> Prosperity may attend conduct of the very worst ... but let this cruel and fatal truth cause no alarm .... Independent of the punishment most certainly reserved by Providence for those whom success in crime has seduced, do they not nourish in their souls a worm which unceasingly gnaws, prevents them from finding joy in these fictive gleams of meretricious well-being, and instead of delights, leaves naught in their soul but the rending memory of the crimes which have led them to where they are?   (p. 466)

But, as Isobel Murray points out in his Introduction to the Oxford edition of *Dorian Gray* – and this holds for Dorian's inner life as well as for the mix of characters – 'The influences for evil are only notionally counteracted by influences for good, because the positively good characters in the book, the artists Basil Hallward and Sybil Vane, are weak and passive compared to the attractive corruption of the others' (p. xiii). Murray points out too, in relation to this question of Dorian's anti-Semitism, that the novel is based philosophically on Arnold's 'division of life into Hebraism and Hellenism' and that Wilde, via Lord Henry, is distinctly more partisan to the latter, which Arnold described as 'spontaneity of consciousness . . . giving force to every feeling, expression to every thought, reality to every dream', than to the former, described as 'strictness of conscience . . . self-denial, guilt feelings, ideas of sin . . . all the maladies of medievalism'. *Dorian Gray* shows Wilde's longing for a revival of pagan joy. His affinity for Christ, however, separates him from that Nietzschean type whom Sade prefigured: 'What is Christ but a leprous Jew who, born of a slut and a soldier in the world's meanest stews, dared fob himself off for a spokesman of him who, they say, created the Universe? . . . . Such lofty pretentions! . . . . Fanaticism for laborers, artisans, streetwalkers . . .' (*J*, p. 514). Wilde's Christ is 'Hellenic', derived from Renan, noble, an exponent of Love over Law. His Hellenism, however, is that of Oedipus, Orpheus, Marsyas and other victims of legend; not of Zeus, Apollo or other overly licensed gods who, on mere whim, are able to wreak destruction on hapless lesser beings.[10] In this, he links to the type of the Wandering Jew; and generalizations about Wilde's attitude towards 'Hebraism' must balance this against Dorian's distaste for a more entrenched, exploitative type.

Because of his very *goodness*, Wilde's Christ is doomed. Perhaps the memory of him can be transformational in the short term, but his triumph in the world as it exists is forfeit to another: the ruthless, hedonistic, Sadean spoiled child. This is shown with conscious artistry in *Salomé*, where Christly Iokaanan is destroyed by the terrible young princess. It is shown too, perhaps not quite consciously, in *De Profundis*, where the Christly Wilde is offered as a counterforce to the sadistic Bosie. But the latter remains free and will live to disagreeable old age where the former is rotting from cruel punishment and will shortly die. Wilde's messiah, in spite of what *De Profundis* proposes, is a model less for living than for dying. He could only have been created with such self-identification by a Wilde who had been substantially crushed. As we have seen in *Dorian Gray*, the Wilde of 'great health'[11] at the height of his powers was seeking a 'saviour' so unselflessly expressive that he could commit any sin without repentance. 'Perditi?' 'No!' Don Giovanni proclaims. Salomé is the persona Wilde created who fulfils this absolutely. An anima figure of aristocratic authority – a 'natural man' in the sense of Baudelaire's quote about Sade – she embodies Wilde's supreme value of 'Beauty' and reveals what in moral terms that value signifies: a type of evil. 'I am a born antinomian', Wilde writes in *De Profundis*: 'Morality does not help me . . . . I am one of those who are made for exceptions' (p. 80). Only as a kind of afterthought from the conscience does Wilde make ideal Beauty love *good*. Salomé is attracted to Iokaanan less for his spiritual purity than for his imperviousness to the fascination she is able to exercise over other men. (Wilde identifies with Christ in part because He shares this Iokaanan-like imperviousness.) Beauty, slighted, will take its Sadean revenge. The type it cannot control – Christ, Iokaanan, Basil Hallward, Wilde – becomes the martyr-masochist.

It is important to remember that the first half of *De Profundis* is an attack on the character of 'Bosie'. Only after having vented this is Wilde able to attain the high ground of his abstractions about Christ. Taken as a work of art, the letter 'creates' Bosie as a creature of terrible, unconscious power. But, whereas in *Dorian Gray* Wilde glorified such a type, in *De Profundis* he – like Hallward victimized by his ideal – scourges it for its 'selfishness', 'shallowness', 'lack of imagination'. Bosie, as Wilde paints him, is above all a damaged soul in whom 'hate was always stronger than love' (p. 47); whose progress is 'sinister in its concentration of aim and intensity of narrowed will power' towards a 'great catastrophe', namely the destruction of a 'drunken, déclassé, and half-witted' yet terribly powerful and bestial father (p. 48). In Bosie, Wilde has chosen to love a supreme – and, as he describes it, supremely worthless – embodiment of the superid; and it remains a mystery to him how he could have thrown away the greatness he ascribes to himself for someone so steeped in *hate*, which is 'intellectually considered, the supreme negation' and 'considered from the point of view of the emotions . . . a form of atrophy, [which] kills everything but itself' (p. 53). What

are the answers? That 'along with genius goes often a curious
perversity of passion' (p. 61)? Yes. That to love the vicious
makes the virtuous feel his virtue the more? Sade might have
said so. That the Orphic–Christly nature cannot exist except
in relation to an outside force which destroys it? Marcuse
might have wished not, but his book does not prove otherwise.
That Wilde still semi-consciously yearned for the Nietzschean
'master morality' which Bosie embodied and only reverted to
the 'Hebraic' authority of Christ when it was conclusive that
it was not in his capacity to achieve the other? This, I suspect,
is closer to the point than Wilde, with his unslakable thirst for
self-propagandizing, could have borne to admit; and the
discovery is portentous for our thesis.

Wilde wanted to dominate. In *De Profundis*, he talks about
his status as 'King' in the world of 'Art' (p. 72) and the
superiority of Art to other human pursuits; and he claims that
his incarceration was because of his temerity in suing the
Marquess of Queensberry, which constituted an act of symbolic
and actual *lèse-majesté* against the 'system' (p. 62). In the
comedies, he had shown a similar temerity by making the
wit and individualism of the dandy triumph over the
smallmindedness of Society.[12] In *Salomé*, he raises Iokaanan
out of the pit in order to castigate the decadence and privilege
of Herod, Hérodias, and their court, which fawns on Roman
power and consumes its intellectual energies in disputes over
religious prophecy and superstition. Iokaanan more than
any other of Wilde's personae focuses his contempt for the
material world and hypocritical order in which he lived and
thrived; and *De Profundis*, with its cult of Christ, reaffirms this
contempt and Iokaanan's longing for a new order to come
replace it. The messiah Wilde presents may be weak – not for
this world – but the urge he represents is for strength, stoicism,
resistance to all temptation. Orpheus–Narcissus longs for
release from his career of drifting sensuality, a career which –
if unchecked – can only lead back through melancholy towards
mystical marriage with the primary 'mother': womb–tomb,
Nirvana, death. Yet the irony remains that the only personae
in Wilde's scheme who break out of Orphic drift into mastery
are those who opt for ruthless self-indulgence. Wilde's longing
for *goodness* is not fulfilled in this world. The ascent of the
sonorous chords of Iokaanan over the cacophony of the Jews

and Nazarenes of Herod's court in Richard Strauss's operatic adaptation has more to do with the raising of a phallic Superman than with *imitatio Christi*; and the mystical marriage of Salomé's passion with its puritanical nemesis in death sounds notes more memorable and ominous for the historical future than any previous lyrical reflections on 'the pale Galilean'.

A few further thoughts, 'out of season':

One of the attractions of apocalypse, whether cultural or personal, is that it may bring life 'back to basics' – ergo, the comfort Wilde derives in *De Profundis* from romanticizing himself as an 'outcast' wandering from 'grey town' to 'green field', sleeping in the long grasses in summer or the shelter of some barn in winter (p. 79). To have done with civilization and commune only with 'the mystical in life' – this is both a Celtic and a universal dream of return to primal innocence. Crime can provoke it, by destroying a man's career in the conscious world; revolution is the analogous catalyst for the mass. Art – especially dramatic art – will hold up the image of it more than it exists in bourgeois life, because art by its nature tends to emphasize the Manichaean, the dialectical: opposition and contrast.

Prison itself is a form of development, distinction, progress along the path to non-materialist mysticism. Crime too has a blessing here: it forces a man down upon himself, to the roots of his individual character. Can he survive prison at all? Art loves this question and deals with it almost as much as it deals with the fascination of crime: from the legend of Socrates, to *The Count of Monte Cristo*, to the concerts of Johnny Cash for the inmates of Folsom Prison. The experience is an emblem of man's romantic striving towards freedom, and transcendence. *Fidelio*, the musical illustration of Goethe's ultimate romantic precept ('Das Ewig-Weibliche/Zieht uns hinan'*[13]) is echoed in the devoted attendance of Constance Wilde on her husband in jail – she came from Genoa to deliver personally the news that his mother had died[14] – or of Renée-Pélagie de Sade, who even went to the Leonoran extreme of dressing up like a man

* *Translation*: 'The Eternal Feminine/Lures to perfection'

in order to get in to her husband when he was confined at Miolans.[15]

These are archetypal romantic situations; they have an attraction in themselves. Nor does the romantic artist from Villon to Pound dare going to prison without being conscious that the 'experience' may lead authority to his mystical–messianic artist–priest authority. Prison from the gifted may extract the *voyant*. Prison too may distort vision: blind the prisoner as surely as Oedipus's self-retributive putting out of his eyes. We see Sade raging at Renée-Pélagie, imagining her lover – even the size of his penis (finding arcane numerological 'signs' in her letters of its exact dimensions[16]) – when all the evidence suggests that the poor woman, in spite of years of abuse and rejection, was doing nothing but trying to cheer and help him, both because she loved him (a classic case of *le monstre sacré*) and because he was the father of her children. How much might Wilde's picture of Bosie be coloured by a similar psychological warp: abuse of the most deeply beloved (cf. primal mother) because of intolerable punishment from the world? Wilde himself admits[17] that he is obsessed and can only circle back and back on the worst aspects of his lover and their relationship. Might the Bosie of *De Profundis* not be a compensatory fiction? – just as the Bosie of Wilde's life was a compensatory fulfilment of the ruthlessness Wilde could not achieve in himself?

What a man conceives in prison, Sade's opus shows us, is bound to be more terrible than what he has lived in life. Reformation is impossible; the antinomian urge can only grow. Wilde's yearning for the penitent cowl of the monk is, by his own admission (p. 79), a further way to symbolize his alienation from a society he has come to deplore.

And the antinomian is a homosexual, or bisexual; a practicer of sodomy; a misogynist, or in any case – in *these* cases – a man periodically and progressively more estranged from women, children, family life. Barthes makes much of Sade's libertines' habit of making their female victims cover their 'fronts' (*Sade, Loyola, Fourier*, p. 124); Yeats enjoys telling a story in *Autobiographies* about Wilde being forced to visit a whorehouse in France after release from prison and remarking, on coming out, about 'cold mutton' and not having had any in ten years.[18] What is the relationship between love of women and this whole progression: art, messianism, crime? Antinomianism, 'against custom', *à rebours* – is it not metaphysically related to 'going the wrong way'; the 'left-hand way', as Joseph Campbell describes it,[19] in philosophical tradition; the 'back door'[20] or conscious preferment of anus to vagina, which, Barthes points out in connection with Sade, is a theatrical act of *choice* (cf. Mailer's Rojack with Ruta in *An American Dream*), which separates its practitioner from mere doctrinaire pederasts?

The anus: locus of decay, death, the repulsive and forbidden – the antinomian journey is linked, surely, to all Faustian exploration of dark spaces, the Unknown, and not just the high but the low. *Curiosity* is the motive force here: the Pandora function in man, which motivates his pact with Satan. Christ resisted knowledge of the Cities of the Plain which was offered him from the top of the hill. Wilde, like Dorian Gray, went down, down, down, and is still going in *De Profundis*, trying to find his way back to the dark cavern of Gethesemane, from which, he hopes – once having entombed himself – he will be able to be resurrected one day in purified, utterly elemental and blameless form.

But in order to get there he must go down. And, managing semiconsciously to have known this all his life, he pursues his career in the spirit of 'Eat, drink, and be merry . . .', a philosophy which in less clichéd form had been preached by Walter Pater in the famous finale to a book which – like the one Lord Henry gives Dorian Gray – had 'such a strange influence over my life', Wilde confesses in *De Profundis*:

> How shall we pass most swiftly from point to point, and be present always at the focus where the greatest number of vital forces unite in their purest energy?
>
> To burn always with this hard, gemlike flame, to maintain this ecstasy, is success . . . .[21]

This is the great credo of 'decadence'. And the Wilde discussed here belongs to that company of artists who, having sold their souls to the great god *energy* – the Blakean emanation[22] which in Shelley rages with the force of the West Wind and in Jack London palpitates with the euphoria of Paula Forrest's 'living living living'[23] – damn the consequences, and, like Byron at

Missolonghi or Janis Joplin with her fix, end, having teetered on the tightrope of 'exhaustion'[24] as long as they can, by burning themselves out.

5 Political Interlude: Anarchism

In his admirable 'history of libertarian ideas and movements', *Anarchism*, George Woodcock notes that Wilde in the 1890s answered a questionnaire for the Symbolist review *L'Hermitage* by remarking that 'he had once been politically a supporter of tyrants but now he was an anarchist' (p. 285). Woodcock later suggests that 'the most ambitious contribution to literary anarchism during the 1890s was undoubtedly Oscar Wilde's "The Soul of Man Under Socialism"' (p. 423). This essay, written shortly before Wilde's pathology of the New Hedonism in *Dorian Gray*, so impressed the Fabians that George Bernard Shaw wanted it reprinted under their aegis, along with William Morris's *News from Nowhere*[1]; and Jack London would not only refer to it admiringly but also lift arguments from it for his most radical novel, *The Iron Heel*.[2] Clearly the split between authoritarian and libertarian socialism had not become marked in the English-speaking world of this period. If it had, these doctrinaire socialists might have been more reluctant to express such enthusiasm for a work whose most impassioned plea is for an 'Individualism' at odds with any system, party, or outer authority. Wilde's *Soul of Man*, in spite of its full title, is only marginally 'socialistic' in the sense that we have come to use that term; and Woodcock is surely correct to recommend it as a representative libertarian statement.

Wilde begins by asserting that man must be freed from the 'sordid necessity of living for others'.[3] Charity is degrading and demoralizing both to those who dole it out and to those who receive it. The former are deceiving themselves into thinking they are reducing a problem, while the latter are further confirming for themselves their lack of control over their lives. Using private property to cure a disease caused by private property is immoral; the only solution is to reconstruct

43

society so that lack of property will no longer plague the poor and surfeit of property pervert the rich. The nuisance possessions bring to the latter incapacitates them for spiritual development. On the other hand, to encourage thrift on the poor is insulting. The poor must revolt against their condition. 'It is safer to beg than to take, but it is finer to take than to beg' (*Soul of Man*, p. 11). Disobedience is man's original virtue (Lucifer, Prometheus). If agitators are needed to show the poor their need for revolt, so be it: no group is ever happy to admit its own misery; the freeing of the American slaves would not have been accomplished were it not for the agitations of self-righteous middle-class abolitionists from the North.

Authoritarian socialism will not do; it disallows freedom. To enslave all the people because some of the people are slaves is punitive and childish. Voluntary association is the only acceptable mode. All government is failure. Work should be defined as anything a man wishes to do. Self-perfection is the goal of existence, but the perfect individual should not be confused with some kind of Caesar: 'Wherever there is a man who exercises authority, there is a man who resists authority' (p. 21). The tragedy of history is that most personalities have been obliged to be rebels and waste half their energy in 'friction'. The ideal is to be 'like a little child', or Christ: not to 'know thyself' so much as to 'be thyself' (Marcuse's Orpheus–Narcissus). All forms of moral imitation are marring. Conformity constitutes 'overfed barbarism'; liberal societies are worse than authoritarian ones in that they sap the spirit of revolt. Removing authority will mean removing all punishment, which – along with inequitable distribution of property – is the main cause of crime. It will also mean removing the requirement of manual labour. Such 'slavery' should be performed by machines: 'Man was not made for moving dirt' (p. 40).

By machine, the state will make 'what is useful', while the individual will be free to make 'what is beautiful'. This he will do by 'realizing his individuality' in art. Whatever form that art takes must come directly out of himself. Public opinion must not be allowed to tyrannize, journalism to practise coercion. If taste is to be advanced, art must be allowed to 'educate'; the mass can only demand what it already knows, but the individual soul can offer something new and unique. *Dominance* is anathema. Its only possible legitimate sphere is in the individual's relation to his self-expression. The reign of the people through democracy may be even more pernicious than that of the king through his courts or the pope through the Church. The people must be willing simply 'to live, to listen, and to love' (p. 82). Mankind, in short, should aspire to Orphic–Narcissistic–Christly perfection just as ardently as the individual. Success will be achieved through what Keats called 'negative capability'.[4] Prometheus with his angry cries and bloody sword will vanish. Unselfishness with its celebration of variety will abound.

Wilde believes that 'people are good when they are left alone'. He envisions what Woodcock describes as 'the long summer afternoon of freedom dreamed of by William Morris' (also by Shelley and Godwin and Winstanley).[5] With a faith in the triumph of the pleasure principle which was to be tragically negated by his fate a few years after (though imaginatively negated much sooner in his portrait of Dorian Gray), Wilde suggests that the Christly era of realizing one's own individuality through the 'pain' of abandonment of or resistance to society is now passed. Man no longer needs to become 'a cenobite' in order to be an individual; solitude – 'dropping out' – can only 'realize an impoverished personality'. The modern era, thanks to 'Science and Socialism', offers man means to realize himself not through 'pain' but through 'joy'. The Greeks sought this, but they had to depend on slaves to achieve it; so too did the individualists of the Renaissance. Modern man alone will be able to 'live intensely, fully, perfectly' because he alone – as we have seen Marcuse imagining – can maintain *abundance*.

 Such a brilliant vista! Of course, Wilde would retreat in *De Profundis* to the idea that modern man can only maintain his individuality through Sorrow and Christly 'Pain'. Both modes may be true depending on the situation of one's culture and time of one's life. What is memorable about *The Soul of Man*, written on the verge of Wilde's greatest happiness and success, is the morning glow of the Utopian dream. This lies at the heart of anarchist tradition. 'By simplifying existence so that toil is reduced,' Proudhon thought, 'man can turn his attention to noble activities and achieve the philosophic equilibrium in which death will cease to have terror' (p. 26). The irony is that, because the anarchist must first 'seek to break down, to get back to the roots', the movement 'has always had its links with that shadowy world where rebellion merges into criminality, the world of Balzac's Vautrin and his originals in real life' – that is, the purely ruthless ones, believers in natural impulse and appetite, admitters of no outside strictures of good and evil: Sade's libertines, Salomé, or their brutalized lower-class counterparts, the James Vanes or *Enragés* of the French Revolution, who wanted to strangle at birth 'the social distinctions which marked the hardening power of the ascendant middle class' (p. 51).

Woodcock notes that Wilde was a devotee of Prince Kropotkin, who lived in London in the 1890s. Kropotkin's life was 'among the most perfect lives I have come across in my own experience', Wilde writes in *De Profundis*; he is 'a man with a soul of that beautiful white Christ that seems coming out of Russia' (p. 112). In Kropotkin, Wilde was admiring yet another hereditary aristocrat; only this one, unlike Dorian Gray or Bosie but in the vein of Iokaanan, had 'an innate puritanism in [his] character which made him shrink from the profligacy of court life'. In place of society, Kropotkin elevated a 'cult of the primitive'. As an explorer for the Russian Geographical Society, he had learned – rather like Jack London would in the Klondike – how to live spartanly but with contentment. These explorations, Woodcock says, 'provided him with long periods of solitary thought' and 'brought him nearer to the point where he would sacrifice even his scientific work to what seemed a higher cause' (*Anarchism*, p. 178). Kropotkin came to embody the transcendental, spiritual form of anarchism which appealed to high-minded later Victorians. Besides Wilde, Morris and Swinburne and Leslie Stephen revered him, as did Hugo and Renan across the Channel. To their humanitarian impulses his anti-Darwinian attitudes were attractive, as this one in *Mutual Aid*, in reply to the theories of Huxley and Malthus:

The struggle for existence is indeed important, but as a struggle against adverse circumstances rather than between individuals of the same species. Where it does exist within a species, it is injurious rather than otherwise, since it dissipates the advantages gained by sociability. Far from thriving on competition . . . natural selection seeks out the means by which it can be avoided. (Quoted, p. 201)

Another contemporary with 'a soul of that beautiful white Christ that seems coming out of Russia' was also a nobleman: Tolstoy. 'What Kropotkin meant by "mutual aid"', Woodcock writes, 'was not very far from what Tolstoy meant by "love"' (p. 208). Tolstoy shared and expanded on Kropotkin's view of Nature as productive of harmony and happiness, this too from experience of Russia's vast wilderness; and, from contrast between Nature and civilization, he developed an adamant disbelief in 'the 19th century idea of progress'. In place of this, Tolstoy exalts 'freedom, brotherhood, and the cultivation of man's moral nature' (p. 215). Hatred of luxury and property combine to encourage striving towards the ascetic, simple life. Tolstoy's Christ embodies this; but where His example leads should not be preordained, as 'life consists solely in the search for the unknown and in our work of harmonizing our actions with the new truth'. The ability to become a 'seeker' in this manner depends on abolition of the state, which 'is nothing but a conspiracy to exploit . . . and demoralize' (p. 209). 'I regard all governments', Tolstoy wrote at the end of his life, 'as intricate institutions, sanctified by tradition and custom, for the purpose of committing by force and impunity the most revolting crimes'.[6] Violence by government is wholly evil because it is a self-conscious 'perversion of reason'; violence by a mob, on the other hand, is 'only partly evil because it arises from ignorance' (p. 217).

Non-violent resistance is the proper course for Tolstoy, as 'civil disobedience' had been for Thoreau and his own synthesis would be for Gandhi. But the great anarchist to come out of Russia in this period embodied, by contrast, 'the destructive urge'. Mikhail Bakunin was also an aristocrat; but, unlike Kropotkin and Tolstoy, he believed in dynamic change: *action*. A romantic eccentric, Bakunin moved swiftly, wrote scantily, and became a Promethean legend in his time – the prototype, allegedly, for Wagner's Siegfried. Like Sade, Bakunin was a man of huge appetite; but in him aristocratic contempt merged with an egalitarian bohemianism more characteristic of the age of Baudelaire. In anticipation of the Revolution in which both Baudelaire and Wagner participated, Bakunin declared, 'Let us put our trust in the eternal spirit which destroys and annihilates only because it is the unsearchable and eternally creative source of all life' (p. 139). After the 1848, he became a rallying-point for those who found Marx's vision of a proletarian dictatorship ominous but were not prepared to revert to the nationalistic enthusiasms becoming the most potent counterforce against it. Bakunin's own Slavic nationalism, with its vision of a 'messianic role' for the Russian people, gave way after years of wandering to a programme for a United States of Europe, to be set up by 'spontaneous revolution' and a 'holy war' carried out by 'peasants and the *déclassé* elements in urban society' (p. 155).

With his experiences of poverty and prison, Bakunin brought an explosive tone to the libertarian ideal. Over time, this eroded his position *vis-à-vis* Marx in the minds of working socialists. Bakunin, dauntless, simply became more extreme. This may be the result partly of a perverse passion he developed for a lower-class student from Moscow. As Woodcock writes,

> The fascination that Nechayev wielded over Bakunin reminds one of other disastrous relationships between men of widely differing ages: Rimbaud and Verlaine, or Lord Alfred Douglas and Oscar Wilde. There certainly seems to have been ... submerged homosexuality; indeed, it is hard to find any other explanation for the temporary submissiveness of the usually autocratic Bakunin to this sinister youth. ... *How the Revolutionary Question Presents Itself* and *Principles of Revolution* ... both extolled indiscriminate destruction in the name of the revolution and preached the sanctification of the means by the end. 'We recognize no other activity but the work of extermination ... but we admit that the forms in which this activity will show itself will be extremely varied, poison, the knife, the rope, etc.' ... *The Revolutionary Catechism* (1870) went on to describe the ideal revolutionary as the one who must lose his individuality and become a kind of monk of righteous extermination, a nineteenth-century descendant of Hashishim:

The revolutionary [Nechayev and Bakunin write] is a man under vow. He ought to occupy himself entirely with one exclusive interest, with one thought and one passion: the Revolution. . . . He has only one aim, one science: destruction. . . . Between him and society there is war to the death incessant, irreconcilable. . . . He must make a list of those who are condemned to death, and expedite their sentence according to the order of the relative iniquities. (pp. 159–60)

Here is the bloodthirsty, totally anti-social incarnation with which anarchism was to become identified in the mass mind, through the assassinations in Paris in the 1890s, the Sacco-and-Vanzetti propaganda in America in the 1920s, and the tradition of small armed criminal–anarchist bands in Spain and Italy both before and after fascism. In this form, anarchism comes to seem less a theory than a rationalization: a nihilistic justification for any and all licence. As such, it can be related to Sade (and grows, certainly, out of traditions associated with the French Revolution); but the Sade it relates to is more the prisoner screaming, obsessed with vengeance, than the libertine seeking to dominate all. As it falls from the high-born through middle-class drop-outs to the low, the idea of anarchism becomes increasingly less idyllic, more savage. Actual confrontation with some hashish-crazed, bloody, bomb-toting murderer would no doubt have horrified Wilde, perhaps even Kropotkin. But, however Wilde may have qualified his statements to label crime a means to Individualism inferior to art (because 'it must take cognisance of other people and interfere with them' – *Soul of Man*, p. 38), there is present in them – as in Tolstoy's and others' – a sense of the inevitability of this precipitous descent.

Stirnerite anarchism is the next step down. Johann Casper Schmidt is another man screaming in a nightmare; only for him the prison was an 'unhappy, luckless, and ill-ordered' petty-bourgeois life and the compensatory persona the 'free-standing egoist' (*Anarchism*, p. 89). *The Ego and its Own* by 'Max Stirner' grew out of Schmidt's timid association with the Young Hegelians of Berlin of the 1840s: *Die Freien* – 'the Free Ones'. A disregarded book in its time, its influence began to be felt only fifty years later, after the ground had been readied by Nietzsche. Stirner spoke to the dispossessed little man made the type of an era by literary inheritors such as B. Traven and Brecht. His creed is 'almost complete inversion' and 'draws near to nihilism and existentialism in its denial of all natural laws and of a common humanity' (p. 87). He posits a 'war of each against all', a 'conflict of wills' in which '*force* and *power* and *might*' are opposed to '*right*'. Realization of true egotism requires these qualities, not possessions, which in fact hamper 'uniqueness'. Nor does the true egoist desire 'mastery', as that would involve a relationship curtailing his independence. The only acceptable kind of association would be a 'union of egoists': a 'free intercourse of unique beings each embattled in his power'; a 'kind of equilibrium based on mutual respect' – 'brotherhood . . . emerging from the danger of mutual destruction' (p. 95). One can readily see how such ideas might merge into National Socialism (especially when identified, as by Woodcock, with Bulwer–Lytton's cult of the 'deadly energy' *vril* in *The Coming Race*). Stirner, however, rejects the state as categorically as he does morality, thus can voice this 'rhapsodic' glorification:

> In crime the egoist has hitherto asserted himself and mocked at the sacred; the break with the sacred, or rather of the sacred, may become general. A revolution never returns, but a mighty, reckless, shameless, conscienceless, proud *crime*, does it not rumble in distant thunders, and do you not see how the sky grows presciently silent and gloomy?
>
> (p. 96)

Like Nietzsche, Stirner prefers aphorism to argument. He deals in paradox – 'inversion' or 'transvaluation of values' – to a degree which matches Sade or Wilde. Paradox was also the mode of his French contemporary Proudhon, coiner of the phrase 'Property is theft', friend of Baudelaire, and 'real inspirer of French socialism'. An '*aficionado*' of antinomial thinking', Proudhon wrote in 'a vigorous prose' which appealed as much as Bakunin's example to the heroic spirit of 1848. 'God is evil', he declared, Sadeanly; man realizes his greatness by 'opposing himself to all in the universe that is non-human'. Prometheus, again, is the type here, not Orpheus–Narcissus;

the world is split between Manichaean poles of good and evil; a dynamic society is the ideal, one 'kept in movement by perpetual change and kept alive by perpetual criticism' (p. 114). Proudhon's pre-Maoism did not prevent him from taking part in organized government. But participation produced little; the Second Empire followed the Third Revolution; and, by the 1870s, the insurrectionary urge in France had taken on a more Stirnerite character.

Figures appeared such as Ernest Coeurderoy, who believed that 'disorder is salvation' and wanted to 'set the torch to the old world beginning with his father's house' (p. 261). Again, as with Stirner, one can hear echoes of Sade and forebodings of the apocalypticism of the twentieth century:

> Forward! Forward! War is Redemption! God desires it, the God of the criminals, of the oppressed, of the rebels, of the poor, of all those who are tormented, the Satanic God whose body is of brimstone, whose wings are of fire and whose sandals are of bronze! The God of courage and of insurrection who unleashes the furies in our hearts – our God! No more isolated conspiracies, no more chattering parties, no more secret societies! All that is nothing and can achieve nothing! Stand up, Man, stand up, people, stand up, all who are not satisfied! Stand up for right, well-being, and life! Stand up, and in a few days you will be millions. Forward in great human oceans, in great masses of brass and iron, to the vast music of ideas! Money will no longer avail against a world that rises up! Forward from pole to pole, forward, all peoples from the rising to the setting of the sun! Let the globe tremble under your feet. Forward! War is life! The war against evil is a good war!

'Isolated conspiracies' and 'secret societies' may refer to the Freemasonry Proudhon and Bakunin shared, or to the cult of cabals Bakunin and others were going in for at the time. These evidence the tendency in anarchism to develop small cadres grouped around a single personality, a tendency most evident in the Russians, who had an instinctive yearning for a 'white Christ' of their own kind to replace the Czar. On the other extreme is the tendency of anarchism to spin off quixotic 'angels of retribution': loners such as the mysterious assassin

Ravachol, a dyer whose 'primitive philosophy naively combined a defence of violence in the present with an idyllic vision of future brotherhood' (p. 289). Tried and put to death, Ravachol conducted himself to the end with stoical blamelessness and is remembered in anarchist tradition as a minstrel who made up songs for 'The Cause', which he sang accompanying himself on accordion:

> Pour établir l'Égalité
> Il faut le coeur plein de colère
> Réduire les bourgeois en poussière;
> Alors au lieu d'avoir la guerre,
> Nous aurons la Fraternité.*

This spirit would be resurrected by Brecht in the 1920s and American 'protest' singers in the 1960s – Bob Dylan in 'Masters of War' or 'Blowin' in the Wind' – for, with the energy of its rage and vague utopianism of its message, anarchism has always been supreme among political philosophies in its appeal to the *chansonnier*:

> Nos pères ont jadis dansé
> Au son du canon du passé;
> Maintenant la danse tragique
> Veut une plus forte musique:
> Dynamitons! Dynamitons!†[7]

Indeed, anarchism's appeal to artists is hardly confined to latter-day troubadours. Woodcock points out that it was the political philosophy of painters from Pissaro to Picasso to the Surrealists and beyond; also of writers who 'hovered around the "dangerous flame" in France' – Stuart Merrill, Vielé-Griffin, Valéry, Remy de Gourmont, and so on – and their counterparts in other countries (p. 286). Mallarmé gave evidence on behalf of an anarchist acquaintance at the Trial of the Thirty in 1894, describing him as 'a fine spirit, curious

---

* *Translation*: 'To establish Equality, we must have hearts full of anger and reduce the middle class to dust. Then, instead of war, we shall have Brotherhood'.

† *Translation*: 'Our fathers used to dance to the sound of passing cannon. Now the tragic dance wants a stronger music: Blow it up! Blow it up!'

about everything that is new'. *Curious about everything that is new*. Writers and artists in revolt against old forms (as all original writers and artists must be) can hardly help but be fascinated by the 'spirit of daring and inquiry' which permeated anarchism in its great age of the *fin-de-siècle*. The 'terrible but intriguing sensationalism in the lives of the assassins ... the element of perverted mysticism' – in these explosions, decadent preoccupations and apocalyptic yearnings come together. But then anarchism, repressed by *les lois scélérates* in France and brutal counter-terrorism in Russia and Italy, had to descend further and further underground until – by the second decade of this century – it lived almost wholly in isolated covens and gangs supporting themselves by crime; and high-minded theory tended to retreat towards that point in the great circle of political ideology where anarchism and its opposite meet.

If 'the vast music of ideas' is where anarchist rhetoric links with Symbolist aspiration, 'great human oceans' and 'masses of brass and iron' are where it links to the revolutionary movements of the twentieth century. 'Money will no longer avail', 'War is Redemption', 'War is life' – such phrases would echo in the bootfalls of Nazis and fascists, which would all but trample the utopian songs of anarchism into inaudibility. These movements became to group-man what Stirnerite anarchism was to the individual: the declaration of independence to exercise *force*, *power* and *might*. The 'long summer afternoon of freedom' gives way to blood chants 'from the rising to the setting of the sun' (Coeurderoy's phrase curiously previews the stretch of totalitarian war-fever from the 'land of the rising sun' to the land of Spenglerian 'twilight'). We come up hard against the problem first discerned in Marcuse and implicit, certainly, in the case of Sade and Wilde: how can individual liberty be made compatible with the group? Does expression of one preclude that of the other? Certainly the Wildean ideal of individual perfection is a noble one, but is not the desire of men to live in harmonious societies as well?

To this, the doctrinaire anarchist must answer that the state, the aggregate, the group must always be limited in favour of the individual. But twentieth-century history shows that this is impossible when state or group speaks with sufficient individuality of its own: the Russian proletariat, German racists, Zionists, Khomeini's Islamics. Even in heterogeneous societies the problem exists. Here the antagonist is Public Opinion, as Wilde identified it. 'In America the President reigns for four years, and Journalism governs for ever and ever' (*Soul of Man*, p. 62). Woodcock quotes from Orwell, 'When human beings are governed by "thou shalt not", the individual can practise a certain amount of eccentricity: when they are supposedly governed by "love" and "reason", he is under continuous pressure to make him behave and think in the same way as everyone does' (*Anarchism*, p. 79). Anyone who participated in radical 'affinity groups' in America in the 1960s (or for that matter went to rock concerts where the loudspeakers kept reiterating 'Come on, people, be cool' and 'Let's just love and dig one another') will recognize that what Orwell was concerned about goes beyond the coercions of the press. This is the reality of Wilde's Arcadian vision. As Woodcock says, 'Few anarchists have given sufficient thought to the danger of a moral tyranny replacing a physical one.'

Fourier is a classic example. His utopia would be built on the pleasure principle, but – as Barthes says (*Sade, Loyola, Fourier*, p. 82) – without 'vexation in the Sadean manner'. Whimsical in spirit, the *phalanstère* is designed to 'dissipate' vexation and induce 'general well-being'. Fourier is an antinomian *par excellence*. He 'stands up' against all received ideas and seeks to make a world wholly new. 'The rule of invention is the rule of refusal: to doubt absolutely . . . to be in opposition with everything being done . . . to preach what Opinion holds to be *impossible*' (p. 88). Fourier's deconstructionism is so complete that he repudiates *the writer* even, as Barthes notes, because *the writer* 'guarantees decorative union and thus the fundamental separation of substance and form'. Fourier's programme, thus, is dispensed in broken units of meaning, aphoristic and in conventional terms paradoxical, rather like the lyrics of rock songs: 'The indirect is a profitable mode of language' – mystery – 'nocturnal furnishings', 'hieroglyphics'. The role of social theorist borders on that of magician. Fourier's Harmony – especially in its aspiration to incorporate its members into the great One of the universe, including the stars – bears the marks of a messianic transcendentalism which would be preached by less illuminated types.

Fourier, Barthes says, 'alone is right, and being right is the desirable thing' (p. 84). Previewing more than a century early what the flower child would want, he offers the 'marvellous real' of life as opposed to the 'marvellous ideal' of fiction (cf. the line in the Jefferson Starship song: 'We can *live*/And leave all the stories behind'[8]). Passion is natural. Passion is clean. Passion is happy. Happiness means 'having many passions and an ample means to satisfy them'. Unity-ness – 'Harmonism' – constitutes a series of 'brilliant and countless combinations': a light-world version of Sade's *120 Journées*. 'The system is a closed one,' Barthes tells us; 'theological, dogmatic . . . . It is a strictly paranoid insanity whose path of transmission is insistence, repetition, catechism, orthodoxy . . . a wild system, whose very excess, whose fantastic tension, goes beyond system and attains systematics' (p. 111). *Love*, including both erotic and sentimental attachments, is the long-held mantra note of 'the Harmonian day'. Free and easily orgiastic, with permanent availability of partners, no denial of or refusal to another, that day becomes the navel of all time: 'We shall be witness to a spectacle to be seen once on each globe: the sudden passage from incoherence to social combination' (p. 118).

Man having come into perfect harmony with other men at last, Time itself can end: 'At the era of the planet's death, its great soul, and consequently ours, inherent in it, will pass on to another, new sphere, to a new planet, which will be implaned, concentrated, saturated . . .' (p. 106). Death, Fourier believes, is a 'trivial transition'; moreover, all transitions are good – they destroy that supreme bugaboo *monotony* and promote change. ('Life is change/How it differs from the rocks' – Jefferson Airplane.[9]) One has a disturbing vision of this happy guru leading his sub-Orphic–Narcissistic disciples off towards the blinding bright light of nuclear holocaust. But this too is implicit in the anarchic–romantic aspiration. In fact, such an ending, with its potential for creating a new Atlantean 'lost past' and releasing mankind into a new post-lapsarian struggle with all old orders and inequities swept away, is precisely anarchic in spirit. Out of the chaos may come *ricorso*, as perhaps promised by the finale of Wagner's

Ring. Or maybe not. But at least, if one is a Sadean/Shavian believer in the 'life force', one can comfort oneself with the idea that some form of matter is bound to live on through the black infinity of space and time.

The reader might do well at this point to recall the period in which this book is being written. 1984, we are told, did not bring the totalitarian tyranny Orwell feared it might. 1986 is, however, a year of anxiety. Fear of nuclear conflagration is ever-present; nor is totalitarianism at all at bay in a world rife with terrorism. For the most part, contemporary assassins belong to distinct political groups, Marxist, Islamic or 'nationalist' in character; and the 'freak' killers of America – John Hinckley, who shot Reagan; the man who shot John Lennon – are not identified with idealistic causes. (Squeaky Fromme, who shot at President Ford, was a member of Charles Manson's 'family', the 'political' coloration of which we shall consider later.) Still, the effect of this constant susurrus of disorder is to discourage the 'spontaneous renewal' of idealistic anarchism such as permeated the West to a remarkable extent in the later sixties and early seventies. There is a 'libertarian' party in America now. Some of its backers also invest in the 'Less Government is Better' rhetoric of the Republican Party. 'Freedom' is most commonly extolled by those who have much and want more. 'Liberty' in the West seems to have more to do with the Thatcher government removing restrictions from the Stock Exchange than the individual being able to express himself free of the molestation of public opinion or the care of material impoverishment.

These cardinal antagonists to the anarchist vision – the tyrannies of 'the People' and of private property – have not been defeated by the rule of 'Science and Socialism', as Wilde imagined they would be. Post-war dreams of literary *cénacles* in London, New York and San Francisco, with their neo-surrealism, their New Romantic, New Apocalyptic and 'beat' labels, led to an interlude of civil-rights activism, pacifism, disarmament crusades, hippyism, drug expansionism, environmentalism, feminism, gay liberation, and a general rebellion (reflected in Marcuse) against the coercions of institutionalized psychology. But that 'long summer afternoon of freedom' came to its autumn in the mid 1970s, a 'selfish' period in which the youth of the middle classes turned their nostalgia back from the Eden of a collective dream towards the comforts of elitist privilege. America is where this turnabout happened most distinctly; and Woodcock, with his anarchist traditionalism as a measuring-stick, may have come close to discovering why:

> At times, and particularly in the United States, the broadening appeal of libertarian ideals has also led to their adulteration, so that anarchism often appears as only one element in what can be described as a climate of rebellion, an insurrectionary frame of mind, rather than a new revolutionary ideology. One finds it mingled with strains of Leninism and early Marxism, with traces of the unorthodox psychology not only of Reich but also of R. D. Laing, with memories of the communitarian movement of the American frontier days, and often with large ingredients of mysticism, neo-Buddhism and Tolstoyan Christianity ... refusal to accept a definite theoretical line ... a widespread antagonism to structured thinking ... a tendency to reject not only historicism but also history. ... It is significant that none of these movements produced a single theoretical work in the field of anarchist thought that is comparable to those produced in earlier periods by Proudhon, Kropotkin or even Herbert Read. (*Anarchism*, pp. 458–9)

Perhaps, like Fourier, America of the period had gone so far towards deconstruction in its 'insurrectionary frame of mind' that producing 'theoretical works' seemed itself a 'counter-revolutionary' separation of substance and form. The Andy Warhol group demonstrated this in their 'art'; Ken Kesey expressed it at the Vietnam Day Committee Rally in Berkeley, California, in 1965.[10] Perhaps, too, the 'ordinary working- and middle-class people' of America, sharing with their counterparts in nineteenth-century Europe a disquiet at the anarchist vision, encouraged an establishment not in favour of too much revolution to diminish its efforts at finding, publishing and promoting such works. Anarchist literature has been at least as much a phenomenon of pamphlets and 'underground' presses as socialism; and the reputation of books such as Wilde's *Soul of Man*, Edmund Wilson's *To the Finland Station* or even Woodcock's *Anarchism* (which deserves durable attention as *the* work on the subject) depends in part on the status of their authors within the literary–academic establishment. Perhaps, finally, a representative 'theoretical work in the field of anarchist thought' for this period could have been produced, only – given the vagaries of revolutionary language – without Woodcock being able to recognise it.

This possibility apart, the anarchist urge, in both its destructionist and utopian manifestations, may be in eclipse at this moment of militarism and material preoccupation (record unemployment, record stock-market rises, and so forth); and even the cult of health, which seems the last vestige of 1960s idealism to remain vital in the 1980s, suggests Fourier's cult of the androgynous superman[11] more than Wilde's perfect individual free and in full touch with spirit and sensation.

It is, perhaps, a question of *pace*, which is related to distribution (*abundance*); also, as said before, of general demonstration of what Keats described as 'negative capability'.

6 'Power' and the Occult

The destructive urge we have been tracking has been focused predominantly against an aristocratic tyranny or tyrant: the French, *ancien régime*, Bosie, the industrial plutocracy of the later nineteenth century. If in the case of some anarchists the point of destruction is ultimately to gain a 'long summer's afternoon of freedom', or in the case of an individualist such as Wilde to reach a kind of Orphic–Narcissistic Christly perfection, it might equally be, as the case of Sade shows, to attain to a level of power oneself which matches or surpasses that of the tyrant(s). Brutality incites brutality. In the case of Max Stirner, we see the anarchist as wimp: the man whose urge to destruction is primarily motivated by feelings of his own insignificance. This type is perhaps even more central to our study than versions of Narcissus or Prometheus, with their beatifying and liberating ideals. Ideals, indeed, far from being the motivating force behind the urge to power, may become mere labels by which it declares itself or tools for its promotion. Moreover, power – even tyranny – may become the predominant ideal, rather than some vision of a sweeter life beyond, in the misty pastel aureole around Narcissus's pool. Sade was enraged because he could no longer perform like the malevolent libertines his fantasy life thrived on. Stirner does not envision destruction in order to become Prince Kropotkin. The 'white Christ' may be an appealing, even useful, ideal to a *haut bourgeois* like Wilde. But even Wilde, as we have seen, is forced to confront the fact that, in the end, the lords of this world are more likely to embody a classical, conscienceless code of mastery.

The destructive urge, then, may equally come to be focused against what is perceived as unmasterful in the personality itself. In Marcusan terms, this might be expressed as the superid killing off Orpheus–Narcissus. Sade battering his innocent young virgins is a man forcibly deflowering debilitating 'virtue' in himself. Dorian Gray's murder of Basil Hallward is

one version of Wilde's psychological revenge against his own
'wetness'. Bakunin's escalating violence of rhetoric might be
seen as a subconscious effort to keep at bay the Tolstoyan
saint vying for expression in him. The anti-type, anti-self at
war with the *good* in these figures may, in the end, operate like
the algolagnic devotees of the legend who rip Orpheus limb
from limb.[1] What characterizes the type in all its incarnations
are two things we discovered in the chapter on Sade: (1)
fierce, fiery energy; (2) absence of soul, if we take that term in
the Wildean sense to mean the shadow-image of transcendental
perfection towards which the individual may strive. Removal
of this image creates restlessness and a spirit of revenge, which
the soulless ones naturally tend to turn on those who still cling
to *goodness*. Corruption of innocence – Dorian Gray's 'killing of
conscience' – might be characterized as theft of soul by the
soulless. The motive for this kind of Mephistophelean act is a
form of jealousy: the soulless one does not want to *get* a soul
himself (a virtually impossible task in the tradition of
demonology[2]) so much as remove it in the other. To paraphrase
Sade, only when no souls exist may the soulless rest happy. In
a totally evil world, evil will cease to be evil – there will be no
good to measure it by. Soul defines evil because, as the
shadow-image of potential perfection, it contains – has to
contain – the balancing moral element.

The struggle of good and evil in, or for, the soul is the
battleground of personality. Among individuals, personality is
a prerequisite for power; nor can any programme of ideals
rationalizing pursuit of power fail to take the erection and
maintenance of personality into account. At the start of this
study, I said I was not going to deal directly with Nietzsche.
This was both because I had done so in *Wagner to 'The Waste
Land'* and because, as a theorist rather than man-of-action,
Nietzsche was not the best example of the thing we are after
in its raw state. At the risk of arrogating too much power to
my personality, I must now change my mind. Nietzsche
demands to be considered in this context, at least *en passant*.
The civilized 'Mediterranean' attitudes of his middle period,
prime concern in the Wagner study, are not the matter here;
it is Nietzsche the phenomenon, especially as apprehended
through his more extreme later works, *Also Sprach Zarathustra*
to *Ecce Homo*, in which we find the most eloquent and sustained

rationalization ever for the man-of-power as an end in himself (though Machiavelli and Balzac, in whom Yeats remarked 'all Nietzsche' could be found,[3] are two among many obvious and important precursors). Only after going through the kind of 'awakening' Nietzsche experienced and projected through these books could dreamers-on-power of the twentieth century – all the dazzling or pathetic Walter Mittys playing their own Gods – establish sufficient personality to construct the elaborate structures of artistic symbol, occult rite, political rationalization or what-have-you on which their power was to be erected and maintained.

There are many Nietzsches, but at least one – perhaps the most influential – develops like this.[4] He begins adult life as a mild-mannered teacher of classics, perhaps a little over-intoxicated with the glory of his subject matter and susceptible to the lure of the heroic in contemporary art (he himself is near-sighted and not robust in health or physique) but otherwise hardly an arresting, let alone alarming, young man. He then comes upon Wagner, *Tristan* and *Siegfried*, engages in his 'stellar friendship' discussing Greek culture, suffers a covert passion for the elder-sisterly Cosima, and writes *The Birth of Tragedy out of the Spirit of Music*. This glorifies the orgiastic and ecstatic impulse in man – pre-individual, Natural, and demanding its lofty, self-mastering Apollonian counterpart – and shows Nietzsche's first signs of revolt against Schopenhauer's 'cult of Nirvana and resignation' with 'an intellectual predilection for what is hard, awful, evil, problematic in existence, owing to well-being, to exuberant health, to fullness of existence'.[5]

The heroic silhouette on the far horizon is in inverse proportion to the shadow cast by the young philosopher's literary début. *The Birth of Tragedy* fails to make the desired impact. The same is true of the essays comprising the following volume, *Thoughts out of Season*. Restless, malcontent, mentally aggressive, Nietzsche, having already had to give up lecturing for reasons of health, now falls out with Wagner, castigates the 'decadence' Bayreuth augurs for Europe, and begins expatriate wanderings which will not end until his complete mental collapse over a decade later. 'Did my loathing itself create for me wings and fountain-divining powers?' the author will ask himself via his most inflated mouthpiece, Zarathustra;[6] but a syphilitic infection and consequent chronic struggle against time and for health provides a less exalted explanation for his development. To some, he seems bent on reducing philosophy to 'a weapon in a fight for self-preservation'. Modified Darwinism infects the Hellenic ideal. Machiavelli also intrudes. Truth might be a 'kind of error', the man declares with perverse glee. What matters, it seems, is not the difference between truth and falsehood so much as the psycho–physiological power emanating from one or the other. 'You should have power over your pro and contra,' he goes on, 'and learn how to put them forth and withdraw them again in accordance with your higher purpose.'[7]

What higher purpose? Far from the Christly Love Wilde was shortly to brandish against his opponents, this equal lover of paradox proposes the 'breeding' of a superior type of man. As if in self-defence for his own weakness and failure, Nietzsche as writer develops ever-more astonishing vitality. He dramatizes himself into an exceptional being in the grand style, speaks in barbed epigrams or from mountaintops, now an heir to Voltaire, now a neo-pre-Christian prophet. Western culture has 'long been writhing in expectation of a catastrophe,' he declares, 'restless, violent, helter skelter'.[8] Out of the mix of his multiple personae – atheist, mystic, romantic poet, professor, preacher, warrior, and meekest of men – he proposes to offer one voice as 'the evil conscience of the age'.[9] When he falls in love, he hastens to kill the sensation. When he falls ill, he flagellates himself back into health. Every symptom of weakness in his character he lashes out against with 'the severest counter-measures'. The result is the self-knower, perhaps the self-torturer ('self-hangman'[10]), but in the end the utterly propless, illusion-free, naked spirit of thought, which – thus self-crucified – feels eminently justified in setting itself up as the fount of a new religion.

God is dead. Christianity has brought about the psychological ruin of man not so much through the example of Christ, whose heroic asceticism is moving, as through its contempt for the body and its perpetuation of the old Judaic shibboleth of a single, vengeful God. Better to be one's own God than to be restrained by such antipathetic dogma. Man must prepare to become his own 'saviour'. The tradition of mystical union is scuttled in favour of magical self-assertion. Descent into pandæmonium is welcomed. Lucifer falls through a 'chaotic universe, without any goal or meaning. And since the process is a blind one, there can be no difference between crime and virtue, or even between life and death.'[11] In the midst of his fall, Nietzsche grasps out towards a vision of what might mediate a new morality, strength with sure measure, *sans* weakness, a new 'middle way'. But the dominant affirmation of his *magnum opus* turns out to be ruthlessness more than nobility: the essence of life is a struggle for power, Zarathustra proclaims from his solitary eyrie; all that comes from strength and elevates life is good, all that comes from weakness and the negation of life is bad; with every degree of growth towards greatness and loftiness, there must also be a growth downward into the deep and terrible; 'the modicum of power which you represent decides your rank, all the rest is cowardice';[12] he who wants to cure, lead and rule others must first prove that he is fit for such a task; only through victories over himself can he do this.

The new morality is a new spartanism, an 'ultra-severe yoga system', puritanism in favour of instead of against Nature (for Nietzsche a more Rousseauesque than Sadean force). Nietzsche's medallion – his only 'love' in the end – is for the 'farthest one': man of the future, vengeful species of the Noble Savage. In the shadow of this Superman, common humanity appears just so much clay; and, out of the traditional moral dialectic, Nietzsche leaves little doubt about which antipode he sees as most likely to lead to the goal:

Man no longer requires a 'justification of evil': justification is precisely what he abhors; he enjoys evil, *pur*, *cru*; he regards purposeless evil as the most interesting kind of evil. If he required a God in the past, he now delights in cosmic disorder without a God, a world of accident, to the essence of which belong terror, ambiguity and seductiveness. . . . In a state of this sort, it is precisely *goodness* which requires to be justified – that is to say, it must either have an evil and dangerous basis, or else it must contain a vast amount of stupidity: *in which case it still pleases*. Animality no longer awakens terror now: a very intellectual and happy wanton spirit in favour of the animal in man is, in such periods, the most triumphant form of spirituality. . . . [Man] may now play the devil's advocate afresh. If in practice he pretends to uphold virtue, it will be for those reasons which lead virtue to be associated with subtlety, cunning, lust of gain, and a form of lust of power.[13]

Thus he would declare, Sadeanly, in his posthumous book, *The Will to Power*. The passage echoes and extends an *aperçu* by a younger, less certain, more curious yet no less instinctively antinomian Nietzsche:

Evil – Test the life of the best and most productive men and nations, and ask yourselves whether a tree which is to grow proudly heavenward can dispense with bad weather and tempests; whether disfavour and opposition from without, whether every kind of hatred, jealousy, stubbornness, distrust, severity, greed, and violence do not belong to the *favouring* circumstances without which a great growth even in virtue is hardly possible? The poison by which the weaker nature is destroyed is strengthening to the strong individual – and he does not call it poison.[14]

In sum, Nietzsche's instinctive bias is toward the antipode indicated by this characteristic apostrophe at the end of the book which gives a name to the problem: 'My old beloved – *evil* thoughts!'[15]

Throughout the opus 'evil' as word and concept is invoked to designate a force which is dynamic: the 'unavoidable and perhaps necessary antagonism to good without which good itself might (in his opinion) grow static and sterile'.[16] At the most extreme reach of 'transvaluation of values', *evil* for this inspired neurotic becomes *good*. More significantly perhaps, it proves itself (or so it seems to one who after all remains a man of thought, not action) the surest means to that most sought-after end: power. That Nietzsche never draws close to power – or even self-mastery – in his conscious lifetime seems only to strengthen the element of 'Promethean barbarism' in his message. *Zarathustra* earns little more notice than *The Birth of Tragedy*; and the man who describes himself as 'the first philosopher of our age, yea – perhaps even something more than that, something fateful and decisive on the very threshold dividing the two millennia'[17] is regarded by friends as an increasingly 'painful case'[18] and by the disinterested as a crank. The rhetoric of his last two, most self-obsessed books, *The Antichrist* and *Ecce Homo*, reaches a high keen of cosmic mockery and incitement as now, quite openly, he 'aims at a revolution as great in the history of mankind as the one achieved by Christ, only in the opposite direction'[19] and goads himself onward in 'drug-like exultation', taking 'stronger and stronger doses' of 'demonic self-assertion' as distinct – in spite of self-challenging asides about 'how much *truth*' one can 'take' – from 'true self-realization'.

Mein Kampf may be the most dramatic literary (if we may call it that) example of Nietzsche's influence on the early twentieth century; but his dreams of power infected many less obvious minds than that of the artist-*manqué* of Linz and Vienna, whom we shall come to in the next chapter. Yeats's was one. According to Denis Donoghue, Nietzsche's philosophy was a – perhaps *the* – principal influence on Yeats's mature (if we may call it that) personality: a Nietzschean struggle for self-mastery forms a kind of bridge in the long career which begins with evocations of rarefied mystical beauty, part ancient Celtic, part Rosicrucian, and ends with what W. H. Auden would characterize as the 'Southern Californian' preoccupations of *A Vision*.[20] Donoghue's little book, published in 1971 and no doubt coloured by the *Zeitgeist* of that period, gives an extraordinary, eccentric picture of a man whom academics like to portray in his house-broken form as the model Irish writer, statesman and Nobel Prize winner. Out of this tepid brew, Donoghue extracts a fiery essence. His Yeats the dreamer-on-glory is an energized, Faustian incarnation of the tower-bound scholar–alchemist who comes over in most of the prose writings. This Yeats has a truth and is of definite interest to our study. Still, from the outset one should recognize that this is less Yeats as he was than as he might have been – or imagined he could have been – had he finally been able to wrestle himself free from the kind of paralysing diffidence which made him impotent with Maud Gonne, and had less of the *fin-de-siècle* over-refinement which made him a welcome guest in *comme il faut* drawing-rooms in Dublin and London, even into the ragged, black-shirted 1930s.

Donoghue begins by pointing out that there remain critics who reject the common view that Yeats was a major poet (*Yeats*, p. 13). He thus reminds us that, for much of his career, Yeats lived on the fringe of literary celebrity rather than in the mainstream. Was Yeats an artist-*manqué*? Certainly many of the figures he mixed with might be consigned to that category: Symons and Beardsley and Pound perhaps; most of the *dramatis personae* of the 'Irish literary renaissance'; all of his colleagues in the Order of the Golden Dawn and Madame Blavatsky's groupings. In the fashion of these types (also perhaps in semi-conscious imitation of his early mentor and fellow Irishman, Wilde), Yeats deliberately adopted the manner and dress thought befitting a 'poet' and sought to conduct his life in a pattern consonant with the high romantic aspirations of *l'art pour l'art*. All this posturing had its reflection in his work. Donoghue speaks of 'an empire of feeling', styles which are 'imperial', words 'for the music of trumpets', a 'revival of oratory' (pp. 14–15). 'He wrote as if he were leading a charge of cavalry', the critic suggests; 'we recognize his style by its tone of command' (p. 21). Such descriptions no doubt would have thrilled Donoghue's Yeats as he liked to see himself. 'Yeats's poems draw an entire life ... toward a centre of power ... passion, energy, will, or imagination' (p. 16) – the area of 'kinship', in short, with Nietzsche. Indeed, echoing Nietzsche's famous formulation about 'slave' and 'master' morality, Donoghue sees the relation between Yeats's experience and his poetry as that of 'servant and master'. 'The reader, too, is kept in his place. .... The words are tokens of mastery.'

In reference to both Sade and Wilde, we have noted the phenomenon of a writer using his pen to try to *dominate* in a situation where he otherwise has no control. This is a tendency Donoghue's characterization suggests. The very self-consciousness of Yeats's erection of his authority, as described, implies latent insecurity, even defensiveness. 'Some poets deem themselves sufficient authority, but Yeats is of the other fellowship, of those poets who must join the visionary company and declare themselves in good standing with the muse before they can gather their talents about them' (p. 37). Thus he makes elaborate invocations of tradition, literary in *Ideas of Good and Evil*, occult in activities associated with Madame Blavatsky and the rest, political in the clamour for Irish independence. Only following all this can Yeats proclaim with full resonance what he is for and against: 'Poets and beautiful women are in league against "the noisy set / Of bankers, school-masters, and clergymen" '; the 'left-hand way' is opposed to conventional authority; ancient Celtic values are set up against modern Englishness. A cult of 'genius', in short, is posed against grey-faced Reason. Thus he plunges into the chaos of the new century in much the same spirit as the D. H. Lawrence who wanted to 'ride with a raw beef-steak for [his] saddle to see the red cock crow all over Christendom', yet on other occasions identified himself with a 'Druidical' Christ.[21]

'The signal merit of the dramatic as a way of life', Donoghue writes, 'is that it allows its adept to retain his chaos; it is as impartial in the employment of chaos as of order' (p. 40). Blakean excess is invited. Passion is 'holy'. Through magic and symbol, angels or devils may be called up from 'the Great Memory'. Happiness 'depends on the energy to assume the mask of some other self' (p. 43). God becomes 'a great dramatist', romantic art God's 'holy fire'; and the poet 'can make himself anew, become his own God'. In this world of change and struggle the poet, in short, has complete licence. 'Yeats delights in conflict because it is a mode of power', Donoghue says (p. 16) – meaning, one supposes, Yeats the poet, not the man, who found conflict quite problematic. 'His imagination loves to cause trouble, starting quarrels between one value and another' – meaning that the poet thrived on the synthesis of antitheses while the man, like other men, suffered from controversy and tried to avoid it. 'It is foolish, then, to recruit Yeats to a cause, [as] he will go over to the enemy, if only to prolong the quarrel' – a true-enough statement if one adds the qualification that Yeats usually went 'over to the enemy' less out of delight in tricky paradox than out of doubts about his own position or persona. In sum, Yeats the active demiurge whom Donoghue presents always is held in restraint by Yeats the Aeolian harp, a passive medium registering the 'wind of love and hate' apprehended in Shelley or the Sidhe. Thus the critic is at least as close to the mark when he depicts his subject not as proponent but presenter: 'As for truth itself,

[Yeats] believed that it could not be stated, could not be known, but it might be enacted.'

Nietzsche's description of the Great Man is advanced as approximating Yeats's heroic ideal:

> He knows he is incommunicable; he finds it tasteless to be familiar; and when one thinks of it, he usually is not. When not speaking to himself he wears a mask. He rather lies than tells the truth; it requires more spirit and will. There is a solitude within him that is inaccessible to praise or blame, his own justice that is beyond appeal.[22]

The solitariness and sphinx-like quality here do sound notes Yeats struck often enough. But Yeats himself was never a glib liar, and basic sincerity is reflected in his personae. Nor, given his precept that 'all dreams of the soul / End in a beautiful man's or woman's body'[23] and his lifelong fixation on a female figure of Destiny mixed of Salomé and Maud Gonne, will it do to suggest that Yeats was 'in love' like Nietzsche with the shadow-image of a warrior on the far horizon. Though he admired, as Donoghue argues, Nietzsche's encomium to 'live dangerously' and 'build your cities under Vesuvius', Yeats risked no revolutionary action in his own life.[24] Though his 'will' may be described in Nietzschean terms as 'thrusting forward again and again to become master over that which stands in its way', no sense of the happy 'yea-sayer' in these efforts predominates. Yeats's career may reflect Nietzsche's idea that 'the feeling of pleasure lies precisely in the dissatisfaction of the will, in the fact that the will is never satisfied unless it has opponents and resistances', but only if one establishes beforehand that no Sadean resonance is implied by the term 'pleasure'. In the end, the medallion can only be found for Yeats out beyond the western wave, where Forgael and Dectora sleep their eternal sleep of lovers in peace; and this is what divides Irish poet from German philosopher more than any other motif. In Nietzsche, an early Tristan-yearning was eclipsed by the dream of triumphing as Siegfried–Superman. In Yeats, the cult of the 'blond beast' would only ever attain the status of one of various wish-motifs in the mouth of one of the many characters in the play:

The stars had come so near me that I caught
Their sighing. It was praise of that great race
That would be haughty, mirthful, and white-bodied,
With a high head, and open hand, and how,
Laughing, it would take mastery of the world.[25]

Donoghue quotes this speech of Seanchan in *The King's Threshold* in order to underline that element in Yeats which is 'pure Nietzsche, the simultaneous presence of joy, triumph, and death, the hero laughing into the face of death' (p. 58). He goes on to argue that, in Yeats as in Nietzsche (and Blake and originally Heraclitus), 'energy replaces knowledge as "the good", action replaces concept'. Again, this is truer to Yeats's dream of the man-of-action than to that figure's opposite, the man-of-thought, which to the end the poet remained. Donoghue does show how in the later poems the urge to action becomes more insistent, even pathetic, so that the old-man persona in 'Lapis Lazuli' makes Lear-like promises to 'do such things, what they are yet I know not / But they shall be the terror of the earth' (p. 126); and he describes nicely how Yeats's feelings of frustration, even 'hysteria', lead to enthusiasm for imposition of order from above along the fascist lines. What this reveals in Yeats, though, more than a final 'liberation' into unalloyed Nietzschean faith in the ruthless, is a creative artist's perpetual need – especially in times of diminishing inspiration – for ever-more violent pendulum swings between order and chaos. Yeats was at last as at first an essentially bourgeois romantic with an essentially bourgeois, Shelleyan resistance to an overarching ideal of savage strength. So much may be apparent in Cuchulain's vision of his own afterlife in the final play Yeats wrote about that mythic hero, the poet's nearest realization of a personal version of the Superman:

There floats out there
The shape that I shall take when I am dead,
My soul's first shape, a soft feathery shape,
And is not that a strange shape for the soul
Of a great fighting-man?[26]

The precious inner vision – sweet, cirrus-cloud-flecked, fairytale in origin – may help motivate blind joy in power; but equally, in the end, it puts a mysterious limit upon it. Mixing with a never entirely extirpated attachment to civilization, this creates the fundamental disquiet – even fear – which Yeats experiences in observing the headlong flight of his culture toward strange, Nietzschean final conflicts. Yeats's ambivalence is nowhere better summed up than in that remarkable poem of 'antithetical revelation', 'The Second Coming', which – in spite of its quotation and anthologization in so many places – I repeat in its entirety here to emphasize its weird relevance to what was, and is, to follow:

> Turning and turning in the widening gyre
> The falcon cannot hear the falconer;
> Things fall apart; the centre cannot hold;
> Mere anarchy is loosed upon the world,
> The blood-dimmed tide is loosed, and everywhere
> The ceremony of innocence is drowned;
> The best lack all conviction, while the worst
> Are full of passionate intensity.
>
> Surely some revelation is at hand;
> Surely the Second Coming is at hand.
> The Second Coming! Hardly are those words out
> When a vast image of *Spiritus Mundi*
> Troubles my sight: somewhere in the sands of the
>   desert
> A shape with lion body and the head of a man,
> A gaze blank and pitiless as the sun,
> Is moving its slow thighs, while all about it
> Reel shadows of the indignant desert birds.
> The darkness drops again; but now I know
> That twenty centuries of stony sleep
> Were vexed to nightmare by a rocking cradle,
> And what rough beast, its hour come round at last,
> Slouches towards Bethlehem to be born?[27]

It is one thing to dream about power, quite another to achieve it. Nietzsche, as we have seen, had to content himself with visions of apotheosis after death, Yeats with being 'kicked upstairs' to the status of national monument in life. Neither came close to commanding the hosts of disciples or Sidhe summoned in imagination, nor with consistency mastering the self. Apart from inspired destruction and struggle, Nietzsche had virtually no system to offer for maintenance once *Wille zur Macht* had achieved its end. Yeats, by contrast, enunciated an elaborate system; but this paradoxically has the effect of negating any idea of one individual attaining lasting power: it posits an intricate cosmic determinism which even the most multifaceted personality would be lunatic to try to pose himself against. However, fortunately for the drama – comic or tragic as it may be – of history, fools rush in where angels fear to tread. One such was Yeats's fellow adept in, and later rival for the leadership of, the Order of the Golden Dawn, Aleister Crowley. In various letters, Yeats recalls the spectacle of this consummate eccentric appearing at the door of the London temple of that occult organization clad in full Highland regalia and brandishing daggers.[28] Yeats, Crowley claimed, had 'usurped' the mantle of the no-less eccentric founder of the Order, MacGregor Mathers, and he, Crowley, had come to take it back. With full support of the other adepts, Yeats 'won' in this bizarre struggle; Crowley was 'barred' from the temple; and ever after, when the subject would come up, the Scots 'magician' would maintain that the Irish poet had maliciously manipulated the other adepts' 'bourgeois' unease over his, Crowley's, 'experiments in sex-magick' in order to discredit a poet whom he, Yeats, knew had superior talent.[29] This implausible assertion would find echoes in statements which marginal 'artistic' characters who came under Crowley's spell periodically made: that he was the greatest poet, greatest genius, greatest so-on-and-so-forth of the day, or perhaps the age, or perhaps ever.[30] Evidence suggests that Crowley himself recognized the element of comedy in such extravagant claims – indeed, perhaps in all of his antics (his outlandish pro-German propaganda, written to feed himself in America during the First World War, indicates the fundamental, even redemptive, presence of the Trickster in him).[31] But this has been lost on all but the odd renegade among his followers. Likewise, it remains a muted note in the cacophony of his remarkable utterances. The fact is that, if 'Crowleyanity' has always seemed 'Crowley inanity' to the normal, healthy sceptic, it has been something else to the true believer; and the story of this occult heretic's system and following has a typological relevance to the larger phenomenon of lunatic group-movements, bound by leader messiahs and their dogmata, throughout the century.

Let me say here that it is beyond my competence to deal in depth with the occult; however, the case of Yeats shows that even within the 'safe' confines of literary criticism, the matter cannot be ignored. In life, if not art or academe, the activities of a 'prophet' such as Crowley may be more influential than conscience-racked truth-seekings of more tidy minds. Unlike Yeats, Crowley was a 'man of action'. His writings from a literary point of view are largely inconsiderable (in fact, nearly incomprehensible, for, if evil speaks its own language, in Crowley one often finds the purest mumbo-jumbo); and the obscurantist paeans of various disciple gospellers are of little help in pinning down significant aspects of the man. John Symonds's *The Great Beast* (1951) was the first really readable book about Crowley; Francis King's more recent biography is mordant, detached, sprightly but essentially sound; and, as I invoked Denis Donoghue's eccentric picture of Yeats to bring out one aspect of that ambivalent dreamer, so I depend on King to elucidate the facts about this spiritualist crank.

Crowley felt threatened artistically: from an early age he recognized that no sensible literary tradition was going to accept him as the 'great poet' he aspired to be. He was also *manqué* socially from the age of about thirty, by which time a reputation for sexual irregularity and sadistic personal relationships had begun to stick. Add to this the fact that he ran rapidly through all sources of money – his own and later those of whatever wealthy or even moderately well-to-do disciples appeared – and one establishes a picture of a fallen angel who was bound to a career outside all acceptable means to 'power' in a bourgeois society. Such a 'body of fate', as Yeats might call it, is determinative; and Crowley appears to have accepted with the kind of *amor fati* Nietzsche lauds that there was no way forward but the 'left-hand' one.[32] Expulsion from the Golden Dawn must have been a blow. However ripe (or rotten) for collaboration the Nazis might have imagined that group in its decadent later years,[33] it had a degree of reputability in the 1880s and 1890s: besides Yeats, its members included arts patron Annie Horniman; several notables who later went on to the Fabian Society and other more public-spirited organizations; and even Wilde's wife, until her husband (one eye always cocked towards reputation) suggested that perhaps it wasn't a highly creditable attachment.[34] However, realizing from the first that – as Symonds remarks – 'a magician needs an order as a politician needs a party',[35] Crowley proceeded undaunted to collect neophyte adepts around him. In some ways, his method might be seen as an application of Wilde's 'anarchic' ideal of Individualism through Joy but without slaves (though, as stated, he lived off the money of those he dominated, and of course the phenomenon of discipleship always implies a kind of willing servitude); also manipulation of the need Marcuse defends for 'disturbed' individuals to achieve 'liberation' through the activities of antinomian groups. At the least, Crowley's career proves Wilde's assertion that the Pain of 'dropping out' no longer had to be solitary. His oscillation between retraction into rhetoric and thrusting-out into ritual interrelations suggests Fourier's 'sudden passage from incoherence to social combination'. It also brings to mind the constant pendulum swing between philosophizing and fucking of one of Sade's libertines.

In association with his first important disciple, Victor Neuberg, Crowley performed experiments in astral projection (King, *Magical World*, p. 46). He believed that one could 'rise on planes' through a form of meditation inducing hallucination. An 'ecstasy' could be attained in which one could experience 'past lives' and the 'eternal life of the soul' before wafting off into an 'ultimate ocean of Nirvana'. (Among his own 'past lives' and precursors, Crowley would later include Mahomet, Luther, Alexander VI Borgia, Christian Rosenkreuz, Adam Weishaupt, who founded the Illuminati, Cagliostro, Éliphas Lévi, a miserable boy who hanged himself, a wickedly satanic Dutchman, and a peasant adventurer in Poland whose beloved would perform sadistic rites on a burgomaster while he watched – p. 122). In their own interpretation of the relation between the Hindu god Shiva and his Shakti, master and disciple would perform rites of sodomy and fellatio designed to bring 'intelligence and spirit' into embrace with 'mindless universal energy'. During one of these rites performed *al fresco* on a trip to Algeria, Crowley drew some 'words of power' in the sand and shortly became possessed, in a weird anticipation of Yeats's vision of a monster–god stirring to life in the desert,[36] by the obscure deity Chronozon, an inhabitant of the Abyss representing (as Crowley would elucidate later) 'Dispersion'. Through a frenzy of blaspheming, a sort of epileptic fit of naked cavorting, and sudden pranksterish acts of violence, Chronozon made his presence apparent to the credulous Neuberg. 'Crowley', King comments, 'became the first magician in occult history to offer his body to an evil manifestation' (p. 58). After the rite, magician revealed to adept that, whereas before he had thought that sex was 'not bad', now he realized that it could be 'positively helpful'. This was a convenient *aperçu*. Whatever mystical secrets sex might have vouchsafed him, it is clear that it provided Crowley with his most dependable method of scrambling the egos of followers and establishing authority over them.

Back in London, armed with the new powers Chronozon had bestowed, Crowley conducted satanic versions of Yeats's rarefied theatrical *soirées*. Into darkened rooms referred to as 'temples', personally invited audiences would be ushered. After a suitable period for sniffing incense, 'experiencing' silence, and preparing the soul for 'ecstasy', the performances would begin. They involved free-form dancing, god-invocation, macabre violin-playing, tom-tom thumping in a weird heartbeat rhythm, and poetic incantation, all washed down with draughts from a 'loving cup' or 'grail' of an 'elixir' concocted of fruit juices, alcohol, alkaloids of opium and mescal buttons (these Crowley had discovered on an early trip to Mexico and regarded as 'sacramental' for the rest of his life). The point of all this was to 'rend away the veil' and 'show there is no God' and that 'man can do as he likes', a message delivered in the slow monotonous chant of the high priest (Crowley) once a suitably Dionysian atmosphere had been reached:

'There is no good. Evil is good. Blessed be the Principle of Evil. All hail, Prince of the World, to whom even God Himself has given dominion . . . .' [A less-than-sympathetic viewer reports on the proceedings:] Men and women danced about, leaping and swaying to the whining of infernal and discordant music. They sang obscene words set to hymn tunes and gibbered unintelligible jargon. [Perhaps what Swedenborg called 'infernal language' and Berlioz uses to magnificent effect in a chorus of demons at the end of *The*

Damnation of Faust, or what Crowley described on occasion
as 'Enochian language – the lost tongue of Atlantis.'[37]]
Women tore their bodices; some partially disrobed. One fair
worshipper, seizing upon the high priest's dagger, wounded
herself in the breasts. At this all seemed to go madder than
ever.[38]

Such diabolical 'happenings', to borrow a term from a later
era, would be repeated in various permutations throughout
Crowley's career, whenever he could gather sufficient celebrants
together. His ability to do this seemed to flag during the lean
years of the 1910s, mostly spent in America; yet Crowley's
faith in himself (or his spirits) remained remarkably high. By
the twenties, he had established himself with the two 'Scarlet
Women' (the name he gave to his main female sex-partners of
the moment) in the 'Abbey of Thelema' in Sicily (an
establishment whose Klingsorian resonances suggest to occult
writer Trevor Ravenscroft resurrection of the tradition of the
wicked, Sicily-based seducer of lost Crusaders, the Landulf of
Capua[39]). Here Crowley entertained a stream of 'pilgrims',
including minor Hollywood actresses and London literati,
who participated in his 'Gnostic black mass', which now
incorporated ingestion of heroin, cocaine, strychnine, ether,
brandy, blood, a new 'sacred elixir' mixed of the fluids of male
and female orgasm (the latter best at time of menstruation),
and on rare occasion even faeces.[40] Drugs were now vying with
sex as the principal agency by which Crowley sought to
engender 'energized enthusiasm'; and, while his method in
this respect directly anticipates certain 'Southern Californian'
mass cultural practices in the 1960s and 1970s, it also recalls
the 'poisoned' pastilles and obscene predilections of Sade.
Various proposed acts of Crowley's were blatantly Sadean:
'the supreme act of sexual magic involved the rape, ritual
murder and dissection into nine pieces of the body of a young
girl', the pieces to then be 'offered to the gods' (p. 85). On the
other hand, the glorification of the Sun (the 'great god'), the
phallus (its 'vice-regent on Earth'), the sex act, and the Great
Goddess force beyond all (to be apprehended through mental
masturbation) have more in common with a large body of
'neo-pagan' notions typical of the *Zeitgeist* of Crowley's period
and often associated with D. H. Lawrence.

Like Lawrence and other *avant-garde emigrés*, Crowley also
touched base in Paris of the 1920s. There he dabbled with
the idea of starting a newspaper with Frank Harris, erstwhile
sex memoirist and biographer of Wilde. This association
provided him with one of many occasions to express his view
of his own modest place in the great scheme of things:

> I am destined to bring to Earth the Formula of the New
> Aeon, the basic Word in which Mankind will work for
> the next 2000 years or so – the word 'Do what thou wilt' . . . .
> You must take me seriously . . . .
> To put it crudely, Industrial-Capitalism is heading for a
> cataract. The only alternative yet is Bolshevism, which won't
> do either.
> Now, the Law of Thelema offers a third way. These last
> years I have been training various people to act as a Brain
> for the human race.   (p. 148)

Even as eccentric a character as Harris could see plainly
enough reason to dismiss Crowley as dotty. Crowley, however,
carried on, dauntless. When the *Express* newspapers attacked
him, he proposed to sue Lord Beaverbrook for libel – this not
out of any hope of success, merely to gain publicity. Notoriety
Crowley did increasingly enjoy. His return to London was
marked, as once before, by a trial which degenerated into an
inquisition about his morals. His book *Diary of a Drug Fiend*
(1922) was compared to *Ulysses* for 'lubricity and obscenity'
and labelled 'a book for burning'.[41] Rumours spread that he
had instigated, through magic or otherwise, the injury, mental
breakdown or even death of various apostates and opponents.
Meanwhile, on returning to Sicily, he found that the Mussolini
government had put into process measures to deport him and
his retinue.

Much of the following decade Crowley spent in Germany.
There he was variously elevated to and dismissed from
positions of power in branches of the indigenous occult
movement, the A∴A∴, the Fraternis Saturni, and notably an
offshoot of Rosicrucianism called the Order of Oriental
Templars (OTO), a 'sanctuary of the Gnosis' which regarded
Crowley's *Book of the Law* as 'reconstructing a primitive world

order which suggests the blackest days of Atlantis' (p. 150) and had anticipated him in enunciating grades of initiation through 'sex-magick' (gradations which, *sans* the sexual aspect, are strikingly similar to contemporary Scientology's 'Operating Thetan' system, with its highest grade, 'free' or 'clear', of 'OT 8'). Other Crowley sects popped up. One was run by a woman who went on to admire Hitler, describing him as her 'magical son' and an obvious student of Crowley's *Book of the Law* (p. 161). This assertion seems all the more improbable when one considers the element of licentious hedonism in Crowley's message. Still, taking the cue from it, King has occasion to discover 'significant similarities between the doctrines of Crowley and Hitler. . . . Both men were drawing upon the demonic emotional forces which took refuge in the unconscious during the high noon of European rationalism' (p. 162). Be that as it may, the Nazis, whether out of antipathy for his decadence (the stated reason) or (as some dedicated Crowleyans might wish to claim) fear of a rival aspirant to universal occult domination, banned Crowley at the same time as they snuffed the candle on the OTO and A ∴ A ∴ and began their extirpation of Freemasonry.

Meanwhile, though none too successful in his attempt to 'conquer' America in the 1910s, Crowley was now working to effect there through a growing number of disciples. These particularly (and fittingly) seemed to aggregate on the West Coast. Unfortunately, at such a distance they tended eventually to slip beyond the Master's control. Thus the 'genius from Cal Tech [California Institute of Technology]' who became head of the 'church' in America at Crowley's death (in 1947, of cardiac arrest, an old man retired to the south coast of England, bronchitic and 'bored') transmitted naïvely much of the 'secret knowledge' and method of initiation to a watchful young frequenter of introductory *séances* whom King dares only to call 'Frater H' ('he has now found fame in another sphere') but a knowledgeable reader will not fail to recognize as L. Ron Hubbard,[42] founder of the 'church' of Scientology (pp. 164–6). After this indiscretion, the 'genius' went on to discredit himself with all but the lunatic fringe by producing a *Manifesto of the Anti-Christ*, which declared war on 'all authority that is not based on courage and manhood', demanded an end to 'the authority of lying priests, conniving judges, blackmailing police', cursed all restriction, called for an end to 'conscription, compulsion, regimentation, and the tyranny of false laws', and proposed to spread Crowley's ideas to all men until 'in his law I shall conquer the world' (p. 171). Such extremism overtook Crowleyanity in America in the 1960s. Another enthusiast, the 'discontent wife of a philosophy professor at the University of Southern California', set up her own cult through the 'Eye of Horus' bookstore, recruiting students and drop-outs, and conducted 'sex-magick' operations using violence and ample bathings of chicken blood. Some of these sessions were allegedly attended by Charles Manson. All of them ended in June 1969 (two months before the Manson murders) after a fire broke out in a replica of the Abbey of Thelema in the California desert (Death Valley was the nearby locus of the Manson family's principal coven). In this conflagration, various rare Crowley manuscripts were destroyed. Afterwards, a child who reputedly started the fire was so maliciously abused that the woman and her followers were forced to flee to Mexico in order to avoid arrest (pp. 185–7).

Today 'Crowleyanity' lives on, in Germany, Switzerland and England as well as America, in isolated covens of diminishing potence and size since the wave of occult revivalism crested fifteen-odd years ago. The received view is that the sect's founder was a 'false messiah', to use Symonds's gentle formulation, or a 'satanic occultist', to use Mario Praz's harsher one.[43] But there are those who still subscribe to Crowley's own claim that he was a great 'prophet of a New Age'; and, by the end of his narrative, King is sufficiently under the spell to propose that '*The Book of the Law* is a more accurate prophecy of the century than Wells or Shaw' and that Crowley himself was 'a man in whom good and evil were as mutually existent, and as closely blended, as in the human race itself' (p. 169).

Probably only by comparison to that sum of 4000 million parts can a megalomaniac be viewed favourably: certainly in comparison to the overwhelming number of individual humans, Crowley must seem a kind of demon, however fascinating. In the end, he depended on a personal magnetism of a kind evidently lacking in our other two, book-bound 'dreamers-on-power'. King repeats accounts of how Crowley's eyes could become black pupils of stony, menacing intensity (p. 74); how his body and face could seem to change shape and character altogether to perceptors subject to his spell; how by powers of concentration and perhaps disguised hypnosis he could make a complete stranger trip and fall over in the street; how as a man of nearly sixty he made love to a nineteen-year-old new Scarlet Woman forty-seven times in as many days, blaming the smallness of the number on a regimen of furious travel back and forth across Europe (p. 155); how an even older Crowley was approached by yet another nineteen-year-old begging to have his child (his unflagging appeal to women he put down to his smell, 'Ruthvah, the perfume of immortality', made up of three parts civet, two parts musk, and one part ambergris) and how he thus allowed one of his several entirely unthought-about offspring, Aleister Ataturk, to come into the world (p. 158). Bald as a crystal ball, paunchy yet emaciated in upper musculature, with rotting teeth and unwashed dirt as often as not on his hands,[44] this alternately whirling and immobile dervish in caftan and beads could by some truly 'occult' personal magnetism speak to suppressed impulses in a peculiar strain of lost soul. In 'liberating' this type into new realms of amorality, Crowley was a precursor. Unfortunately, as is often the case with charismatic upper-class eccentrics, many whom he 'precursed' would prove insufficiently civilized to see the degree to which it may all have been a species of cosmic joke.

7 Hitler

Whereas Nietzsche yearns for a kind of self-glorification as the warrior on the far horizon and Yeats has a romantic wish vision of Forgael and Dectora beyond the western wave, Hitler's 'medallion' is an image of himself as hero protecting the abstraction of a whole nation, the 'mystical concept' of *ein Deutsches Volk*. In tandem with this comes the remarkable shadow-image of the Jew, whose ruthless megalomania as described in *Mein Kampf* represents not only what 'the hero' fears as directly inimical to his 'beloved', but also, paradoxically, the perverse ideal into which he feels Nietzscheanly compelled to forge his own personality in order to defend 'her'. For Hitler, an impression of Jewish hegemony becomes a satanic programme for power, coeval in status with Wagnerian staging and quasi-religious prescriptions on how to regenerate the race. The 'hero' pursues power with the vengeful energy of one whose adolescent dream of being a painter, and later an architect, has been frustrated by what appears to him a hostile, 'decadent', Jewish-dominated establishment; and who, thus fallen from a kind of bohemianism acceptable to his bourgeois origins, has inhabited a world of proletarian rancour, where the grey existence of dosshouse and work-gang is only enlivened by bright political slogans painted on walls, sensational pamphlets, and conspiracy-theory arguments to be 'won' by whoever can harangue the longest and most vehemently. Add to this the boyhood diet of Karl May novels about Indian struggles in the Wild West, the Wagner idolatry, and the exposure to racist occultism via turn-of-the-century Viennese cranks such as Lanz von Liebenfels, and one begins to gather the elements contributing to the alternately fanatical and stoic illusion of mastery achieved by the man most often advanced as the archetype of 'evil genius' in our time.[1]

Too much of what we 'know' about Hitler is disparaging hearsay. This is perhaps because the man proved a disaster not only to those whom he opposed but also to those with whom he appeared to be in some kind of sympathy. German nationalism and Prussian militarism were crushed by him; the reputation of German 'culture' and romanticism was debased. Socialism as an ideal was put into question by his 'nationalist' version of it, fascism (not after all his original concept) thoroughly discredited. Neo-Gnosticism became identified with its Manichaean dark half in part because of him; the Roman Catholic Church was tarnished by its apparent non-opposition; sects as disparate as Lutheranism and Theosophy were tainted by association; and any legitimate basis there may have been for ethical anti-Semitism in the period was incinerated with the bodies in the concentration camps. What Hitler proposed was a universal hierarchical order ruled by blood, strength and valour; what he produced was precisely what he opposed – a world dominated by rival 'materialisms' of capitalism and communism, becoming increasingly 'mongrelized', anarchic and spiritually impoverished, and having no anagogical 'third force' of potence to guide it otherwise.[2] If some positive aspects of the present-day health-and-body cult reflect unintentionally precepts of 'strength through joy', the predominant legacy of the Nazis to the post-war world must seem negative: various techniques of propaganda by states and parties; a more pervasive acceptance of the idea that the way of the world is ruthlessness.

Given all this, it is not hard to see why Hitler has been viewed generally as a devil and 'admired' only by those with a taste for antinomian sensation, thus that most of what is written about him continued to be marred by obfuscatory prejudice. The most damning charge advanced to discourage growth of Hitler idolatry may be that the man was 'banal': a sort of Austrian Richard Nixon: bourgeois, socially uncomfortable, flatulent, insecure.[3] This characterization is familiar enough and has a truth (a reading of *Mein Kampf* reveals the 'genius' to be about as great a master of literary style as the author of *Six Crises*); but at the same time, it is misleading. As there were several Nietzsches, so there are many Hitlers. If the mild-mannered professor contained the germ of the new Prometheus, so this 'evil' leader conjured out of Teutonic 'banality'[4] contains flashes of the Son of Light. What we are concerned about here is how a superficially unlikely, rather

wimpish young man travelled the road from art to messianism
to crime. But first, in consideration of the fact that we have
reached this point directly from Crowley, it seems appropriate
to say a few words about the matrix of the occult which has
increasingly been argued to have provided a mythic context
for the Hitler 'phenomenon'. I depend here on Jean-Michel
Angebert's *The Occult and the Third Reich*, subtitled 'The
Mystical Origins of Nazism and the Search for the Holy
Grail'.[5] Studies of this sort are dangerous ground for sound
academic analysts to tread on; however, as with Yeats, the
well-known interests of many Nazis make at least a brief sortie
towards the territory unavoidable. Thus, trying not to perform
the sort of dance on the head of a pin which characterized a
recent bestseller, *The Holy Blood and the Holy Grail*, I shall
summarize Angebert's argument.

Nazism, it is contended, is 'the most recent manifestation of a
militant neo-paganism locked in a death-struggle with its arch-
enemy, traditional Christianity' (p. x). It is also a selective
resurrection of traditional Western Christian heresy, for
convenience labelled 'Gnosticism', locked in a similar struggle
with 'the Jewish faith, which wants to use the mysteries of
integral knowledge for its own advancement' (p. 5) and, to a
lesser extent, with 'white magic' strands of the 'great tradition'
of the occult, such as Rudolf Steiner's Anthroposophy and
international Freemasonry. As defined, Nazism could, and did
to many, appear as a martial order defending the central body
of older, suppressed Indo-European values against authority
(an-archy) as invested in the liberal, materialistic institutions
of the modern West. As such, it could, and did, appear to
provide an historical and quasi-religious justification and
binding-force for a wide-ranging variety of antinomian impulses
as inherent and eternal in the character of group-man as in
that of the 'disturbed' individual.

The aspiration to create a new, hard race of Supermen had
only been restated by Nietzsche, Angebert points out (pp. 119–
29). The Nordic pagan origins of the idea had been resurrected
by Wagner, particularly in the *Ring*, with its glorification of
the rise of the sun-god–hero Siegfried and its final battle of the
forces of good and evil leading to *Götterdämmerung* (pp. 130–

55). In Wagner's opus, especially the 'fifth part of the *Ring*', *Parsifal*, are also embedded 'secrets' of the Gnostic 'wisdom', which is the less obvious but, to analysts such as Angebert, more potent strand of covert tradition contributing to the Nazi sense of mission. Catharism is the Gnostic manifestation the French occultist wants to concentrate on; but that twelfth-century and thirteenth-century heresy, geographically concentrated in the land of the troubadours, Aquitaine, and of their German counterparts, the *Minnesänger*, in southern Germany, in turn derives from a body of ideas going back to the origins of all Indo-European religion in Zoroaster (pp. 69–88). The Provençal *gay saber* (Nietzsche's 'Gaya Scienza') had its roots thus in the struggle between Ahura Mazda and Ahriman, the principles of light and darkness, good and evil, first enunciated about 4500 BC by the Aryan holy hermit on his mountaintop, companioned only by his emblematic eagle, from whom Nietzsche takes the title of his great work. Through various incarnations, including the Middle Eastern cult of Mithras, the doctrines of the Essenes, the Johannine gospel, the heresy of Manes, who regarded Christ as 'the Sun of this world', the Paulician and Bogomil heresies (the latter centring in Bulgaria and providing, according to Gibbon, the origin of our term of opprobium 'bugger'[6]), Zoroastrian ideas passed to the West, where they merged with indigenous mysticism originating in the cults of Isis and Osiris in Egypt and passing through metamorphoses at the hands of the 'great initiates', Orpheus, Plato, Pythagoras and others, and also incorporating elements of the other great, ancient Indo-European religions, Hinduism and Brahmanism, which were themselves in other ways derivative from the same 'prehistoric' body of cosmological ideas.

Historians concerned to discover occult tradition behind otherwise apparently unprecedented movements are apt to pile Pelion on Ossa: 'proving' the point becomes less a matter of specific evidence than of quantity of suggestion. Still it is clear that, whether Angebert's 'great tradition' actually gave birth to the movement or merely provided a range of suggestions and symbols after the fact, it became a significant feature of Nazi personality. In the Cathars above all (also their supposed heirs, the Knights Templar), Hitler in particular could find sympathetic motifs of sexual purity, male brotherhood, vegetarianism, insurgence against Roman (transposed to liberal) hegemony and corruption, anti-materialism, worship of the Sun (itself a legacy, according to Angebert, derived in part from the Druids), mystical meditation, distaste for this world, aristocratic detachment, elitist communion in high places (Eagle's Nest–Montsalvat), secrecy, initiation, love of animals (related to theories of metempsychosis), the cult of blood (the central relic of the Grail, whose Christian significance overlays a pagan tradition of the cup which catches the blood of the sacrificial bull), the nobility of suicide or *endura*, the tradition of involvement in holy war against Semites (the Crusades), and most of all the legacy of mass martyrdom (the slaughter of all remaining known heretics by the pope's armies in league with the king of France in the first half of the thirteenth century) (pp. 23–39). Angebert also recognizes the Cathar tripartite division of pures, adepts and mass in the tripartite hierarchical structure of the Nazi state into leaders, party and people (pp. 200–6). Both in turn he sees as application of time-honoured pyramidical structurings of occult organizations, deriving originally, as stated, from the mysteries of Egypt. In addition, he finds in the non-metropolitan (Rome–Paris) orientation of Catharism common ground with the anti-urban element in Nazism and in the 'fixed' feudal structure of Cathar society, with its mystical value put on such crafts as weaving and pottery, a link-up with the nostalgia for medieval tripartite division of craft (master, journeyman, apprentice) in Nazi industrial practice.

Further behind all this stand the legends of a 'lost world', either Hyperborea or Atlantis (pp. 57–65), which can be found in such disparate sources as Plato's *Timaeus* and the Tibetan *Book of the Dead* (cf. the importance of classical Greece and the Himalayan plateau, among other places, in Nazi geographical metaphysics). Hyperborea, whose capital was Thule, was situated, so mythological tradition states, in the ice lands of the North Atlantic, and its inhabitants were harsh stoical giants – prehistoric versions, as it were, of Nietzsche's Supermen. Atlantis, situated in the middle of the ocean which bears its name, was the first and greatest civilization of science and bureaucratic order; also the first to fall because of that ubiquitous bugaboo, 'decadence'. The Nazis, so Angebert would have it (I use irony here to re-emphasize the need for caution, though what we know of the intentions of Himmler, for instance,[7] suggests that no smoke has been sent up without fire), sought, as did various occult groupings of the time and the past, to find modern ways of breathing new life into the race of Hyperborea and civilization of Atlantis – an aspiration sufficiently mesmerizing yet vague as to seem to justify a wide range of experiments in eugenics, manipulation of 'culture', and police-state practices. The immediate connection between Nazism and all this apparently innocuous lore is identified as the Thule Society, one of numerous occult–political groupings which flourished in Germany, particularly Munich, after the 1918 defeat, and which numbered among its members or associates Dietrich Eckart, Anton Drexler, Hans Frank, Rudolf Hess, Hitler himself, Alfred Rosenberg, and others prominent in the subsequent creation and rise of the National Socialist German Workers Party (pp. 163–70).

The Thule Society had been founded by 'a strange character named Baron von Sebottendorf' in 1912 to continue the tradition of racist German occultism begun perhaps with the Illuminati in the eighteenth century but certainly established with the appearance of the Vril Society, or Lodge of Light (a group which had ties with Theosophy and the Order of the Golden Dawn), in the latter half of the nineteenth. Sebottendorf had declared the Society's goal to be the usual occult one of 'rediscovering the thread of lost knowledge', or *gnosis*. But from the first this was more specifically defined as an attempt to 'reconstitute, page by page, the Great Book of Aryan Mythology'. Work towards this goal had been begun by the Rosicrucians, alchemists and early Freemasons (the racist ones who rejected the Kabala). Now, however, Sebottendorf declared, it had to be approached with a new fanaticism, because

A vast organization of disbelief, of monstrous proportions, intends to bend to its will the civilized world. The religious institutions have been so gravely weakened that they are not capable of pulling themselves together, let alone putting up a united front. If spiritual leaders do not come forth in the West, chaos may bring down everything into the abyss. (pp. 166–7)

Sebottendorf's 'vast organization of disbelief' is, of course, that international materialist 'conspiracy' which Hitler would reduce simply to *Jew*. The Thule Society was, accordingly, formed only by German males able to demonstrate purity of blood (women were admitted solely as 'auxiliaries'). Its logo, shortly to be adopted by the Party, was 'the swastika with the symbol of the god Wotan'. The significance of this Sebottendorf conveyed in a speech given two days before the 'betrayal' of the 1918 armistice:

> I intend to commit the *Thule Gesellschaft* to this combat [against the 'betrayers', socialists and Jews], as long as I shall hold the Iron Hammer. . . . I swear it on this swastika, on this sign which for us is sacred, in order that you hear it, O triumphant Sun! And I shall keep my faith with you. Have confidence in me as I have in you. . . . Our God is the father of battle and his rune is that of the eagle . . . which is the symbol of the Aryans. And to call attention to the fiery-nature of the eagle, he will be shown in red. . . . Such is our symbol, the red eagle who reminds us that we must pass through death in order to live again. (p. 169)

Into this sort of Grail Order the young Hitler was ushered, the 'paraclete' whom a range of thinkers-*manqué*, shadow Nietzsches and Crowleys, imagined was 'the only man possessing the wherewithal for rousing Germany from its lethargic sleep'. Cast as the hero by those who subscribed for mystical reasons to a *Führer-Prinzip*, young Siegfried–Parsifal was set up from the first to throw off the authority of what Angebert calls his 'unknown masters' (these men? Liebenfels? Wagner? the Tibetan monks later said to be imported to Berlin?) once he was able to imagine the full force of all necessary 'occult' power concentrated within his individual, specially sanctified personality. Angebert claims that Hitler did this in the later 1920s and 1930s and, as a result, increasingly fell prey to the tug of the Klingsorian half of the occult antipodes: black magic. Whether or not this is so, it is clear that the 'left-hand' tradition was a significant part of the *Zeitgeist* which allowed him to reach power and one of the effective tools he was able to manipulate to maintain his position there. (This was perhaps even more true of a fellow-

traveller such as Hess, whose status as Deputy *Führer* and
designated successor is said to have had to do with his high
level of 'initiation' – p. 172). If Hitler finally sought to demote
this strain of antinomianism in his entourage, it was not with
the overtness that he did away with, for instance, the
homosexual cult around Ernst Röhm. It is true that
industrialists became closer to him in the 1930s and military
men during the war, and that the conscious-world manipulator
Goebbels, *aparatchik* Bormann and technocrat Speer were his
most-favoured cronies by the end. But even after Hess
undertook his bizarre Grail-seeking peace-mission to Britain
and was declared insane, no purge of occult undercurrents in
the movement took place. Indeed, Himmler was busy creating
for himself and a new inner elite shadow-status as first knights
of the Grail.

Hitler's account of his own early development, *A Reckoning*, the
first volume of *Mein Kampf*, superficially takes the structure of
a *Bildungsroman* of the period – Hamsun's *Hunger* and Joyce's
Portrait of the Artist as a Young Man spring to mind – and thus
indicates his bourgeois origins and early education. But a swift
falling-off in every chapter towards polemical digression, indeed
ranting, impresses the reader even more with the fact of the
young man's descent into what a working-class writer of the
period – Jack London is a fine example – might most fear and
avoid: the urban proletarian 'abyss'. The book must modify
anyone's notion that young Hitler was poorly read. References
to Schopenhauer and obvious gleanings from Nietzsche combine
with evidence of study of less exalted thinkers fashionable at
the turn of the century to suggest that he shared in the
general attitude that any young man who wanted to rise
above the ruck had to 'light out after knowledge with a club',
as London had put it, and that – for the 'hero' – eclectic self-
education was ideal. Like Stephen Dedalus (whom Joyce
originally called 'Stephen Hero'), Hitler early on proposes to
'be his own father'. Respect and contempt for the order-loving
civil servant become in turn respect and contempt for the
proletarian type who supplants him as the figure of male
strength the young 'hero' must confront and best. After his
parents' death and his failures as student and artist in

Vienna, Hitler proposes to 'leap into this new world [of proletarian labour], with both feet, and fight my way through'.[8] Here, however, he finds the typical development a horror like that which London had reported in *The People of the Abyss*; and he describes it in similar terms:

> Now he walks the streets hungry; often he pawns and sells his last possessions; his clothing becomes more and more wretched; and thus he sinks into external surroundings which, on top of his physical misfortune, also poison his soul. ... And so this man, who was formerly so hard-working, grows lax in his whole view of life and gradually becomes the instrument of those who use him only for their own base advantage. (*Mein Kampf*, p. 25)

Those who 'use him', in Hitler's view, are not only the capitalist masters but also the social-democratic agitators; for, if Hitler's picture of these 'unfortunate victims of bad conditions' is almost identical to London's, his solution is hardly a form of Christian socialism. Explanation for this must circle back to the fact that Hitler was a bourgeois fallen without apparent means of escape into the very 'trap' which London, a proletarian, had consciously pulled himself up from. As a workman, London had been in his element; Hitler by contrast, on the one occasion he describes of actually 'leaping in with both feet' and joining a work party, comes across as, at best, an inspired misfit and, at worst, a querulous wimp:

> Our discussions at work were often very heated. I argued back, from day to day better informed than my antagonists concerning their own [socialist] knowledge, until one day they made use of the weapon which most readily conquers reason: terror and violence. A few of the spokesmen on the opposing side forced me either to leave the building at once or be thrown off the scaffolding. Since I was alone and resistance seemed hopeless, I preferred, richer by one experience, to follow the former counsel. (p. 38)

It cannot have been lost on Hitler subconsciously, anymore than the reader, that this painfully vulnerable youth had proved unable to meet his 'mates' on the time-honoured, working-class male ground of *physical* self-expression; and his violent resistance to their demand that he join their union suggests the petulance of psychological hurt as well as precociously held, 'granite-hard' conviction. Intellectual contempt and patronization of the working classes mask feelings of inferiority and threat. Boasts of 'superior' ability to 'see through socialist thought-processes' and discover the manipulating hand of the Jew behind all are part of compensatory efforts to establish his own equal 'strength'. Nor can Hitler's later fanatical admiration for physical toughness be unrelated to an old twinge of desire to have in his unimpressive, bourgeois frame just those attributes which hostile workmen were able to flex against him. Hitler's peculiar version of the cult of the blond beast must be seen in this light. His undertaking to imitate the dark, Machiavellian ways he ascribes to the 'beast's' opposite and historical enemy, the Jew, is a means of setting himself up to dominate these strong men he had secretly admired but whose admiration he had not been able to earn.

As he describes it in *A Reckoning*, Hitler went through two principal modes of 'initiation'. The first was mental and took place on these 'mean streets' of Vienna: he became, in his estimation, an exceptional observer of men – specifically, of the interaction between dominated and dominator, Nietzsche's 'slaves' and 'masters'. The second was part physical and part moral and took place in the trenches of France, where he felt for the first time comfortable male comradeship, faith in his own will, and the anagogical power of a 'higher ideal':

> The Goddess of Destiny begins to weigh peoples according to the truth and steadfastness of their convictions. . . . I had so often sung '*Deutschland über Alles*' and shouted '*Heil*' at the top of my lungs, that it seemed to me almost a belated act of grace to be allowed to stand as a witness in the divine court of the eternal judge and proclaim the sincerity of this conviction. . . . Now began the most unforgettable time of my earthly existence. Compared to the events of this gigantic struggle, everything past receded into shallow nothingness. (pp. 149–50)

But, as the unspeakable slog through the trenches drags on,

the romance . . . . had been replaced by horror. The
enthusiasm was gradually cooled and the exuberant joy was
stifled by mortal fear. The time came when every man had
to struggle between the instinct of self-preservation and the
admonitions of duty. I, too, was not spared by this struggle.
Always when Death was on the hunt, a vague something
tried to revolt, strove to represent itself to the weak body as
reason, yet it was only cowardice. . . . Yet the more this
voice admonished one to caution, the louder and more
insistent its lures, the sharper resistance grew until at last,
after a long inner struggle, the consciousness of duty emerged
victorious. . . . At last my will was undisputed master. . . . I
was now calm and determined. And this was enduring.
Now Fate could bring on the ultimate tests without my
nerves shattering or my reason failing.   (pp. 151–2)

The self-respect gained in such 'initiations' hardens the
instinctive, self-defensive contempt for all external forms of
authority, save the handful of abstractions about blood, valour
and strength the experience of war has vouchsafed. Now
German politicians join Viennese journalists and bankers,
socialists and decadent proletarians against whom the younger
man had developed a rationale of animosity. In the shattered,
chaotic post-war homeland, public life offers no reverable
masters. The demobbed soldier, feeling no more a 'hero' than
Vietnam veterans would in America five decades later, prowls
the streets of brawling 'Red' Munich with the cynicism of
some character out of Brecht (p. 186). Against his ideals of
Wagnerian culture, *Deutschland über Alles*, and the great Nordic
race, real Germany seems to be peopled by sheep being led
around by clever propaganda. The *Volk*, he declares, lacks
perspicacity, is guided by emotions, and may be swayed by
simple fundamental principles, 'love or hate, right or wrong,
truth or lie, never half way this and half way that, never
partially, or that kind of thing', reiterated over and over with
dramatic emphasis and 'unflagging attention' (p. 167). From a
lecture of Gottfried Feder's, he takes one useful slogan: 'against
international capital' (p. 194). From the vilification of
Ludendorff by the 'Jewish' press, he reminds himself of the
evil fact that 'something of even the most insolent lie will
always remain and stick' (p. 211). From the scurrying of mice

for crumbs on the floor of his cell-like barrack room, he remembers the importance of fear of hunger and poverty in stirring up fight in the small-town bourgeois (p. 199). Money is the great anxiety in an era of hyperinflation: thus, he plans to play on instinctive reactions against 'money as god' and 'the economization of the nation' (p. 213). Nature is better than civilization. 'Half-education' and journalism, which is 'education continued in adulthood' (p. 219), have duped the people and led them away from 'instinct' and 'the fundamental necessity of Nature's rule', which is 'these laws of eternal fight and upward struggle' (p. 223). From German peasant stock and early marriages based on 'emotion' rather than 'financial expediency' let a new flowering of the race begin (p. 225). A 'Greek' model of healthy mind in healthy body must be engendered, as 'the first reason for personal cowardice lies in physical weakness' (p. 230). The Jewish–urban plagues of syphilis and tuberculosis must be stopped; so too must the hideous trap of prostitution. 'A struggle against the poisoning of the soul must begin', for 'our whole public life today is like a hothouse for sexual ideas and stimulations' (p. 231), these inculcated into the mass mind by pornography, decadent art-forms such as Cubism and Dadaism (p. 235), and criticism which 'mocks' truly fine work and renders the mass 'uncertain in judgment of good and bad' (p. 239).

In line with his belief in the need for single, simple reductive ideas and the efficacy of the bold lie, Hitler lays all these horrors of modern life at the doorstep of the Jew. This Machiavellian manipulation of truth is without question the outstanding achievement (if one may call it that) of *Mein Kampf*; and the chapter of *A Reckoning* entitled 'Nature and Race', once it gets through the pseudo-Darwinian cant about the inequality of human 'species' and the *précis* of historical race competition borrowed from Houston Stewart Chamberlain's *Foundations of the Nineteenth Century*, launches into a typology which, if it were concentrated into a single character in a drama, might constitute one of the great literary demons, worthy to stand alongside Richard III or Mephistopheles. At once Uriah Heep and the most exalted Machiavellian prince, Hitler's Jew is able to manipulate the poor, simple, virtuous masses from all directions until, thoroughly confused and demoralized, they can only accept perpetual servitude to him.

No typology of the capitalist–establishment 'pig' in the 1960s could surpass this characterization for its concentration of the despicable and unacceptable in humankind. Hitler's Jew is purely selfish, ignoble, lacking in ideals. Behind his veneer of civilization, he is brutally exploitative; and the only way to oppose him – for, as much as he is a chameleon, he is also a coward – is by courage and 'the fist'.

In seeking to convince his audience, Hitler becomes uncharacteristically seductive. He contends that as a youth he had nothing against the Jew, and that it was only against the great resistance of his innate tolerance and scepticism that he was finally, through experience and the above-mentioned 'superior' powers of observation, compelled to see the dark truth. This, however – as indeed all of *A Reckoning* – is an elaborate set-up for the promoting himself as the messiah come to initiate a mass movement for the 'liberation' and regeneration of a *Volk* whom he boldly, and quite accurately, assumes will not resent his 'fatherly' contempt amid the triumphal flow of strident oratory. In the last chapter of *A Reckoning*, he talks about the leader, who must have 'the highest unlimited authority, also with the ultimate and heaviest responsibility', and about how 'only the hero is cut out for this' because of 'the genius and energy of his personality' (p. 313). Then, rather in the vein of an apologist for Ron Hubbard rationalizing the hierarchical gradations of his cult, he goes on,

> Some idea of genius arises in the brain of a man who feels called upon to transmit his knowledge to the rest of humanity. He preaches his view and gradually wins a certain circle of adherents. The process of the direct and personal transmittance of a man's ideas to the rest of his fellow men is the most ideal and natural. With the rising increase in the adherents of the new doctrine, it gradually becomes impossible for the exponent of the idea to go on exerting a personal, direct influence on the innumerable supporters, to lead and direct them. Proportionately as, in consequence of the growth of the community, the direct and shortest communication is excluded, the necessity of a connecting organization arises: thus, the ideal condition is ended and is replaced by the necessary evil of organization.

Little sub-groups are formed which in the political movement, for example, call themselves local groups and constitute the germ-cells of the future organization. (pp. 314–15)

Here, underlining the myth that all energy radiates from the leader as rays from the sun, setting the stage for his own reluctant ascension from the people towards higher duties, and taking full account of his target audience's instinctive antinomian disquiet with 'the necessary evil of organization', the paraclete ends his prelude. Now the curtain may rise and performance begin of perhaps the most ambitious referred artwork of all time: the creation of the National Socialist state.

The second book of *Mein Kampf* presents the first acts of this creation. Neither them nor later acts shall we analyse here – obviously this has been done before and will be done again so long as fascination with this epoch continues. What should be pointed out, though, is that *Mein Kampf*, like Sade's opus, *De Profundis* and many of Charles Manson's 'songs', was written in a prison cell; and the paranoia and rigidity which characterize it (as they do less Hitler's later, also dictated, *Table Talk*) must emanate in part from the fact. This is important. The element of militant 'men's lib' which biographer Joachim Fest identifies in Hitler[9] derives from twenty or more years of living in meagre, confined conditions with no one but malcontent males for companions. First we have the doss houses of Vienna, then the trenches, next the modified barracks of Munich after the war, finally Landsberg Prison. Not until the mid twenties did Hitler enjoy the company of a 'better class' of person, women, and less than the meanest digs. Nor is it surprising that, if his boyhood bourgeois tastes and aspirations coloured the atmosphere of his entourage in the thirties, in the forties, when pressed, he would revert instinctively to the environment and attitudes of encampment and bunker. We shall see a parallel development later in Manson, who spent almost the exact same period of his early life in the even more cramped, all-male condition of prisons. The mentality such an atmosphere breeds is no doubt as significant a cause of criminality in these figures as psychological traumas of childhood. A 'soft' Orphic–Narcissistic dream of original mother-love is brutally, forcibly and repeatedly battered, until perhaps fully eclipsed by proofs of the necessity of at least Promethean, perhaps Luciferian or even Satanic strength. Throughout *A Reckoning* the spectacle of the *victim* is countered by that of the *survivor*. These twin types, born of hardship, dance their way through Hitler's imagination to the end. Symbiotic as Yin and Yang, they sum up for him – much as Nietzsche's 'slave' and 'master' or Sade's dominated and dominator – the eternal antipodes of human nature.

It is the view of a man who has had, and will have again, his 'back to the wall'. It also has remarkable similarity to the experience of the Jew as history has depicted him, alternately fleeing persecution and building palaces of gold out of the pawnshops of the ghetto. In his sentimental attachment to such an interpretation of life, Hitler, as *aficionados* of paradox have sometimes pointed out, seems more Jew than Aryan – at the least more the archetypal complainer than the neo-pagan 'yea-sayer'. While his 'keen observation' of the powers of manipulation he ascribes to the Jew becomes a basis for his programme of dominance, the 'tragedy' of the Jew as 'scapegoat' becomes a basis for his characterization of the contemporary German condition. It is perhaps going too far to say that his formulation of a German 'master race' is a conscious mockery of the Jewish tradition of a 'chosen people'; yet Hitler does, explictly in *Mein Kampf*, propose imitation of Jewish methods for racial survival as a step in German liberation from 'victimization'. The Jew against hostile indigenous European races becomes transposed into the German against a hostile, Jewish-manipulated world. If the Jew has created the concept of group antinomianism, now the German must adopt it. If the Jew has employed a vast web of covert organization to advance himself, so the German must not hesitate to employ gangsterism, taking his models from the *Protocols of the Elders of Zion*, American (Jewish-made) films, or wherever he can find them. If on the one hand the German may view himself as the new 'pure', holy outcast, and potential martyr like the Cathar, so he must also learn to fight in the context of the new urban world-order, whose 'cathedrals' are department stores and banks (p. 241), and whose most knowledgeable adepts are indicated by a contemporary Anglo-American poet thus:

> The rats are underneath the piles.
> The Jew is underneath the lot.[10]

This is the dark side of the formula victim-survivor, the one originating in doss house and prison, which Hitler, like Manson, would revert to in times of stress. Unlike with Sade, though, there is a bright side. Dominance after all can be achieved: Hitler is not thrown back again and again into Vincennes or Charenton. If in his megalomania and cult of self he regards the rest of mankind, even his own people, as a dog, experience will show him that the animal can, at least for a time, be mastered, brought to heel and petted. At his zenith, 'Uncle Wolf' impresses Winifred Wagner, millions of Germans, and even some Jews with his kindliness. Like some Alpine gentleman out of an idyll of *Edelweiss* and *Lederhosen*, he seems the essence of calm and lofty good nature, throwing flowers to women but never making sexual overtures to them, chucking children under the chin but never having any of his own or claiming a single one as his favourite; for he is the equally just and attentive suitor and father to all. To simple needy souls such as those who would find their 'father' deity in Manson, faith in such a figure mitigates the horror and incomprehensibility of a hostile world. If on the dark side Hitler could provide the protection of the gangster, on the bright he could offer the warmth of the sun – of which, as we have seen, his sign, the swastika, is the symbol. *Primum mobile*, generator of all energy, god of love and light for the chosen as of wrath for their enemies, the *Führer* becomes mythically the embodiment of the Johannine Christ, Siegfried–Wotan, the Cathar priest–king, and even, subliminally, the phallus of Crowley or Lawrence, 'vice-regent' of the Sun here on Earth. As such, in his eyrie, he must spend many hours in solitude, dreaming, meditating, even mentally masturbating on the vast forces behind all: ambiguous Nature, the great mother Erda, the cosmological and metaphysical abstractions out of which – according to his mentor Chamberlain – the Germanic race draws the distinction of its 'feminine' soul.[11]

This is the dramatic role Hitler conspires with the archetypal yearnings of his disciples to create: the mountaintop dreamer on 'Das Ewig-Weibliche', who will descend when called upon to lead his people in a battle to the death with the 'masculine' principle of materialism which threatens their existence in the 'lower' world. The end is good if the means are perhaps only rationalizable with reference to classical values of war, Machiavelli, and the exigencies of all-too-real modern life. Hitler offers no less than a return to Eden after the final conflict – very much what Manson would seem to offer his hippy cadre, with similar characterization of the enemy, located now not in Vienna, Paris, London or New York so much as multiracial, 'decadent' Los Angeles. In both cases, disciples are set up to respond favourably to such a siren song by their own recent fall from bourgeois order into lumpen-proletarian chaos. Against this, a spectacle of free, 'natural' life in the open air seems the most ready escape. From sentimentalization of beatific Nature to acceptance of the 'laws' of natural ruthlessness is a small step; and, to people who have either lost or never found the talent to make money, the challenge of 'competing' by the more 'natural', less 'clever' method of spilling blood may become the 'great initiation'. Once baptized in this element, the initiates are bound to and paradoxically exalted by their new status in conventional view as 'criminals', 'outlaws'. The scales have fallen from their eyes now; at last they can 'see' (have they not demonstrated it by their actions?) that conventional morality is nothing but a system of 'lies' designed to maintain power by those who manipulate and exploit, and that there is an older, more primal morality – again, that of survival. In going beyond conventional good and evil, risking as well as giving death, they have also drawn closer to the first principle governing existence: Life–Death – the ineffable gift of some unknown Destiny and final proof of the vanity of all conventional strivings. In bringing them into contact with this mystery, the great father–*Führer* has, too, allowed them new insight into the *pathos* of all things: he has initiated them into deeper understanding of Pain and thereby, in some interpretations, of Love.

One should not miss the element of *Schadenfreude* in the Nazi appeal: the tears and blood of those who must be 'sacrificed' feed an increasingly insatiable longing in those who, 'but for fortune', live on. The bond between victim and victimizer is as apparent as in Sade; only, in the Nazis as in the case of Manson's followers, the spectacle of victims suffering seems to have stimulated something akin to the mystical Sorrow Wilde talks about in *De Profundis* rather than just provoking more effusions of bully-boy glee on the part of the victimizer. This is an ambiguous point: certainly there is an element in the Nazi *Weltanschauung* which followed Sade (via Nietzsche) in militating against that 'Christian' emotion, pity. On the other hand, mass butchery could not have been initiated and taken to such lengths had the German population not been moved subliminally by some neo-Cathar, if not Christian, idea that the souls of the victims were being dispatched from this imperfect, material world to some 'better place'. Heaven, Valhalla, some form of reincarnation – whatever the view of where the energy of life escapes to after death (or even if death is comprehended as no more than a *Tristan*-like release from terrestrial 'pain'), there is no doubt that the mystery of *das Ende* holds a positive allure for a certain type of mind and that the 'releasing of souls' may thus be rationalized as a 'good', or at least quite moving, act. We have noted the value put on suicide by the Cathars. This was also characteristic of the Druids, who are said to have practiced blood sacrifices as well. The classical virtues of death in battle and suicide after defeat are well-known, time-honoured traditions in the West, as *harakiri* is in the East. Transcendence of this 'vale of tears' is a recurrent motif in Indo-European mysticism, and ascent to Wotan's hall was the noblest fate to which the Nordic hero could aspire. All these notions stand behind the Nazi cult of death, dignifying it. Most important of all, perhaps, is the image of the death of Christ, undertaken to prove his Love, which animated the mind of those medieval centuries for which the Nazis had such nostalgia and permeates the metaphysical value-system of the West to this day, Nietzsche notwithstanding. Hitler benefited from this in mesmerizing his 'beloved' *Volk* into pursuing their own and other peoples' *Götterdämmerung*. He also, true to the supreme 'captain' role he had designed for himself, did – in spite of the cowardice in the face of death which he apparently exhibited in the 1923 *Putsch* and which must have preyed on him subsequently as he drafted *Mein Kampf* – accept the 'responsibility' of unleashing the cult of death on himself too and, like the last Cathar 'pures' in their beseiged Montségur or Wotan at the end of Wagner's tetralogy, 'go down with the ship'.

The survivor then, in the end, gives way to the victim –
always the more tragic antipode of the two, and the one which
ultimately had to appeal to the 'artist' in Hitler's mentality.
Here the whole thrust of Romanticism, and specifically
Romantic opera, comes into question. Plenty has been written
about Hitler and Wagner, even a little by the present author;
and there is no need to go into the matter again in detail here.
Suffice it to say that, from the time he attended a performance
of *Rienzi* in Linz in 1906 with his boyhood friend Kubizek[12]
until the last time he sat by the side of the composer's
daughter-in-law at the Bayreuth Festival, Hitler remained
under the spell of 'Old Klingsor'. And what did he see on the
Wagnerian stage? A glamorization of an 'eternal' struggle
between Germanic – pagan or Cathar – orders against dark
forces of materialism, sex and magic? Yes. Representations of
the glories and dangers of the life of the heroic individual?
Yes. The 'magic power' of words, of music, of spectacle, of
staging? Yes indeed; and so much more emotionally potent
than in mere spoken theatre. An intellectual Idea: triumph
through strength, redemption through Love, purification by
renunciation, sacrificial death? Yes, and this last was finally
most important. 'The supreme expression of opera to him was
the finale of *Götterdämmerung*', Joachim Fest tells us.[13] 'I need
something enabling me to do away with the established order
of things in the world and to *overcome history by destroying it*',
Hitler told Hermann Rauschning.[14] 'Do you understand what
I'm getting at? *The world must be freed from its historical past.*' In
Wagner, such an act is romanticized as 'redemption through
Love': an apocalypse which returns Earth to primal innocence.
The reality of 'scorched earth', however, is something else,
just as the butchery of German youth in a futile quest for
Lebensraum is not the same as the spectacle of Siegfried burning
on his pyre after his adventures and slaying of the dragon of
the East. Any attempt to 'aestheticize' politics can only lead to
war and its horrors, Walter Benjamin wrote.[15] Hitler is the
great proof of this. His attempt to create in the Nuremberg
Rally a mass political counterpart to the Bayreuth Festival
succeeded all too well. Inevitably, such celebration of the
'forging' of the national Siegfried's 'sword' would have to be
followed by its testing in 'heroic' deed.

Whether 'art' was using politics to achieve some epic design or politics was using 'art' to advance worldly aims remains a moot point. Fest tells us in connection with Hitler's pilgrimages to Bayreuth that 'music meant little more to him than an extremely effective acoustic means to heighten theatrical effects'.[16] On the other hand, Rauschning tells us, most startlingly, that, in connection with the above-quoted remarks on *Götterdämmerung*, Hitler confided, 'I am as aware as all your intellectuals, all your founts of knowledge, that there is no such thing as race in the scientific sense of the word' and that he had merely utilized 'the notion of race' in order to help National Socialism '*establish a new world order*'.[17] If Hitler's prime political idea was indeed so empty and his prime artistic love likewise superficial – if, in short, neither politics nor art was the ultimate motivation, then what on earth after all was? Sheer Machiavellian opportunism? This does not sit comfortably with the 'appalling sincerity' of the man, complained of in a review of *Mein Kampf*.[18] Nor does it square with what we know of Hitler's personal conduct – his relationship to Eva Braun, for instance, and the rest of the domestic scene at Berchtesgaden. Opportunism was there, of course: in the 'real' world anti-self Hitler adopted, which we have identified with his picture of the Jew. Sincerity, however, is the stronger motif – indeed, a major source of the problem – in the private man. Here was a spirit which had wandered the fields as an adolescent dreaming of being Rienzi, later dreamed of being an architect, then and later drew and painted competently but with neither distinction nor genius,[19] and finally became decorated for bravery in war. In it, we see the precise pageant of Wagnerian development: dreamer to bohemian to artist to hero. To *Meister*–messiah is but one more step; and Hitler's medallion of hero–Jew defending his beloved *Volk* might be further defined as a version of the great precursor himself, with his ideally *sincere* Parsifal and necessarily *opportunistic* Klingsor elements.

I have written elsewhere about Wagner as the type imitated by a generation of artists and artists-*manqué*. That Hitler falls into the latter category is revealed more than anything by the absence of evil, the grotesque, the experimental, or the new in such 'artworks' as we know he produced or commissioned.[20] It may seem surprising that someone so conscious of evil in politics and life should have been so beatifically insipid in the kind of images which drew his aesthetic–emotive attention. But that is the fact; and in it lies a major explanation for Hitler's awkwardness and hostility to most of what was modern in contemporary life. This was not a debilitation Wagner suffered from in his day. But then Wagner was not an artist-*manqué*. Hitler was as a painter. Rosenberg was as a philosopher. Hans Frank and others were as poets. Goebbels was as a novelist. The typology is clear enough. As Louis Lochner tells of the young man who later became chief propagandist of the Reich:

> He was rejected for military service during World War I because of a deformed foot [the Byronic touch].
> He managed to secure a number of Catholic scholarships and attended eight famous German universities – Bonn, Freiburg, Wuerzburg, Munich, Cologne, Frankfurt, Berlin, and finally Heidelberg, where he took his Ph.D. degree in 1921 at the age of twenty-four. He studied history, philology, and the history of art and literature.
> His ambition was to be a writer. The year of his graduation at Heidelberg he wrote an unsuccessful novel, *Michael*, and followed it by two plays, *Blood Seed* (*Blutsaat*) and *The Wanderer* (*Der Wanderer*), which no producer would accept. He also applied, unsuccessfully for a reporter's job on the *Berliner Tageblatt*, internationally famed liberal daily [which he would later excoriate as 'Jewish'].
> All these experiences, together with the loss of the war and the collapse of the German Empire, embittered him and kept him restlessly wandering from Rheydt to Cologne, Berlin, and Munich, until, rather by accident, he heard Adolf Hitler speak in 1922.
> Young Joseph Goebbels first tried to interest university students in Hitler's message and thereby discovered that he had the gift of eloquence.[21]

And so they came under his sway, men whose patterns in life had been much like his own, or could have been 'but for fortune': mystics who had once believed the *fin-de-siècle* notion of 'Salons de la Rose-Croix' –

Artist! You are a priest: Art is the great mystery.

> Artist! You are a king: Art is the true empire.
> Artist! You are a magician: Art is the great miracle[22]

– but now imagined that their dreams of power and hermetic secrets could be absorbed into politics against the forces which had failed to recognize them for the 'geniuses' they imagined themselves to be. They gathered around Hitler because, in spite of all the qualifications which might be raised about his personality, he seemed to embody the artistic–mystic ideal of heroic charisma:

> He had, man to man, such radiance that you were more or less forced to follow him and share his ideas. He was absolutely the same, whether speaking to just one man or to a million. He swept you along with him and convinced you in spite of yourself. His personal magnetism was tremendous. He had an enormous power of suggestion.[23]

Something 'occult', as in the case of Crowley, was clearly in this; for Hitler was neither physically powerful, as we have said, nor compellingly handsome. But he had a voice which Angebert describes as 'a harsh torrent rolling over the boulders of the Austrian Alps';[24] and he had eyes 'so strange that at first they were all that I saw', as the historian Benoist-Méchin reports:

> They were of a clear, transparent blue, striated with gray. One might have said that they were empty as though lifeless. But very quickly you changed your minds. What made them seem empty was their motionlessness. You might have said that his pupils, instead of observing the outside world, were turned inward and followed a drama unfolding somewhere deep within him. Unlike most people, who look at you – or even through you – the chancellor had a way of looking at you which drew you to him, and swept you into his hidden interior. You felt a sort of dizziness, which it took some doing to shake off.[25]

Perhaps an element in this strangeness might be blamed on the injections of drugs and vitamins which Hitler had started in mild doses by 1941, when this encounter took place, and later were partially to debilitate him. Also involved here may be his adolescent trick of the stare-down, which Speer makes light of, having 'won' against it during a lunch at the Eagle's Nest.[26] Still, the man's mesmeric power cannot be dismissed or joked away readily; and it is a significant, imponderable element in the whole equation – one we shall meet again in the case of Manson. To what extent may there be something strictly internal and never medically or intellectually identifiable which gives a man exceptional powers? and to what extent may this, rather than theory or experience, be what leads him to present himself as a destiny, ready to remake morality in his own image and take on the given order as an apparent arch-demon of crime? Mystery shrouds the answers, as in the end it does the man who provokes the questions, making him all the more attractive to groups who long for something beyond the ordinary to exalt their own trampled-on, insignificant-seeming lives. Eccentricity, unpredictability, a 'neurasthenic craving for sheer movement';[27] enormous resources of energy which seemed 'multiplied by every fresh disaster' combined with a 'somnabulistic calm' which seemed 'entirely divorced from the real world'; authoritarianism combined with anarchic propensities; order and chaos; icy hate and fiery love; misanthropy and Christliness; 'wild fantasies of destruction' alternating with visions of constructing great new imperial monuments – these antipodes were embodied in Hitler, making him effectively the incarnation of some dream or nightmare of completely unleashed human licence. They secured him in power for so long as he could inspire the dreamers and balance one element against another. Fear, however – that emotion which animates every nightmare and which had been the 'overwhelming experience of his formative years'[28] – provoked the ultimate error: overcompensatory aggression. Moreover, his adoption of the paradoxical character he ascribed to the demon he proposed to defend honest mankind against ('Great liars are also great wizards'[29]) has assured that posterity – the 'following' he was ultimately playing for – must recognize the 'evil' Klingsor part of his personality in as high or higher relief than the 'good' Parsifal he apparently fancied himself primarily to be.

8 Sixties' *Zeitgeist*, I: Mysticism

Hitler imagined himself to be initiating a new epoch when he unleashed the Second World War. Aleister Crowley had beaten him to such a claim, as various others, when he asserted through his persona Simon Iff in *Moonchild* that he had done likewise with the First World War:

> The people think [the war's] about violation of solemn treaties, and the rights of little nations, and so on; the governments think it's about commercial expansion; but I who made it know that it is the baptism of blood of the New Aeon. How could we promulgate the Law of Liberty in a world where Freedom has been strangled?[1]

Hitler and Crowley share belief in the need for purposeful destruction. They are almost identical in the faith of megalomaniacal *voyants* that only they are equipped to *see* world-historic imperatives. Where they are not at one is in their views of the 'new order' to be initiated. Crowley's 'liberty' is an exuberant chaos. Hitler's state is almost precisely the opposite: an apotheosis of bourgeois fixity. But, as Simon Iff says, with echoes of Wildean 'individualism',

> The bourgeois is the real criminal, always. .... Look at the testimony of literature. In the days of chivalry our sympathies go with the knight-errant. ... When kingship became tyranny, and feudalism oppression, we took our heroes from the rebels. ... It was always the Under Dog that appealed to the artist. Then industrialism became paramount, and we began – in Byron's time – to sympathize with brigands and corsairs. Presently these were wiped out, and today or rather, the day before yesterday, we were reduced to loving

absolute scoundrels ... or the detectives who (although always on the side of society) were equally occupied in making the police look like fools. ... And you must remember that the artist always represents the subconscious will of the people.   (p. 270)

As the young victim, would-be artist, and rebellious espouser of dangerous ideas, Hitler fits into this knight-errant–underdog–scoundrel persona. As the erector of a new absolutism, however, he becomes the arch-enemy and rival of the type of New Man whom Iff's description previews. Prometheus–Lucifer becomes Caesar–Napoleon; the primal energy of youthful protest gives way to an entropy of power; liberation from the hegemony of 'Jewish materialism' leads to a tyranny of blood so much worse that any *Eroica* dedication must be ripped up. The conqueror's destiny is to consume himself in the manner of a black magician. As Crowley goes on,

The truth is that, as [black magic's] intimates advance, their power and knowledge becomes enormously greater; but such progress is not a mark of general growth, as it is in the case of the White Brotherhood; it is like a cancer, which indeed grows apace, but at the expense of the man on whom it feeds, and will destroy both him and itself in the long run. The process may be slow; it may extend over a series of incarnations; but it is sure enough. The analogy of the cancer is a close one; for the man who knows his doom, suffers continual torture, but to this is added the horrible delusion that if only the disease can be induced to advance far enough, all is saved. Thus he hugs the fearful growth, cherishes it as his one dearest possession, stimulates it by every means in his power. Yet all the time he nurses in his heart an agonizing certainty that this is the way of death.   (p. 116)

One might recall here Hitler's worsening insomnia and nightmares during the War.[2] Black means may lead to total control for a time, but not to permanent mastery any more than to the Liberty Simon Iff extols. These come from discipline in forms of 'white magic' derived from ancient Egypt and the East. Iff himself is a Taoist. His way of dealing with forces which disturb him is to gain mystical unity with them. Thus, when the black magician Douglas (based on MacGregor Mathers[3]) sends an evil 'thing' into his sphere,

> Iff [sets] himself to complete assimilation of that Thing; he [makes] certain that it should be part of himself for ever. His method of doing this [is] as simple as usual. He [goes] over the universe in his mind, and [sets] himself to reconcile all contradictions in a higher Unity. Beginning with such gross things as the colours of the spectrum, which are only partialities of white light, he [resolves] everything that [comes] into mind until he [reaches] such abstractions as matter and motion, being and form; and by this process [works] himself up into a state of mind which [is] capable of grasping these sublime ideas which unite even these ultimate antinomies. That [is] all.   (p. 145)

The black magician seeks to combat Iff by opposition. 'Divide and rule' might be his motto. Any force which confronts him he attempts to fix into a Manichaean scheme:

> Douglas was too blind to see the way – an acquired blindness resulting from repeated acts whose essence was denial of the unity of himself with the rest of the universe. . . . The result was that his whole mind was aflame with the passion of contrasting things, of playing forces off against each other. When it came to practical decisions, he divided his forces, and deliberately created jealousy and hatred where co-operation and loyalty should have been the first and last consideration.
>
> Yet Simon Iff had used no spell but Love.

The battleground between Iff and Douglas ultimately is Cyril Grey, an adept magician embodying characteristics of the young Crowley. That Iff will win Grey's allegiance is a foregone conclusion: the two are in substantial alliance from the beginning of the book. At the same time, by the end, Grey's maturation involves recognizing that 'the corpse of Douglas was his own' (p. 301). As the cannibal warrior eats his defeated foe in order to take on his strength, so the white magician must absorb the dualistic spirit of the black to perfect his own unity. Fully realized 'magic' of either sort must contain evil; the difference lies in when and how it is used. Though a 'white' magician, Simon Iff is, as we have seen, not averse to 'promulgating' a world war in order to bring on a better (as he views it) era. Crowley himself would repeatedly justify bizarre means by such ideal ends. Moreover, in *Moonchild*, in spite of a structural bias towards Iff, the liveliest portion of narrative energy is devoted to Douglas and retinue; and anyone tempted to see the book as a refutation of Crowley's legendary wickedness might wish first to consider the extent of slander against Mathers, Yeats (depicted as the adept Gates, who falls from a tower and dies while trying to subvert Cyril Grey's 'experiment'), Isadora Duncan and others whom the author felt badly done by in 'real life'.

'Love' as proposed by Crowley in *Moonchild* and elsewhere is clearly ambiguous. Inasmuch as the doctrine is life-celebrating and universal, it could appeal to generations growing up in the wake of two world wars more readily than some death-yearning parochialism such as Hitler's. Still, Crowleyan Love aspires towards power as much as Hitlerian hate. Simon Iff's relationship to Cyril Grey is analogous to Lord Henry Wotton's to Dorian of a similar surname (Crowley, who had moved in some of the same circles as Wilde when a young man, was no doubt aware of this); like Lord Henry, what Iff exercises is *influence*; and, as the Wotton–Gray relationship has shown, this may be a supreme form of mastery. 'Love' is proposed not so much for its Christly qualities of kindness and self-sacrifice as for its erotic powers of attraction and adhesion (cf. Grey's power over Lisa la Giuffria, the 'Scarlet Woman' of the book and focus of his experiments in creating an homunculus: the 'moonchild' of the book's title). In short, Crowleyan Love is a kind of magnet: a mesmeric 'unifying' force, ultimate tool in the 'magician's' bag of tricks; an all-effacing and sublimating drug – one whose effects, however, are not able to last even as long as it takes for mother to incubate foetus.

The reader may have already begun to recognize the similarity of this to the 'Luv' of the 1960s, which degenerated into various kinds of pursuit of power by the 'selfish' 1970s. Before we get to direct discussion of that phenomenon, however, we should take occasion to consider how various ideas we have been discussing transferred to the American scene. The sixties, after all, was a peculiarly American decade: arguably the moment in which a young nation burst out of its bucolic, bourgeois sleep into a Nietzschean 'dawn' leading directly to Spenglerian 'twilight'.[4] This transference might be glimpsed through the eyes of an English author who was born in the year before Crowley, knew him in Paris as a young man, wrote a novella about him, and then – in the decade when Hitler was wreaking his 'purposeful' destruction on Europe – sat down to write a mature novel which returned to scenes and issues of that early encounter, but in transformed guise and to thoroughly different effect.

I am speaking of Somerset Maugham, his novella *The Magician* (1907) and his great novel *The Razor's Edge* (1944). The latter, which takes its title from a line in the *Katha Upanishad*, is a light-world counterpart to an exploration of dark, subterranean Western mysticism in the former. Larry Darrell, an American expatriate of modestly comfortable means, replaces Oliver Haddo, a Scottish (like Crowley) 'alchemist' of aristocratic pretensions. In terms of the dialectic Crowley sets out in *Moonchild*, Darrell is a 'white magician' where Haddo was a 'black'. While the latter anticipates Douglas (*Moonchild* was written a decade after *The Magician*) and destroys himself in the course of one of his plots, the former follows the path of Simon Iff towards the wisdom of the East. In Darrell, Maugham, with his remarkable 'third eye' as a novelist, anticipates a whole generation of Americans, 'beats' and 'hippies', which would reject the apparently inescapable materialism of their time and place for a Protean spiritualism mixing partially digested bits of Hindu and Buddhist philosophies with indulgent, quasi-Wildean 'self-realization': 'flower children' or 'magic Christians' who would turn their backs on their birthrights and aspire to an ideal of the truly 'liberated' individual, 'crown of creation' in all humanist philosophies, whether of West or East.

Larry Darrell represents this ideal. Conceived in a period in which America seemed to be saving old Europe from 'dark forces',[5] he embodies a sense of 'becoming' far more hopeful than the actual 'being' of his 'real life' successors would ultimately justify. The most striking distinction between him and his counterparts perhaps is his instinctive acceptance from an early age of the solitude necessary to 'realize his genius'.

This is surely a romanticization of a seventy-year-old expatriate novelist's achievement more than an accuraté *aperçu* of the coming American man. What solitude lies naturally in the American soul – memory of loneliness on the frontier – was diminishing in the period Maugham was writing. An urbanized society more eager for Fourier's 'group joy' or Crowley's 'energized enthusiasm' was growing up. Nevertheless, Maugham somehow foresees that a sort of 'rear-guard action'[6] was shortly going to challenge the forward march of 'manifest destiny' and, for over a decade, force it to turn inwards and 'eastwards' towards the real 'last unconquered frontier': not Vietnam so much as knowledge, self-mastery, *gnosis*.

While his Chicagoan peers are going to Henry Jamesian (or perhaps more properly Scott Fitzgeraldish) parties, young Darrell reads William James in the quiet *sanctum* of an all-male smoking-club. Later, at the cost of having to break his engagement to a latter-day Isabel Archer, he takes his studies to twenties' Paris, where he lives in a modest hotel room like the one where Oscar Wilde died. From the Bibliothèque Mazarin and cafés of the Left Bank, he goes on to Germany, divesting himself of cash and worldly goods, and pursues fortune as an itinerant workman. He links up with a Polish aristocratic revolutionary exile, one Kosti, who mixes the bonhomie of Bakunin with the sad sagacity of Stanislaus in B. Traven's *The Death Ship*. A devout Catholic, a drunk, harsh, caustic and cynical, Kosti extends Darrell's education in Western mysticism by lectures on Ruysbroek, Plotinus, Denis the Aerogapite, Jacob Boehme and Meister Eckhart, among others. From him Darrell learns, as he later reports to Maugham (author appears unfictionalized as narrator in the novel), 'the ultimate reality of things' and 'the blessedness of union with God'.[7]

For a time, Darrell stays with monks and imagines he should have lived in medieval (perhaps Cathar) Europe: 'Like Rolla, I've come too late into a world too old' (*The Razor's Edge*, p. 249). But eventually, like the hero of Hermann Hesse's *Narziss und Goldmund*, he grows impatient with world-denying asceticism. Too much praise of God goes on in the monastery, he decides, and too much preoccupation with sin. At the same time, there is too little attention to the overarching moral question: how could a supposedly benevolent God have found it necessary to create evil?

In pursuit of an answer, Darrell goes to India. There he lives in an ashram and 'spends time in the infinite'. In quest of 'saintliness' (which Maugham later remarks 'requires just a touch of ruthlessness'), he learns of the tripartite division of godhead into Brahma the Creator, Vishnu the Preserver and Siva the Destroyer. He develops Brahmin sympathies, which are in line with an older American ('Boston Brahmin') tradition, as Maugham points out with a quotation from Emerson:

> They reckon ill who leave me out;
> When me they fly, I am the wings;
> I am the doubter and the doubt,
> And I the hymn the Brahmin sings.
> (p. 262)

But it is in the 'lower' tradition of Hinduism that Darrell finds the most satisfactory, if still inadequate, explanation for the moral nature of the universe. This he reveals to Maugham in a conversation in a café in Montmartre some years later. The conversation, Maugham tells us, is the reason he wrote the book; however, since in terms of the story line it is extrinsic, any reader who becomes bored may be excused from reading on.

Seldom has an author been so disingenuously diffident about his moral purpose. But of course Maugham, unlike so many we are speaking of – indeed, unlike his hero, who ultimately ends his career of study by publishing a rather *manqué* little book on an eccentric selection of precursors – is an artist before all: a man of delicate feints and charms, having much in common with the secondary 'hero' of the novel, an aging American expatriate aesthete. As such, Maugham obviously finds it awkward to interpolate philosophy into high-art fiction. But *The Razor's Edge* belongs to the anxious era which produced *Doktor Faustus*, not to the 'golden age' of Maugham's obvious model in the effort, Henry James; and, as with the septuagenarian Thomas Mann's novel, spiritual dialogues demand our attention precisely because the author has felt compelled to 'violate' his art to present them.

'Do you know anything about Hinduism? [Darrell asks Maugham] I should have thought it would interest you. Can there be anything more stupendous than the conception that the universe has no beginning and no end, but passes everlastingly from growth to equilibrium to decline, from decline to dissolution, from dissolution to growth, and so on to all eternity?'

'And what do the Hindus think is the object of this endless recurrence?'

'I think they'd say that such is the nature of the Absolute. You see, they believe that the purpose of creation is to serve as a stage for the punishment or reward of the deeds of the soul's earlier existences.'

'Which presupposes belief in the transmigration of souls.'

'Yes ... Has it occurred to you that transmigration is at once an explanation and a justification of the evil in the world? If the evils we suffer are the result of sins committed in our past lives we can bear them with resignation and hope that if in this one we strive towards virtue our future lives will be less afflicted. But it's easy enough to bear our own evils. What's intolerable is the evil, often so unmerited in appearance, that befalls others. . . .'

'But why didn't God create a world free from suffering and misery at the beginning? . . .'

'The Hindus would say that there was no beginning . . . .' (pp. 264–5)

We are close here to the Celtic Yeats's suggestion that 'the living give life to the imaginings of the dead';[8] and the apparent morbidity of such an imperative makes the worldly Englishman sigh. Wearily, Maugham remarks on 'the weary wheel of becoming' which characterizes mystical doctrine. Darrell gazes at him with his powerful blue eyes. In a 'musical' voice and faintly ironical tone (the elements of personal charisma are here, as in Hitler and Crowley, only Maugham insists always on casting them in a positive light), Darrell remarks *en passant* on a phenomenon we first encountered with Crowley but shall find cropping up again as we draw towards

Mexico and Los Angeles – that the strain of antinomianism we are tracking may have to do with climate, or at least cults of the sun: 'When the Aryans first came down into India they saw the world as beautiful and delighted in it. It is only later when the climate had sapped their vitality that they began to see matter as evil' (p. 278). But leaving this provocative *aperçu* aside, the conversation passes on to that central problem which had plagued Maugham at least since his encounter with Crowley four decades before:

> 'Larry, old boy ... This long quest of yours started with the problem of evil. It was the problem of evil that urged you on. You've said nothing all this time to indicate that you've reached even a tentative solution to it.'
>
> 'It may be that there is no solution, or it may be that I'm not clever enough to find it. Ramakrishna looked upon the world as the sport of God. "It's like a game", he said. "In this game there are joy and sorrow, virtue and vice, knowledge and ignorance, good and evil. The game cannot continue if sin and suffering are altogether eliminated from the creation." I would reject that with all my strength. The best I can suggest is that when the Absolute manifested itself in the world evil was the natural correlation of good. You would never have had the stupendous beauty of the Himalayas without the unimaginable horror of a convulsion of the earth's crust. ... In some ways the values we cherish in the world can only exist in combination with evil.'
>
> 'It is an ingenious notion, Larry. I don't think it's very satisfactory.'
>
> 'Neither do I', he smiled. 'The best to be said for it is that when you've come to the conclusion that something is inevitable all you can do is make the best of it.' (pp. 279–80)

Darrell thus avoids Cyril Grey's conscious absorption of evil into himself. The American soul, to paraphrase Walter Rathenau, has not yet 'consented to recognize' evil as inherent.[9] In the political sphere, Darrell will therefore shortly reappear as Graham Greene's 'Quiet American', who wanders into Vietnam along the path of good intentions. Eternally boyish, not doubting for a moment his own merit, the type indeed has 'powers'; and there is a touching nobility in his aspiration to use them to 'free people of pain and fear' (p. 246). When his old friend Gray Maturin develops migraine as a result of losing a fortune in the 1929 crash, Darrell 'heals' him through a combination of hypnosis, concentration and suggestion. Maturin, like Maugham, becomes a kind of believer in Darrell's Christliness. His wife, however – the Isabel Archer-type to whom Darrell was once engaged and who remains in love with him – is not so beneficently effected. Isabel Maturin (she is in fact called by the same Christian name as James's archetypal American heroine) watches and waits. Though the essence of *haut-bourgeois* decorum on the surface, she is determined to get back at the man who once threw her over for *gnosis*. Her chance comes when Darrell becomes engaged to another old friend, Sylvie MacDonald, who has turned to alcohol, drugs and footloose living since a motor-car accident killed her husband and child. Darrell, predictably, is attracted to Sylvie by a desire to 'save' her. Isabel, on the other hand – at least according to Maugham (but here his narration becomes suspiciously redolent of the misogynist homosexual's mistrust of women) – takes the first opportunity to jostle her rival back into desperate ways. Sylvie runs away. Ultimately she dies a whore's death, knifed by a sailor or pimp in Marseilles. Meanwhile, Darrell, having published his slim volume and given away what money he has left, sets off, rather like Dick Diver at the end of his European quest and romantic disaster in Fitzgerald's *Tender is the Night*, for the great, enwombing heartland of America. There, as a mechanic or pilot or truck-driver – indeed, somewhere out on the American road where technology and philosophy ride in tandem – he remains optimistic that he may yet find the answer he has been looking for.

Thus the end of Maugham's novel becomes a starting-point for our quest. Larry Darrell with his rejection of bourgeois America in the form of Isabel, his indefatigable desire to develop a fresh, unprejudiced system of belief, and his sentimental attachment to fatality as shown by his engagement to Sylvie, becomes the new American man of the Jack Kerouac era: a Lawrence Ferlinghetti returning from expatriate literary youth in Paris; a Bob Dylan declaring, in the words of the title to one of his early albums, his intention to 'bring it all back home'. What happens to Darrell in these incarnations we shall discuss further on. First, something more needs to be said about the 'wisdom' a generation began to pick up as it imitated him in leaving indigenous materialism in favour of the spiritual 'journey to the East'. To get a wider perspective on this, I turn to a celebrated All Souls' College scholar of mysticism, R. C. Zaehner.[10]

Alienation is the fundamental 'problem' of the modern period, Zaehner says. This stems from man's loss of his feeling of oneness with Nature, which formed the basis of his earliest belief systems. The philosophy of India, specifically the *Upanishads*, is 'the fount and origin' of religious expression of this primal unity:

> First the teaching concerning the infinite.
>
> This is below, it is above, it is to the west, to the east, to the south, to the north. Truly it is the whole universe.
>
> Next the teaching concerning the ego.
>
> I am below, I am above, I am to the west, to the east, to the south, to the north. Truly I am the whole universe.
>
> Next the teaching concerning the Self.
>
> The Self is below, the Self is above, the Self is to the west, to the east, to the south, to the north. Truly the Self is the whole universe.
>
> The man who sees and thinks and understands in this way has pleasure in the Self, plays with the Self, copulates with the Self, and has joy with the Self: he becomes an independent sovereign. In every state of being freedom of movement is his.[11]

Such freedom and beatitude were lost in the West through failure of the Christian Church and triumph of scientific dogma. An urge to recapture them is reflected by fascination with mystical experience in various writers of the late Romantic period (Whitman, Proust, and William James are three Zaehner cites). The keynotes of such experiences are 'total aloneness with the universe', 'cosmic consciousness', and 'ecstatic joy because death and time are transcended and all the opposites are melted into One' (*Drugs, Mysticism*, p. 63). This 'One' Zaehner recognizes as the same as that of medieval

heresy, the neo-Platonists, and Meister Eckhart. It is also the
state yearned for by pursuers of 'instant Zen': what he calls
'the current drop-out cult' (p. 40).

This cult is made up of four 'ingredients': Eastern mysticism,
drugs, pop music and sex. The mixing of the first two Zaehner
credits to Alan Watts and even more to Aldous Huxley, whose
late book *The Doors of Perception*, written after the author had
expatriated himself to Los Angeles, constitutes a paean to
LSD. Taking its title from the poet the 'beats' most admired,
Blake ('When the doors of perception are cleaned, man will
see things as they are, infinite'), and later passing it on to the
most sensational rock group sharing period and locale with
Manson, the Doors, Huxley's book forms an essential cultural
synapse. Perhaps even more than transported teachings of
Crowley, *The Doors of Perception* exercised *influence* over the new,
naïve and receptive 'Southern Californian' 'counter-culture'.
In consideration of massive abuses of LSD which followed,
Zaehner finds it hard to forgive his fellow Englishman for this.
Nor does he make more than passing reference to Huxley's
qualification of the drug-enthusiasm in a subsequent volume.[12]

The real culprit for fraudulent enlightenment, however, is
Dr Timothy Leary. Disregarding the spontaneous and multiple
origins of the movement he is tracking, as well as the
opportunism in Leary's claim to guru-status, Zaehner discusses
The Politics of Ecstasy as if it were the 'drop-out cult' bible. In
it he finds mixed the other 'ingredients' Huxley left out: pop
music and sex. The latter for Leary, as for Crowley, is a
version of the love of the god Shiva for his Shakti, or 'power'.[13]
'Sexual union is the sacramental re-enactment of an eternal
truth'. LSD, 'the most powerful aphrodisiac ever produced',
derives its importance as host in the rite:

> The three inevitable goals of the LSD sessions are to
> discover and make love with God, to discover and make
> love with yourself, and to discover and make love with a
> woman. You can't make it with yourself unless you've made
> it with the timeless energy process around you, and you
> can't make it with a woman until you've made it with
> yourself.

It would follow from this that, as Leary puts it, 'the real trip is the God trip' (*Politics of Ecstasy*, p. 223); and here is where that fourth element, pop music, enters (it must properly be labelled 'rock' to distinguish it from the 'safe', or in a word of the era 'plastic', pop music of the middle-brows, from Frank Sinatra to Tom Jones): 'God is a hipster, he is a musician, and he's got a great beat going. You'll never find him in an institution or in an American television stage set. He's never legal! And he's got a great sense of humour.' You may find him in informal *séances* of conga-drum beating around lakes or creekbeds where nude 'brothers and sisters' cavort, playing flutes and braiding flowers in their hair; at 'electric kool-aid acid tests' where free-form jazz–rock bands such as the Grateful Dead 'jam', or perhaps at open-air 'happenings' in Golden Gate Park. As Ken Kesey would show in his contemporary *One Flew Over the Cuckoo's Nest*, you could not find this 'hip' God of Freedom in even such liberal 'institutions' as hospitals. You would be more likely to find Him in jail, or out on the road made mythical by the great 'buddy' Kesey inherited from Kerouac: Neal Cassady. The model of the 'outlaw' is a fifth, and for our purposes perhaps the most significant, 'ingredient' in the 'drop-out' formula. This type whom Leary suggests when he says that God is 'never legal' is the peculiarly American, Wild Western version of the knight-errant–underdog–scoundrel persona Simon Iff predicts will triumph in the New Aeon.

Zaehner hardly recognizes this. What concerns him is how Leary's LSD gospel reflects the pervasive lack of appeal of established culture. America is 'an insane asylum' (p. 241) and 'an air-conditioned anthill' (p. 198), Leary declares, echoing as we shall see the final rantings of Artaud. Traditional religion has become entirely hollow. American Protestantism with its 'formal preaching and censorious ethic' never really was a religion in the sense of having any 'interest in the experience of the divine'; the Catholic mass, which should ideally be 'the place of meeting between man and God', has lost its effect (p. 211). In this situation, it is neither surprising nor inappropriate that a generation should turn to mystical paths. What Zaehner deplores is that this should happen without the neophytes' being properly forewarned of the pitfalls for which orthodox religion has historically opposed all but a few of these paths: (1) the mystic who 'triumphantly realizes his essential oneness with God commits in this sublime way the root-sin of all mankind – "to be like God" – or, in other words, he *"repeats the Fall"* ' (*Drugs, Mysticism*, p. 85); (2) mysticism in any case almost always tends to 'blur differences', with the result that the gentle oscillation between dualism and unity on which civilization depends gives way to extreme espousals of the one (Manichaeanism) or the other (Eastern philosophy, or what Crowley calls 'white magick'); (3) mystical heresies are 'for ever speaking of a state which is beyond good and evil, right and wrong', a fact which can only, at best, lead to imitation of 'the Semitic God', not to observance of the laws of the Pentateuch, let alone faith in a benevolent Christ.

It is only in 'Love' that practitioners of Leary's 'spontaneous mystic faith' seem to approach harmony with a positive Christian tradition; but to Zaehner this Love is 'hypocritical': a slogan based on 'neurotic need and wishful thinking', involving 'self-deceit and self-delusion with consequent damage to the individual' (p. 94). Zaehner chronicles several examples of the kind of 'mystical revelation' members of the 'drop-out cult' have experienced. 'I am the universe', one woman rhapsodizes; 'I am Love. Love. Love. Love. Love' (p. 95). This is a 'positive inflation' coming very near to 'a more or less conscious megalomania', Zaehner remarks; at the same time, it is also a 'negative inflation', felt as 'annihilation of the ego' (p. 97). In either form, such states of mind appal the scholar, just as they did the psychologists Jung, who invented the term 'inflation', and Freud, whom we have noted (via Marcuse) described it as 'the oceanic feeling'. As with these fellow intellectuals, what seems to annoy Zaehner most is the cheapness of revelation *en masse*: after all, if every man can attain enlightenment easily and readily, what need does society have for high-priced psychotherapists, let alone university dons? 'True religious contemplatives', Zaehner points out, experience their mystical revelations in silence and solitude: after the ordeal of a 'dark night of the soul', if, say, a follower of St John of the Cross; after exposure to mild sensory aids – music and ritual dance – if, say, a medieval Sufi (p. 99).

The LSD 'session', with its visual, auditory and tactile stimuli, reminds Zaehner of those latter-day, decadent Sufis who took to smoking hashish and *ma'jun* and disregarded the injunction that appreciation of youthful beauty in the ritual dance was not to pass the stage of contemplation. For him, the new mystics are practising a kind of Dionysian diabolism. Even adepts of Krishna, he points out, must search for integration through 'cleansing of the soul' and 'living apart' (p. 102). The Christian mystic, moreover, properly finds 'Love' to be a spirit directed beyond himself and all Earthly creatures towards apprehension of the Divine (p. 104). As for Zen, Zaehner quotes an ancient saying to the effect that 'becoming attached to one's enlightenment is as much a sickness as exhibiting a maddeningly active ego' (p. 98). 'Authentic Zen', he claims, 'must remain the privilege of the few'; and 'those who take drugs in an attempt to experience *satori* [a word Kerouac threw around liberally] are not practising authentic Zen at all' (p. 115). With more than a hint of academic snobbery he concludes, 'LSD sessions are so far removed from anything the present author has come across in his quite extensive reading of the mystical writings of most of the religious traditions that he cannot possibly class it as specifically mystical' (p. 107). More tellingly, he points out that the 'drop-out' who experiences 'revelation' by means of a drug will discover, even more than the conventional mystic, that his dominant sensation once the experience has ended is not 'ecstasy' so much as 'paradise lost' (p. 117).

'Paradis artificiel' is how Baudelaire described the mystic realms opened to him by opium and hashish; the 'Void' or 'Emptiness' is how Mahayana Buddhism describes the state the seeker enters once he has reached the goal of his quest. Revelation involves by its nature all-annihilating disillusionment. 'Die while alive, and be completely dead', the seeker must learn; 'then do whatever you will, all is good.'[14] This becomes the hippy's hope once he has passed through the 'doors of perception': to become spontaneously good; like a little child, in Wilde's image;[15] 'gratefully dead' to *samsāra* and all frustrations of the material world. Here he may achieve a benign nihilism, or so it would seem. But his 'charter', however quiescent, is implicitly anti-intellectual. Moreover, as Zaehner points out, it might be taken from the same source as Simon Iff's formula for mastery, the farther-East doctrine of *Tao Te Ching* –

Banish wisdom, discard knowledge,
And the people will be benefited a hundredfold.
Banish human kindness, discard morality,
And the people will be dutiful and compassionate.
Banish skill, discard profit,
And the thieves and robbers will disappear.
If and when these three things are done they find life too
  plain and unadorned,
Then let them have accessories;
Give them simplicity to look at, the Uncarved Block to
  hold,
Give them selflessness and fewness of desires.[16]

– and here hides a hint of militant destructiveness as well. It comes in the word 'banish' and is cognate with Iff's blithe suggestion that he would 'banish' the old era by unleashing world war. (One might also hear an echo of Sade's contention that mankind could free itself of Vice by 'banishing' Virtue.) Zaehner does not develop such an argument; but later on, when he cites the boast of the Vedic god Indra, the Universal Self, of his evil deeds ('I killed . . . . Transgressing many a compact, I impaled . . .'[17]) and the revelation of Krishna to his disciple Arjuna that 'a man who has reached a state where there is no sense of "I", whose soul is undefiled, may slaughter all these worlds yet paradoxically slay nothing',[18] he indicates the kind of apocalypse towards which hippy 'integral wisdom' may lead.

The book from which I am taking these arguments was published in 1972, thus benefiting from its author's observation of the new enlightenment from its dawn to its twilight. One cannot fault Zaehner for facts, but his understanding surely suffers from an imbalance of knowledge over experience. More than once one has the sense already remarked on of an academic defending armchair inquiry over the hurly-burly of 'real life'. Yeatsian caution opposes Crowleyan clowning again; only here the devil's part is defended by the 'drop-out' from high academe, Leary, rather than from the Golden Dawn. The irony is that Zaehner is in substantial sympathy with the rebellion, and even quest, of those he looks down on. That orthodox contemporary culture is antipathetic to him becomes increasingly apparent as the book goes on. Indeed, at the beginning of his antepenultimate chapter, 'Beyond Good and Evil', he launches into a critique which might have elicited a 'right on!' from Charles Manson, to say nothing of more politically attuned 'outlaws':

> With ever-increasing urbanization and the progressive mechanization and dehumanization of urban life ... the vast majority of urban jobs mechanical and dull, man is more and more dependent on distractions which the mass media are all too ready to supply. ... In previous ages work was distraction and only the privileged had leisure. As Pascal said, leisure was dangerous. ... 'There is nothing so intolerable to a man as to be completely at rest, without passions or occupation ... a black mood, listlessness, worries, rancour, and despair. ... How hollow is the heart of man, how full of filth!' ...
>
> Ideologically we are bankrupt. God is dead, in his place is Mammon. Man turns to science, then away from it once he recognizes its power to destroy not only bodies but the soul itself. Pseudo-scientists – astrologers, occultists, witches, social 'scientists', psychiatrists – all these are 'broken reeds'....
>
> We are a sick society. ... We, following the USA, are the real materialists, much more than the Communist bloc, for, though some of us may still pay lip-service to spiritual values, basically we care for nothing but material welfare and material comfort. We have grown flabby and rotten inside.   (pp. 138–42)

'Have you seen the little piggies in their starched white shirts?' the Beatles had sung[19] and Manson's followers would scrawl in blood on the walls of the houses of their decadent, *beau monde* victims; and, when a man at the pinnacle of establishment intellectual life can describe his world in such damning terms, is it any wonder that 'low' voices should clamour for cleansing?[20] Yet Zaehner's personal vision is even more bleak than the above grouse reveals. He quotes from his favourite novelist, Bernanos: 'The modern world is ruled not by God, nor by science, but by Satan, the prince of this world' (p. 145). He goes on to summarize Bernanos's 'masterpiece', *Monsieur Ouine*, a book written to demonstrate that, 'with the progressive dehumanization of man, you will see all manner of beasts emerge whose names men have long since forgotten, assuming that they ever had been given one' (p. 144). Monsieur Ouine's own name combines *oui* and *non*, 'yes' and 'no', and thus represents the 'eternal enigma', the 'union of opposites'. But this unity is not sympathetic, like Simon Iff's. On the contrary, Ouine embodies 'the yawning abyss of pure ambiguity where everything is relative and evil wears the mask of good' (p. 149). A youth Ouine cultivates as a disciple initially imagines the man might be a 'a saint'. Later, however, Ouine is revealed as 'an incarnation of the Cold, and it is the absolute Cold that is hell, the fixed, still cold of eternal, loveless solitude, beyond the reach of good and evil' (p. 154). (Note the reversal here, whereby hell is cold, not hot, and marked by solitude, not Bosch-like swarms of demons: a particular hell of the cloistered intellectual who has failed to come out into the gregarious world of Wilde, Crowley and Leary, where Individualism promises to be achieved through group Joy, rather than solitary Pain.) Ouine's microcosm is a village 'dying of boredom'. In it, as in him, 'everything is ambiguous, there is no ground to stand on, you can only sink' (p. 150).

Depressing? But then one man's devil is another man's god. Christly divinity may be dead in this avatar post-Einstein; religious embodiments of other types are not. Zaehner links Ouine to philosophic Hinduism, which 'regards Brahman as being totally beyond right and wrong since every *right* action binds you to the wheel of *saṃsāra* from which again you must escape' (p. 165). He also cites Zoroastrianism and its offshoots, whose 'two spiritual principles are *twins* who respectively *choose* to do good and evil' (p. 166). Ouine has a similarity of ice to fire with Yahweh of the Old Testament, who is 'indeed beyond good and evil, and the author of both' (p. 164): an 'immoderate' deity who gives way to his emotions and suffers thereby in his treatment of Job (and possibly too of his son, Christ) and who arbitrarily favours a 'chosen people' whose members, in Bonhoeffer's words,[21] 'kill, deceive, rob, divorce, fornicate, doubt, blaspheme, and curse'. Last but not least comes the God of materialistic Protestantism – 'good-and-evil, light-and-darkness, indeed he is Monsieur Ouine, not split but an *antinomy*: a totality of inner opposites' (p. 167). Zaehner sums up his feeling towards this deity via a 'revelation' Jung had as a twelve-year-old and reports in *Memories, Dreams, Reflections*, another text sacred to seekers of the period:

> I gathered all my courage as though I were about to leap forthwith into hell-fire, and let the thought come. I saw before me [a] cathedral, [a] blue sky. God sits on His golden throne, high above the world – and from under the throne an enormous turd falls upon the sparkling roof, shatters it, and breaks the walls of the cathedral asunder.[22]

Thus 'Monsieur Ouine' can be transformed into a figure of comedy: God as the 'merry prankster' of halcyon LSD days. Zaehner, however, clings to intellectual sombreness. Life is in chaos; the centre has not held. Fine figures such as Pope John XXIII may seem momentarily to be reviving the kind of Christian spirit he dreams on in his own medallion, but they pass all too swiftly from this fallen world. And so Zaehner must end by following Bonhoeffer in the sentiments that 'death is the supreme festival on the road to freedom';[23] 'death is God's greatest gift to man, a gift we should accept not in fear and trembling but with joy' (p. 194); and 'to die to self so that you may live in God' is the ultimate happiness and goal (p. 210).

These are nice paradoxes to voice when playing 'glass-bead games' in the *sanctum* of All Souls' College. But when brought down from Castalia and applied to the 'real world', do they really hold superior moral value to the encomiums of a Leary to live life to the fullest and attempt to achieve moments of mystical *satori* thereby? Which, we might ask – deeply thought pessimism or shallowly proclaimed optimism – ultimately provides the better rationalization for dispatching souls out of this 'vale of tears' through self-shocking acts of murder?

That Leary was once a Harvard professor is no doubt one explanation for why Zaehner concentrates on *The Politics of Ecstasy* rather than works more closely approximating 'bible' status for the generation in question. In spite of ingratiating spurts of 'hip' argot. Leary writes in language and grammar Zaehner can 'relate to', unlike, say, the great pop Buddhist and 'beat' chronicler, Jack Kerouac. At the same time, Zaehner,

with his elitist distaste for anything new, is a classic example
of the cramped institutionalized thinker Leary left the university
to get away from, while Kerouac, who had long since blazed a
trail out of Lionel Trilling's Eng. Lit. lectures to Walt
Whitman's free-loving road, is godfather to the kind of 'drop-
out' Leary hopes to be guru for. As I suggested earlier,
Kerouac is the true, homegrown Larry Darrell; and, in his
sequence of *romans à clef*, one can see better than anywhere
else the ebb and flow of cult faith in new mystical doctrine.

   In the last chapter of *California Writers*, I discuss briefly
how the 'energized enthusiasm' of *On the Road* eventually
disintegrated into the pessimism of *Big Sur*, yet how what
Allen Ginsberg refers to as Kerouac's 'Bodhisattvic heart'
lived on to become a moral ideal for the 'flower children'.[24]
Riding the great wheel of Eastern mysticism from enlightenment
to *samsāra* to dissolution in 'the Void', taking drugs (marijuana,
not LSD), searching for sex (its comforts, not its 'power'),
always listening for 'the beat' (jazz though, not rock), Kerouac
blends all four of Zaehner's 'ingredients', along with the fifth
one we have noted – that peculiarly Western romantic
attachment to the 'outlaw' (his 'buddy', Neal Cassady). In all
Kerouac's works, these ingredients churn together in uneasy
harmony and come simultaneously to exalt and negate the
revolutionary new 'lifestyle' his kind is determined to invent.
But *Desolation Angels*, a book published well after embarkation
on the road yet before the final drift into liquor-sodden
despair, is probably the best place to see them in full tension.[25]

   The book begins in the Cascade Mountains of Washington
State, where the author (fictionalized as Jack Duluoz) has
gone for the summer to work as a forest-fire spotter. There he
lives simply, reading the *Vedas*, cooking brown rice and
communing with magnificent vistas of blue sky and evergreen.
With no human being around to disturb him, he is free to
meditate on life and the world: a lower-middle-class American
version of Zarathustra, or the Ferryman of *Siddhartha*. Wholly
restored to primal 'oneness with Nature', he is able to feel the
Void in its delightful aspect. When he starts back to civilization
at the end of the summer, he is full of heightened awareness
and spirituality.

   The city, however, puts out different 'vibrations'. Not the
least of them is Duluoz's own desire for time-honoured urban

substitute 'voids' – drink, drugs, music and sex. He checks into a skid-row hotel in Seattle, buys a pint of whisky, and wanders the 'mean streets' looking for kicks. What he finds is Baudelairean: beautiful yet grotesque; 'unreal' yet so intensely of the flesh that he can see it decomposing in his mind's eye. Wildean Sorrow and Germanic *Schadenfreude* mix with Leary-like or Crowleyan Joy in his response to the shabby Dionysian revels he watches. A sad fatality to all human efforts at happiness is his most distinct affirmation, as in this reverie provoked by a stripper:

> Nobody can climb to her snatch except the Sultan organ who'll bear witness to her juices then go to his juiceless grave and her grave be juiceless too in time, after the first black juices the worms love so, then dust, atoms of dust, whether as atoms of dust or great universes of thighs and vaginas and penises what will it matter, it's all a Heaven Ship – The whole world is roaring right there in that theatre and just beyond I see files of sorrowing humanity wailing by candlelight and Jesus on the Cross and Buddha sitting neath the Bo Tree and Mohammed in a cave and the serpent and the sun held high and all Akkadian–Sumerian antiquities and early sea-boats carrying courtesan Helens away to the bash final war and broken glass of tiny infinity till nothing's there but snowy light permeating everywhere throughout the darkness and sun – pling, and electro-magnetic gravitational ecstasy passing through without a word or sign and not even passing through and not even being – (*Desolation Angels*, p. 127)

There is an 'erectile' volubility to this prose not unlike what we saw in Sade; and perhaps one should note in passing the Reichian sexual habits typical of Kerouac's time and place – Neal Cassady, besides his exploits with women (and occasionally men), was said in his prime to masturbate five times a day.[26] Furthermore, the whole passage reflects a post-war and peculiarly American urge to synthesize motifs from all religions into one Oversoul-ish viewpoint. Beatific as this may be, it leads directly (as Zaehner might have predicted) to apprehensions of *Götterdämmerung*, Sadean violence, final war.

The upshot is that, from contemplating the womb and sexual act, Duluoz moves towards a realization of why Cathar and Buddhist monks felt compelled to reject the Earthly body. Later in the book, after sexual frustrations apparent in the above have been temporarily assuaged, he expresses the idea outright (and with misogynist undertones):

> By far the sweetest gift on earth, inseminating a woman, the feeling of that for a tortured man, leads to children who are torn out of the womb screaming for mercy as tho they were being thrown to the Crocodiles of Life. ... The essential teaching of the Lord Buddha was: 'No More Re-birth' but this teaching was taken over, hidden, controverted, turned upside down and deformed into Zen, the invention of Mara the Tempter, Mara the Insane, Mara the Devil. ... Meaning that, for every Clark Gable or Gary Cooper born, with all the so-called glory (or Hemingway) that goes with it, comes disease, decay, sorrow, lamentation, old age, death, decomposition – meaning, for every little sweet lump of baby born that women croon over, is one more vast rotten meat burning slow worms in the graves of this earth. (p. 274)

Kerouac's disillusionment might lead another seeker – would lead some, as we shall see – to fatal 'black magic' divisions. But all remains One for him. Ubiquitous pathos breeds cosmic sympathy. In the eternal present of his stream-of-consciousness, he is forever riding the wheel back to the desire which leads to decay, the hope which dissolves in despair:

> Ah, I think, but somewhere ahead in the night waits a sweet beauty for me, who will come up and take my hand, maybe Tuesday – and I'll sing to her and be pure again and be like young arrow-slinging Gotama vying for her prize – Too late! All my friends growing old and ugly and fat, and me too, and nothing there but expectations that don't pan out – and the Void'll Have Its Way.
> Till they re-establish paradise on earth, the Days of Perfect Nature, and we'll wander around naked and kissing in the gardens, and attend dedication ceremonies to the

Love God at the Great Love Meeting Park, at the World
Shrine of Love – Until then, bums –
Bums –
Nothing but bums – (p. 129)

He dreams of Eden: the hippy Woodstock; the Void of
happiness glimpsed on the mountain. But what he finds down
here in the city is more like the *inferno*: the hippy Altamont;
the vision of junkies, 'wild boys', and human devils in the
work of another incanter of the transported 'ОМ', his friend
William Burroughs. In a restaurant, for instance, Duluoz sees
a pair of young punks stabbing straws against the counter to
remove the wrappers 'as though stabbing someone to death, a
real hard fast death-stab that frightens me . . . probably stab
old men at night'. This makes him feel the Void as awful:
'That's the way it goes, there's your world – Stab! Kill! –
Don't care! – There's your Actual Void Face – exactly what
this empty universe holds in store for us, the Blank – Blank
Blank Blank!' (p. 133).

Later, in San Francisco among his beat buddies and listening
to jazz, he feels the Void as happy again – 'The only meaning
is without meaning'. But each twist of the kaleidoscope of
drunken, exuberant *living* changes the pattern. Great friend
Cassady (here as elsewhere called Cody Pomeray) seems like
'Christ's contemporary frightening brother' as he talks in
'amazing rhythms of [speed-stimulated] talk' about his guru
Edgar Cayce, who became a seer because 'in a previous
lifetime he drank the blood of living human sacrifice', or about
how each man has '*an evil spirit* and *a good spirit* vying for [his]
special entity soul' ('I see them above their heads, see, you
can repel the evil and draw the good by meditating on the
white square of your mind which I see above your head and
in which the two spirits do dwell – sfact'). But, while Duluoz
can 'dig' this Crowleyan gibberish in his eternal tourist-of-
ideas sort of way, a girl Pomeray is trying to seduce by it is
less impressed: 'I'm not gonna be corrupted by his talk! Is
Cody the devil? Is Cody an angel? . . . No! I'm going outside!
The man is evil!' (p. 152).

Duluoz hangs on to the wheel. When Pomeray grabs him
and says, 'Jack sleep read write talk walk fuck and see and
sleep again', he is so charmed that he reaffirms his faith: Cody

is 'the earnest Christ whose imitation of Christ is in the flesh before you sweating to believe that all does really good-and-bad matter – All shining and shaking to believe it – a priest of life' (p. 181). For a moment, sheer physical energy and spirit holds back the encroaching shadow of the Void. But then weariness comes down. Duluoz says to someone, 'I'm too old for young idealism like that' (p. 188). Inevitable entropy slows the wheel's turnings. Presences suddenly seem to contain their ominous opposites. Irwin Garden (Ginsberg) cannot be separated from his famous fatalist line: 'I have seen the best minds of my generation destroyed by madness.'[27] A party degenerates into planning for anarcho–phallic revolution: 'We'll have assholes showing on the screens of Hollywood. . . . We'll show them the golden brain of our cocks' (p. 195). A young poet looks 'like a saint' but feels compelled to pursue his path as 'an evil-seeker', reading the Egyptian *Book of the Dead* and passing joints. 'Your Buddhism is nothing but the vestiges of Manichaeism, Ja-a-a-ck,' he tells Duluoz; 'Manichaen sutras . . . all these Buddhist negatives' (p. 198). Under the burden of absorbing and becoming One with all this reeling life, the latter can only agree. 'O I'm not a Buddhist anymore', he says, denying his gods; 'I'm not anything!'

A hip *Walpurgisnacht* reaches its 'last horrible scene' in a fancy restaurant. There 'the best painter in San Francisco' demonstrates current belief in artistic licence by 'cramming his pockets full with free cigarettes that have been generously left in open boxes made of teakwood' (p. 202). Duluoz is 'turned off'. The great wheel of enlightenment may justify petty theft to some, but for him the 'New Aeon' means quiet departure from bourgeois values, not careless subversion of them. Still, he continues to identify himself with the 'outlaws'. Against the backdrop of order-loving, materialistic America, they remain holy: 'Cody, I had a vision last night of a gang of dark men like Raphael and David D'Angeli and Irwin and me all standing in the gloom with glittering silver crucifixes and neck chains over our dark breasts! – Cody, Christ *will* come again!' (p. 223). Dark, faintly ominous, potentially vengeful, they are the 'desolation angels' of the book's title: spiritual brothers of the lowest of the low – even lumpen-prole dregs, Duluoz intuits as he and his *Führer* among buddies hop a flatcar south to LA and ultimately Mexico:

See cool Negro hoboes on the car next to mine calmly smoking cigarettes in the cars of lashed trucks and right in front of everybody! Poor Cody! Poor me! To L.A. ... and twenty young men sitting among armed guards, on their way to prison, a prison bus, and two of them turn and see me and all I do is slowly lift my hand and slowly wave hello and look away as they slowly smile –
Desolation Peak, what more do you want?   (pp. 225–6)

Indeed, how much further can Larry Darrell go in stripping the givens of Western society off, making himself an itinerant workman or untouchable, learning Stephen Dedalus's 'reality of experience' from the bottom up? In Kerouac, as I indicate in *California Writers* and Frederick Feied has argued in *No Pie in the Sky*, the urge of the American 'seeker' from Whitman to London to Dos Passos and beyond to 'get down to basics', in a phrase of the age, or find 'the bottom line' with that type who on Yeats's 'great wheel' might be identified with the hunchback or fool, reaches its apogee. Nor, in the 'Art-is-Life' decade of the 1960s, with its debt to Kerouac as moral pathfinder, was this sentimental identification with the underdog a minor motif. The musical 'revolution' of the decade grew out of a merger of old poor-white folk songs with black blues (only towards the end was poor-white Country and Western mixed in). This made rock-and-roll in message as different from 'bobby sox' pop as drugs of the 1960s were from Daddy's stolen liquor bottles at beach parties of the previous decade. The entire spirit of the generation Kerouac heralded was antinomian. Its description of its lifestyle as a 'counter-culture' is obvious testimony to this. Almost any kind of activity opposed to bourgeois conformity became *ipso facto* 'hip'. All laws were questioned as segregation statutes were repealed, the Vietnam War came under attack, and drug busts and traffic violations put thousands of middle-class kids behind bars for the first time in history. Overhanging all like a black cloud was the spectre of a rapacious, closed, manipulative establishment: an eternal angry parent whose aim was to limit, even punish, youthful celebration and freedom, and whose agent was the ubiquitous, dark-uniformed brutal nanny of the cop.
Kerouac saw all this coming. He saw it through understand-

ing of the broken outlaws he and Cassady might become – that society would make them turn into – if they persisted on their 'freedom road'. He describes it most poignantly in the famous article 'The Vanishing Hobo', which later became the final chapter in *Lonesome Traveller*. This echoes the kind of doss-house existence we saw the young Hitler living in Vienna. It also suggests the kind of adult expectations an illegitimate, reformatory-educated nobody like Manson (he shared these elements of background with Cassady) might have been content to fulfil had he not been 'born under a bad sign' and 'with teeth'. The opening and closing passages deserve to be quoted at length:

> The American Hobo has a hard time hoboing nowadays due to the increase in police surveillance of highways, railroad yards, sea shores, river bottoms, embankments and the thousand-and-one hiding holes of industrial night. – In California, the packrat, the original old type who goes walking from town to town with supplies and bedding on his back, the 'Homeless Brother', has practically vanished, along with the ancient gold-panning desert rat who used to walk with hope in his heart through struggling Western towns that are now so prosperous they don't want old bums any more. – 'Man don't want no pack rats here even tho they founded California' said an old man hiding with a can of beans and an Indian fire in a river bottom outside Riverside California in 1955. – Great sinister tax-paid police cars (1960 models with humorless searchlights) are likely to bear down at any moment on the hobo in his idealistic lope to freedom and the hills of holy silence and holy privacy. – There's nothing nobler than to put up with a few inconveniences like snakes and dust for the sake of absolute freedom. . . .
>
> The hobos of America who can still travel in a healthy way are still in good shape, they can go hide in cemeteries and drink wine under cemetery groves of trees and micturate and sleep on cardboards and smash bottles on the tombstones and not care and not be scared of the dead but serious and humorous in the cop-avoiding night and even amused and leave litters of their picnic between the grizzled slabs of

Imagined Death, cussing what they think are real days, but Oh the poor bum of the skid row! There he sleeps in the doorway, back to wall, head down, with his right hand palm-up as if to receive from the night, the other hand hanging, strong, firm, like Joe Louis hands, pathetic, made tragic by unavoidable circumstance – . . . 'I don't want to show my hand but in sleep I'm helpless to straighten it, yet take this opportunity to see my plea, I'm alone, I'm sick, I'm dying – see my hand up-tipped, learn the secret of my human heart, give me the thing, give me your hand, take me to the emerald mountains beyond the city, take me to the safe place, be kind, be nice, smile – I'm too tired now of everything else. I've had enough, I give up, I quit, I want to go home, take me home O brother in the night – take me home, lock me in safe, take me to where all is peace and amity, to the family of life, my mother, my father, my sister, my wife and you my brother and you my friend – but no hope, no hope, no hope, I wake up and I'd give a million dollars to be in my own bed – O Lord save me – ' In evil roads behind gas tanks where murderous dogs snarl from behind wire fences cruisers suddenly leap out like getaway cars but from a crime more secret, more baneful than words can tell.

The woods are full of wardens.[28]

Kerouac saw a horror at the end of his road. He saw coming if not already arrived the destruction of his medallion. Yet, for all his knowledge of the phases of the wheel and his forgiveness of evil in the personalities of his peers, he showed no urge to 'purposeful destruction' of the forces which threatened it. Never having 'transvalued values' enough to justify murder, he would sooner have destroyed himself than have lifted a finger against a hostile world. In this, he indeed ends by being like a Cathar 'pure': a soul yearning to be dispatched to a 'better place'. Never aspiring to power either through the occult like Crowley or political manipulation like Hitler, he did not develop exceptional personal magnetism or charisma. His mundane goal was simply to be a good 'buddy'. *Vis-à-vis* Manson, he stands in something of the relation of Yeats to Crowley, though without similar personal connection. But, of figures discussed in this study, he finally has most in common with the 'white Christ' of Wilde, the saintly Kropotkin, or Tolstoy, whose non-violent rejection of extant Western morality became a starting-point for others' more active opposition. Both responses have their time and season in the revolutions of the great wheel Larry Darrell went off to discover. In this way, the American paraclete's quest comes to provide a groundwork for conscientious insurrection and yet more simply vengeful forms of mayhem than Isabel Maturin's subtle, bourgeois precipitation of Sylvie MacDonald's demise.

9 Sixties' *Zeitgeist*, II: Cruelty

One of the themes being rehearsed here is the time-honoured one of the difficulty the intellectual has in coping with 'real life'. Perverse ideology may appear as a defensive rationalization for inability or sheer refusal to cope, or for the 'pain' which results from trying to cope with conditions in basic conflict with 'our earliest picture-dreamings'. This phrase comes from the great German novelist of the period, Thomas Mann,[1] who illustrates the idea in several of his books, notably *Death in Venice*, where inability to cope is manifested in Wildean terms as *amour de l'impossible*; also its fictive successor *The Magic Mountain* (originally intended as a novella and *Death in Venice*'s 'twin'[2]), where contemporary Western civilization is depicted as self-protectively sealed off in a sanatorium of manners and ideas, yet forced finally to go down to the world and 'face the music' (modernist cacophony) of the First World War. The metaphor of coming down off the mountain is a useful one. We have just seen the problems Kerouac encountered in doing precisely that. We have described Hitler's 'myth' in terms of coming down off the Berghof to help his people 'cope' with a hostile Europe by unleashing the Second World War. Both had been suggested as semi-conscious versions of the archetypal descent of holy-man–Zarathustra, which Nietzsche glorifies, and of various heretical traditions derived from it.

Zaehner is the kind of intellectual who does not dare venture down from his 'mountain' (the university): instinctively, he knows that scorn and neglect await his troubled conscience 'out there'. Yeats's self-restriction to elitist groups has similar motivation, though his yearning for the hurly-burly is greater. Wilde's 'slumming' destroyed his authority as wit, aesthete and intellectual in his day. Sade's confinement with the lowest of the low undermined his credibility as a philosopher by amplifying rage beyond sense. Only Crowley and Leary of those we have discussed seem to have been able to 'come down from the mountain' and exist happily, though at the cost of denunciation, exile and (in the case of Leary) incarceration. The success of Larry Darrell we cannot speak for. Maugham leaves his progress in America's heartland unexplored. But, if it indeed merges with Kerouac's, as suggested, then even this idealization ends unfortunately, the paraclete dissolving into an 'oceanic' Orphic–Narcissistic pool of drink, drugs, music, sex, footsoreness and melancholy.

The question of how one comes down the mountain from ideology to action is dealt with from a variety of angles by Mann's friend and fellow German, Hermann Hesse. Born two years after Crowley, three after Maugham, a dozen after Yeats and the same number before Hitler, Hesse was small-town bourgeois in origin and experienced a Baudelairean self-loathing of type. Living as a bookseller and in an uncomfortable marriage, he wrote several novellas in the first decade and a half of the century, all incompletely successful attempts at 'liberating' himself – that is, becoming what in absence of a more exact description we might identify as Simon Iff's New Man. Divorce, a 'breakdown', and therapy with Carl Jung led to a sea-change in his life and art. Simultaneous with this came the First World War, which moved the provincial writer towards an unfashionable pacifism. As in the parallel situation of D. H. Lawrence, Hesse felt obliged to become a wanderer (in his case over Europe rather than the globe). Flying free of Stephen Dedalus's 'nets',[3] he reincarnated as a middle-aged, Old World Larry Darrell. Leaving security and order behind, he went questing through chaos and 'the reality of experience' to find his own 'middle way'.

Demian (1917) is about the Jung-assisted break. *Siddhartha* (1922) is about the peace which might be found along the Eastern 'path'. *Steppenwolf* (1927) tracks a passage from bookish bohemianism to 'decadence'. *Journey to the East* (1931) assesses the value of the 'wisdom' of *Siddhartha* in an increasingly Kafkaesque, bureaucratized West. *Narziss und Goldmund* (1934) presents a dialectic between the cloistered man of intellect and vagabonding man of action in its early-Romantic setting of medieval Europe. Finally, *The Glass Bead Game* (1946) confronts head-on the tenuous relationship of the intellectual with the 'real world': in its ending, the master of a renowned esoteric order goes swiftly to his death (by drowning – he knows everything but how to swim) upon coming down from the mountain to be tutor to a promising but as yet unformed youth. All these books (several in lucid translation by the same man who translated *Mein Kampf*) lined bookshelves in Portobello Road, Greenwich Village, Haight-Ashbury, Topanga Canyon, and other centres of the 'hip' *avant-garde* during the LSD period. Tom Wolfe reports that, while Bob Dylan and the Beatles blasted out from stereo speakers, Kesey's 'merry pranksters' left off pot-smoking and cavorting to consult two 'sacred' volumes – *Journey to the East* and science fiction writer Robert Heinlein's *Stranger in a Strange Land*.[4]

Among things which made (and make) Hesse durable are that he was (1) an intellectual without being cloistered like Zaehner; (2) a man of the road without becoming dissolute like Kerouac; and (3) an artist or at most guide as opposed to aspirant guru like Leary, Crowley or to a lesser degree Huxley or Watts. Puritanism is in his work, but it does not stifle. Licentiousness is admitted but rarely allowed to go too far. Overall, he achieves an impression of Larry Darrell-like mind–spirit balance. All the same, he clearly foresees and is ready to accept in himself periods of daemonic possession. These, he believes, must inevitably (and eternally) recur, so long as one remains committed (as he does) to an ideal of full personality. Circular moral unity in Hesse suggests Yeats's great wheel; but, unlike in Yeats, Hesse's 'evil' characterizations demand to be encountered in the self first and 'tested out' psychologically, not merely dreamed upon with troubled and external point of view. So much is expressed (I use the verb particularly to emphasize a German Expressionist timeliness and flavour) in what was to become Hesse's most celebrated book in the 1960s, one which would give its name to a pre-Doors Los Angeles rock band, *Steppenwolf*.

This novel constitutes an ironic Western sceptical (Nietzschean) obverse to the Eastern quiestistic achievement of its immediate predecessor (*Siddhartha*). As such, it presents as clearly as a literary effort might the steps by which Dionysian 'awakening' could lead to mindless cruelty, and how such cruelty could come to be regarded with sublimely detached coolness as simply part of a larger pageant. The fiction unfolds in layers. First comes an 'Author's Note',[5] written the

year before Hesse died (1961); it warns, with prescience, that
the book may be liable to be misunderstood by 'very young
readers'. Next comes a 'Preface' by a fictionalized 'young
reader', the son of the landlady of the 'Steppenwolf' of the
book's title, Harry Haller (intentional same initials as those of
the author); this suggests that the 'records' which follow must
be understood as a revelation of the mentality which overtakes
a generation in which 'two cultures and religions [classical
versus modernist, Germanic *versus* Jewish, etc.] overlap'. Finally
we arrive at 'Harry Haller's Records', supposedly abandoned
by their author upon leaving intellectual seclusion for the
lively world; these are divided into two interrelated parts, 'FOR
MADMEN ONLY' and 'TREATISE ON THE STEPPENWOLF', and form
the main body of the narrative.

Precisely like his creator, Haller is approaching his fiftieth
birthday. He has studied extensively, both in Eastern and
Western thought, and has written essays and articles on
subjects from Goethe to pacifism. He loves music, Mozart
especially, and describes it as 'the door to another world'
where one may find God, the stars, acceptance of all things
and fear of nothing. At the same time he loathes jazz, the
'Americanized' new man, and 'these soul-destroying, evil days
of inward emptiness and despair . . . on this ravaged earth,
sucked dry by the vampires of finance'. Whereas Sade found
justification for his demoralization in the corruption of the
ancien régime, Haller like Hitler, Simon Iff and the *poètes
maudites*, finds it in that of the bourgeois. Disconsolately, he
wanders the city streets, a version of Baudelaire or Kerouac.
He knows all cafés and concert halls but is apathetic to them.
Then one night he glimpses one he has not seen before: 'MAGIC
THEATRE. ENTRANCE NOT FOR EVERYBODY. FOR MADMEN ONLY.'
This strikes him as 'a greeting from another world' (*Steppenwolf*,
p. 42). He is tempted to go in, but does not. Later, he tries to
find the place again, without success. However, on his way
home, a little drunk with wine, he is confronted by a man
with a placard reading, 'ANARCHIST EVENING ENTERTAINMENT.
MAGIC THEATRE. ENTRANCE NOT FOR EVERYBODY.' The man
gives him the 'companion volume to fortune-telling booklets'
entitled 'TREATISE ON THE STEPPENWOLF', then disappears into
a *crépescule de soir*.

There are several motifs with evident appeal to hippies

here; and readers knowledgeable in the lyrics of rock songs may hear echoes throughout the book – the attempt to find the way back to the Magic Theatre in the Eagles's line 'trying to find the passage back to the place I was before';[6] Haller's longing for a 'glimmer of the golden track again' in the title of the Grateful Dead's first single, 'The Golden Road to Unlimited Devotion'.[7] Such connections are not entirely wild. The transition Haller undergoes when he finally does make his way back is pre-hippy: 1927 German urban, Semitic or 'mongrel' decadence of the kind glorified in *Die blaue Engel*, and later *Cabaret*, and swept away in the Nazi–puritan 'regeneration' of the 1930s. This transition proceeds along all four paths towards 'erotic reality' indicated by Marcuse: fantasy, art, group joy and death. It leads Haller to the 'play impulse' prefigured in Kant and Schiller and a realm of ever-changing identities and partners as if under the spell of the fairies of *A Midsummer Night's Dream*. Simultaneously, it brings him to an understanding of Hegel's principle that true 'Freedom' must involve 'risk of death' – his androgynous 'guide' Hermine tells him at their first meeting that, once she has made him 'mad enough', she will require him to kill her (p. 106).

Steppenwolf, like *Demian*, is a story of psychological awakening. The Magic Theatre and its denizens – Hermine, the jazz musician Pablo, and the 'whore-with-a-heart-of-gold' Maria – represent antithetical, *Walpurgisnacht* therapy for a modern Faust. Haller has been stewing in solemnity and repression. He has described himself as 'belonging with the suicides' and in fact has promised himself death on his fiftieth birthday (pp. 58–9). 'Self-slaughter' has seemed to him a way to 'go back to the mother, back to God, back to the All'; and this bottom-line, existentialist attitude has enabled him also, well before pre-hippy tutelage, to be 'capable of loving the political criminal, the revolutionary or intellectual seducer, the outlaw of state and society, as his brother' (p. 63). Though he 'would not have known how to deplore theft and robbery, murder and rape, otherwise than in a bourgeois manner', he has a proud certainty that 'the vital force of the bourgeoisie resides in such outsiders' as himself: artists – or in fact (for this is what Haller, if not his new comrades in the Magic Theatre, should be described as) artists-*manqué* – who always possess 'two souls', feel 'God and the devil' within, and oscillate

between 'happiness and suffering' (p. 55). Haller, in short, is
from the first a caterpillar yearning to become a butterfly; and
his so-called 'wolf' half – restless, savage, self-mocking, hostile
to the world – exists as a result of his not yet having
accomplished this metamorphosis.

The 'wolf' subverts the man, and *vice versa*. Just before his
first visit to the Magic Theatre, Haller has dinner with a
professor and wife (in some ways suggesting Jung and his
wife) and finds himself almost literally barking with hatred
over their 'safe' interpretation of Goethe, their desiccated quest
for 'analogies between Asiatic and Indian mythologies', their
prejudice against Jews and Communists, their general philistine
chauvinism (pp. 90–3). Tepid dabblers in pre-countercultural
ideas, these 'good souls' provoke Haller to an inner response
as violent as that of the hip hero of Robert Stone's *Dog Soldiers*
against 1970s' trendies eager to dabble in heroin.[8] However,
instead of letting one of them kill himself with an overdose,
Haller flees and – after a disguised psychoanalytical session
with Hermine – immerses himself in a dream of dialogue with
his personal Goethe. Why, he asks the great German artist–
mystic, should he have spent his career 'preaching optimism'
when he had long since discovered 'the hopelessness of life'
(p. 112)? Goethe, who initially appears as 'commanding', with
'a nod like an old raven' and 'the star of a secret order on his
breast', responds by transforming into a dancing, laughing
sprite. The star of his order bursts into flower and he
disappears to melodies from *The Magic Flute*,[9] saying, 'You should
not take old people who are already dead seriously.... You put too
high a value on time' (p. 116).

From the episode with the professor, Haller affirms the
aperçu Siddhartha enunciates (and Crowley and Leary would
assert against orthodox contemporaries): that the received
man-of-knowledge may be the 'enemy of knowledge'[10] (Hesse
also seems to register a protest against what Marcuse calls
Jung's 'spiritualization of want'). From Hermine and the
sprites of the Magic Theatre, he learns further what Siddhartha
tells his boyhood friend Govinda once he has come to rest as a
ferryman at the end of his quest: that a man seeks when he
thinks he needs a goal, but once he has 'found' he needs
none.[11] 'All we learn by heart about heroes and geniuses and
great deeds and fine emotions is all nothing but a swindle

invented by the schoolmasters for educational reasons to keep
children occupied for a given number of years', Hermine tells
Haller: 'Death, eternity, the path to the saints, the kingdom
on the other side of time is what we want' (p. 178).
Anticipating Mick Jagger's line in 'Sympathy for the Devil'
that 'Every cop is a criminal/And all the sinners saints',[12] she
goes on: 'Every sin can be a way to saintliness' (p. 180).
Anticipating the Eden-call of the great slogan song
'Woodstock'[13] – 'And we got to get ourselves/Back to the
garden' – she concludes, 'Our only guide is our homesickness'.[14]

The destiny, then, Haller realizes, is to become an
'Immortal'. This state he ultimately poeticizes thus:

> We above you ever more residing
> In the ether's star translumined ice
> Know no day nor night nor time's dividing,
> Wear not age nor sex as our device.
> Cool and unchanging is our eternal being,
> Cool and star bright is our eternal laughter.   (p. 245)

The transmoral idea is, we might note, 'cool' and delightful
rather than cold and paralysing, like Bernanos's Monsieur
Ouine. Haller, guided by his 'liberated' *alter ego* Hermine, is
not frightened of the post-Nietzschean world order (or
disorder). Not for him to continue a solitary, uncompanioned,
un-conscious-exploring quest like Zaehner's; he must break
out of his All Souls' cloister. Thus he accepts Hermine's
formulations that 'we are children of the devil', 'the devil is
the spirit', and 'we have fallen out of nature and hang
suspended in space' (p. 149). He learns from Pablo that 'a
musician's job is not to think, just to play'; that 'music does
not depend on education' (p. 155); that the jazz-player is no
more or less sublime than Mozart; and that Mozart himself,
being of that 'cool' company of angels, is no more offended by
the idea of *Don Giovanni* being played on a wireless than he is
by Haller's own writings (which are revealed as 'plagiarizings
ill-got' – p.241). Maria, the beautiful lover who brings back
in enriched form memory of all the beloveds Haller has ever
known, shows him further that a street girl may talk of jazz
'with as much admiration and ecstasy as an intellectual over
Nietzsche or Hamsun' (p. 163). Thus we draw close to a

generation's obsession with rock minutiae, down to occult
investigation as to whether 'signs' in the lyrics or on covers of
Beatles albums in fact 'proved' that Paul McCartney was
dead.

Flower-like Maria makes Haller's 'soul breathe once more'
(p. 166). A *gamine* who 'sometimes had furs and grand hotels
and others only the garret', she is 'one of the culture of
women and men who lived for love alone, were simultaneously
innocent and corrupt, in love with life and yet clinging to it
far less than the bourgeois' (p. 162). She never takes money
from Haller; but one day, without warning, she drifts out of
his life. His surprisingly equinanimous response to this is a
measure of the progress of his 'initiation'. Concurrently with
Haller, Maria has been the lover of Pablo; and, on one
occasion, the latter has invited the older man to a bisexual
romp. Haller has refused, though with toleration. Later, his
attraction to Hermine as Herman, a male friend of his youth,
reveals developing openness to sexual freedom reminiscent of
'those years of childhood when the capacity for love, in its first
youth, embraces not only both sexes, but all and everything,
sensuous and spiritual, and endows all things with a spell of
love and fairy-like ease of transformation' (p. 195). It is,
rather shockingly, with such 'fairy-like ease' that Harry later
fulfils Hermine's prediction and kills her. This happens when
he finds her *in flagrante* with Pablo. The act is committed, with
Freudian appropriateness, by knife.

Haller proceeds with the somnambulism of Dorian Gray –
indeed, there is even a resonance of Wilde's fatalist line from
Reading Gaol: 'I had killed my love' (p. 244); 'Each man kills
the thing he loves'. Like Susan Atkins on the murder of
Sharon Tate,[15] Haller describes what happened with chilling
sensual detail: 'I plunged in my knife to the hilt. . . . The
blood welled over her white and delicate skin. . . .' Eros joins
hands with Thanatos, and a mist of *Schadenfreude* occludes
moral questions: 'I would have kissed away the blood if
everything had happened a little differently.' For a moment
fear breaks in, not guilt or even regret for the victim so much
as trepidation that the victimizer may be held from future joys
by his Sadean excess: 'Had I quenched the sun? Had I
stopped the heart of all life?' But then Haller senses 'the
coldness of death and space breaking in'. He is transported to

the presence of the Immortals. They put him on trial – but not for the murder, rather for his failure to 'learn to laugh'. This surreal 'justice' is matched by that of their sentence: Haller is condemned to 'listen to life's radio music and to reverence the spirit behind it' (p. 251).

If one takes Hermine as an *anima* emanation, Haller's 'murder' of her is nothing more than a psychological breakthrough and, as such, justifiable – indeed, quite 'healthy'. But *Steppenwolf* is more than just a psychological case study. It is a novel, a representation of behaviour – as such, imitable by easily *influenced* minds; and here is where the problem begins. The love-murder, lovingly described, might be read on a purely realistic level: Harry Haller goes to the Magic Theatre a last time, participates in a Dionysian *soirée*, drinks, takes a puff or two on one of Pablo's hashish-filled cigarettes (perhaps a sniff as well of cocaine), and goes on to indulge in a kaleidoscope of activities which culminate in this bloody, self-releasing and transcending existential act. There is at least as much 'justification' for his murder as for Camus's in *L'Étranger*; and, of course, the point in both books is that, in the amoral 'New Aeon', no justification for any act is needed. Man has gone beyond Yeatsian debilitation: he need no longer think, he may 'do what [he] wil[ls]'. Hesse is understandably ironic about the whole business, but this does not get him off the hook. Elsewhere on the 'great wheel' of possibilities offered in the Magic Theatre, Haller has found the following:

— JOLLY HUNTING/GREAT AUTOMOBILE HUNT
— MUTABOR/TRANSFORMATION INTO ANY ANIMAL OR/PLANT YOU PLEASE
— KAMASUTRAM/INSTRUCTION IN THE INDIAN ARTS OF LOVE/ COURSE FOR BEGINNERS; FORTY-TWO/DIFFERENT METHODS AND PRACTICES
— DELIGHTFUL SUICIDE. YOU LAUGH/YOURSELF TO BITS
— DO YOU WANT TO BE ALL SPIRIT?/THE WISDOM OF THE EAST
— DOWNFALL OF THE WEST/MODERATE PRICES. NEVER SUR-PASSED.
— COMPENDIUM OF ART/TRANSFORMATION FROM THE TIME INTO SPACE/BY MEANS OF MUSIC
— LAUGHING TEARS/CABINET OF HUMOUR

— SOLITUDE MADE EASY/COMPLETE SUBSTITUTE FOR ALL FORMS
   OF/SOCIABILITY
— GUIDANCE IN THE BUILDING-UP OF THE/PERSONALITY.
   SUCCESS GUARANTEED.
— MARVELLOUS TAMING OF THE/STEPPENWOLF
— ALL GIRLS ARE YOURS
— HOW ONE KILLS FOR LOVE   (pp. 210–36[16])

We have seen what Haller does when he goes through the last
of these 'doors': murder for self-expression is the last stage of
the German Romantic quest, a 'natural' reversal of *Young
Werther*'s cult of suicide, soon to take national form in the
Hitler adventure. Thus the previous 'door', 'ALL GIRLS ARE
YOURS', shows a prior stage in that quest permeated with 'the
fragrance of springtime' and the atmosphere of a pre-*Faust*ian
or *Don Giovanni*an eighteenth-century pastoral love tale (p. 229).
Counting backwards, the 'door' previous to that opens on a
scene which convinces Haller that he may be done with his
split personality (man–wolf) for ever: 'schizophrenia' is a
creation of language; multiple personality is both the fact and
ideal.[17] The 'art of building up the soul', he is told on going
through the next previous 'door', is to disintegrate oneself into
fragments and reform in ever-changing personae, as a playwright
does when creating characters in a drama (according to Hesse–
Haller's interpretation – p. 224). This is the crux of the
matter. If the truly 'liberated' personality can, like an artist,
learn to draw up from his subconscious all capabilities as man
and beast, then it is only 'natural' that in the course of things
he should 'create' himself into a murderer from time to time.
With no moral law to restrain him, the only reason he should
not do so is pusillanimous fear of captivity or death – which
punishments in any case, to the entirely multifaceted soul,
might simply constitute other forms of 'experience'.

   That *Steppenwolf* could appear to be promoting such an idea
is no doubt why Hesse, like Huxley with *The Doors of Perception*,
felt compelled to addend a disclaimer; but, even more than
Huxley's 'sequel' to *Doors*, Hesse's 'Author's Note' is really
powerless to mitigate unfortunate imitations. The most
dramatic and memorable scene in *Steppenwolf* comes when
Haller goes through the first 'door' to the 'GREAT AUTOMOBILE
HUNT' (p. 210). Here he finds armoured cars chasing pedestrians

and crushing them to death. The 'long-awaited war between men and machines has commenced'. Radicals representing contemporary 'reds' and anticipating present-day 'greens' prepare 'to make an end at last of the fat and well-dressed and perfumed plutocrats who use machines to squeeze the fat from other men's bodies'. 'Set factories afire at last!' they cry. 'Make a little room on the crippled earth! Depopulate it so that the grass may grow again.' Sade lived the Terror against feudal hegemony; Haller joins in that against bourgeois. 'In every eye I saw the unconcealed spark of destruction and murder, and in mine too these wild red roses bloomed as rank and high, and sparkled as brightly' (p. 211). Note the glorifying imagery for 'murder' and 'destruction': 'unconcealed spark', 'wild red roses', 'high', 'sparkled . . . brightly'. Joy in unleashed animal aggression is more aesthetically conceived than in Sade, but it is there just as apparently. With a Hitlerianly blue-eyed companion from school days, Haller climbs into a tree (returning to pre-human, Darwinian monkey state[18]) and machine-guns cars over a cliff as they wind up the mountain road. 'It makes no difference what our victims are called', his companion counsels; 'the world is done for and so are we' (p. 214). Apocalypse is welcomed, one's own destruction as well as another's. In an amoral epoch, nothing finally matters. Thus the gunman can tell his victim with Dadaist whimsy that he is killing him for 'exceeding the speed limit' (p. 215). Joy indeed has become a subtle form of brutality:[19] 'We do not kill from duty, but pleasure, or much more, rather, from displeasure and despair of the world. For this reason we find a certain amusement in killing people' (p. 216).

Schadenfreude here gives way to the ghoulish laughter Haller ascribes to his Immortals, those icy 'strange gods';[20] and like black-shirted gangsters of a few years hence – anarchists of before and Mansonites after – Haller-as-terrorist imagines the world so awry that what he is about, however inhumane, is messianically cleansing, *good*:

> 'Yes,' said I, 'what we are doing is probably mad, and probably it is good and necessary all the same. It is not a good thing when man overstrains his reason and tries to reduce to rational order matters that are not susceptible of rational treatment. Then there are ideals such as those of

the Americans or of the Bolsheviks. Both are extraordinarily rational, and both lead to a frightful oppression and impoverishment of life, because they simplify it so crudely. The likeness of man, once a high ideal, is in process of becoming a machine-made article. It is for madmen like us, perhaps, to ennoble it again.'   (p. 219)

'It is a pleasure to drink at such a fount of wisdom', Haller's ruling-class victim replies. The irony is charming and voice likable. But even the most 'adult' reader can have little doubt which side of the dialectic Hesse–Haller's first-person narration favours.

As I sit back down to write, I have just turned off the television. On it was showing *The Life and Times of Judge Roy Bean*, a movie which depicts the Wild West in much the moral terms of Hesse's novel and ends with a group of maverick cowboy 'old-timers' taking on the bourgeois-era oil barons who have replaced a sod-busting, anarchic life close to nature with the tyranny of the machine. This movie was made in 1972, three years after the Manson murders and one after Jim Morrison died in Paris. The director was John Huston. His first success came with Dashiell Hammett's tale of the impact of European amoralism on the American scene, *The Maltese Falcon*, his second with a tale by Hesse's fellow German and contemporary anarchist, B. Traven, about the assault of man on the Earth and his fellow man for greed in Mexico, *The Treasure of the Sierra Madre*. I mention these things here to remind the reader of something so obvious we need hardly dwell on it: the anarchic, antinomian principle we are tracking was present, and had been present, in American life and culture long before the explosions of the 1960s. Indeed, as we draw closer to the destination of LA 1969, we must note that the legacy of the 'Wild West', both in fact and as glamorized through movies – the shoot-'em-up, go-for-broke, you're-only-as-good-as-the-speed-of-your-draw mentality which had permeated indigenous mythology ever since Theodore Roosevelt and Owen Wister conceived of creating the American 'knight' as a cowboy,[21] and which had influenced vulgar European culture through such 'exports' as those Karl May novels to which young Hitler was addicted – was clearly a dominant motif. Underneath this lay the ethos of the Indian, both real and romanticized; also – specifically in the Southwest, where it had been begun to be revived by such sun-cultists as D. H. Lawrence (*The Plumed Serpent*) long before Carlos Castaneda made his 'journey to Ixtlan' – the ethos of old, noble, pagan Mexico.

Antonin Artaud knew this. At the end of his most lucid period, he travelled like Lawrence and Traven and Crowley before him to the 'fertile crescent' of the Western Hemisphere sun-cult and underwent his initiation into the lore of the dark god of peyote. Artaud's records of his stay with the Tarahumaras[22] anticipates Castaneda and the 'Quetzalcoatl' cult of Los Angeles in the late sixties. Jim Morrison made his own 'pilgrimage' to Mexican sun temples, modelling himself on Artaud in this as in other things – most notably his principles of performance. These were taken in some part consciously from the 'theatre of cruelty', which Artaud had theorized and tried to realize unsuccessfully before his Mexican adventure. A 'madman' in his time, Artaud was a prophet for the sixties, when electric amplification and theatrical lifestyles would converge to create the messianic artform of the rock concert. 'Rock-n-roll is pure *machismo*', Mick Jagger has said; and the *auteur* of 'Sympathy for the Devil' is reputed to have regarded Artaud as a prime precursor and wanted to play him on stage or in film ever since pre-Rolling-Stones days.[23] Thus we come on a last, essential Old World progenitor of the New Aeon of the sixties. Artaud once called himself the 'Mômo', which is a play on the French colloquial expression for 'brat' and also a reversal of 'ом–ом'.[24] A mystic, he was in quest of a intensified state of 'bone and fire'[25] rather than riverside quiescence *à la* Siddhartha. A man screaming from a sanatorium rather than prison, he became a modern successor to Sade: embodiment of the victim, angry survivor, genius of destructiveness. His own era never quite seems to have known him, and he stands before and beyond the sixties rather more as a shadow-god than in real flesh-and-blood form. 'Artaud is alluded to far more frequently than he is read', his critical biographer Julia Costich has written in her Preface to *Antonin Artaud*. His 'myth', as that of Nietzsche, may be (have been) more influential than his

chaotic opus itself; and, with considerable debt to Costich's
scholarship, I shall sketch a version of it.

His 'life of crisis' was a history of sickness, frustration and
accident. At five, he nearly died of meningitis. At ten, he
nearly drowned. Almost all his siblings died young. At college,
he suffered from 'deep depression'; for this, as well as
hallucinations and 'sleepwalking', he was discharged from the
army. After a spell in a clinic in Switzerland, it became clear
that he would not be able to enter his father's shipping-
business; thus he set off for Paris to become an artist. It was
the 1920s. He lived in the house of a psychiatrist who
published a review, *Demain*, which provided an outlet for his
first poems, later collected in *Tric-trac du ciel* (*Heavenly
Backgammon*). Declaring himself 'of the race of Baudelaire,
Nerval, and Nietzsche' (p. 12),[26] he rationalized lack of success
with established publishers, assuaged his 'pain' in opium and
laudanum, and joined forces with the Surrealists. He edited a
number of *La Révolution surréaliste* and contributed 'open letters'
under the title 'Fin de l'ère chrétien'; but he broke with André
Breton over the Surrealist 'healthy love of life' and political
activism – he was in too much pain to be other than a
pessimist, too much a *voyant* for journalistic rather than
metaphysical 'solutions', too much an instinctive rebel to
identify with any single 'movement'.

Artaud spent most of the 1920s writing poetry and taking
drugs, both of which, Costich suggests, were 'united in the
quest to overcome fragmentation' (p. 27). With yet more
intensity than previous *poètes maudites*, he felt haunted by a
supervening force of evil: a force of 'malevolent grandeur'
which attacked the body with as much relish as it possessed
the soul. A Gnostic revulsion from the physical life appeared
early on and manifests itself in diatribes against the female
sex, reproduction and even – unusual in the company we are
discussing – the phallus: 'Only when organs, including the
male member, are eliminated, will man be truly free, restored
to wholeness beyond the power of [the evil] God' (p. 105).[27]
Death, he declares in *L'Art et la mort* (1928), is 'not outside the
domain of the spirit'; indeed, it is apprehendable at four
moments in life – in childhood, in the depths of anguish, in
dreams, and under the influence of drugs (p. 33). Death is not

only knowable in this way; it ought to be known, to be discovered by the artist, who is 'seer' for everyman. Ultimately, he may realize (as latter-day 'immortalists' such as Germaine Greer and Heathcote Williams would, at least for a time, argue[28]) that death does not exist but is 'a fraud perpetrated by sinister occult forces or human weaknesses'.

Apprehension of such truths requires, Artaud argues, a state of 'divine terror'. This is brought on by shock and aggravation of the nerves; and a form of 'living theatre' is the most effective means to transmit it. Artaud's love of theatre dates at least from his first years in Paris, when he supported himself by acting. (His performance of Marat in Abel Gance's film *Napoleon* is an early and enduring example of his 'alienation technique' as an actor: when Charlotte Corday murders him in his bath, he expectorates a mouthful of coffee, which in the black-and-white print looks horrifically like coagulating blood.) His theory incorporated ideas of Nietzsche, Strindberg, Gordon Craig and Adolphe Appia; Wagner's *Gesamtkunst* and Mallarmé's Symbolist theatre of the Ideal, though without 'hidden allusions or secret structures'; Japanese Noh and Balinese theatre, with their emphasis on gesture; the clowns of *commedia del arte*, the rhetoric of contemporary Expressionism, the violence and sex of Jacobean drama, and above all the primal conflicts of Greek tragedy. However, wanting to go farther than any previous form, Artaud makes his theatre into an anti-theatre, intending to 'destroy drama as it has been known in France'.[29] In line with his belief that a cosmic force of evil was descending on the world, he wants performance to be like 'the gnostic idea of the life whirlwind': sudden, apocalyptic, transitory. No performance will be able to be exactly repeated. Success depends entirely on the coming-together of actor, spectacle and audience as a 'unified corpus'. The director must reign as supreme as a contemporary dictator, and the play as fixed text must cease to exist. Words should 'have the importance they acquire in dreams'; screams, noise and music will be equally significant, as will breathing, intonation and facial expression. 'All the grand myths are black'; thus subject matter must concentrate on carnage, torture, spilled blood, the war of the sexes – in short, the 'black magical', 'evil', Manichaean divisions. The theatre has three 'doubles', plague, cruelty, and alchemy (the science of transmuting the material into the ideal); but all these 'conjoin in the consummate double which is Life'.[30]

Artaud actually put together an 'Alfred Jarry Theatre' and later a 'Theatre of Cruelty'. His vast plans for production included versions of *The Revenger's Tragedy*, *Woyzeck*, Sade's 'Le Château de Valmont', the story of Bluebeard, *Atreus and Thyestes*, and not least his own apocalyptic, anti-white, anti-colonial *La Conquête du Mexique*. This was to glorify 'an Indian culture in which sacred cruelty is reflected'. Well before embarking on his voyage across the Atlantic, Artaud believed that the Mexican deities embodied 'thought older than the legend of the Grail and cult of the rose-cross', indeed older than the myths of the Deluge and Atlantis itself (p. 74). But the 'Theatre of Cruelty' collapsed before *La Conquête* could be mounted, owing to a generally negative critical response. Artaud blamed a society which stifled new ideas: 'Bourgeois capitalism must give way. It is immoral, being built exclusively on money and gain.'[31] The one major project of his own realized before the end came was a version of the old Italian tale of incest and parricide, of which Stendhal and Shelley had done early Romantic versions. *The Cenci* enabled Artaud to mount a metaphysical attack on the family, society and authority prefiguring that of the sixties 'Generation Gap'. Cenci is a symbol of tyrannical riches and power, corrupt 'justice' and religion; Beatrice, his daughter, is a clairvoyant and exceptionally 'liberated' girl. Beatrice murders her father after having been violated by him. Significantly, though his sympathies are clearly with the murderess, Artaud shows the girl becoming evil through her act. In the finale, as she is being hung by her hair on a wheel, he has her say, 'I fear that death will teach me/That I have ended by being like him.'[32]

Set designs by Balthus and lighting anticipating early acid-rock light shows at the Fillmore Auditorium failed to save the production or, in the end, Artaud's theatre. Thus in the 1930s he became free to pursue his peculiar form of *gnosis* by other means. Rejecting European culture 'because of its reliance on fixed texts, its debased sexuality, and false distinction between the sacred and daily experience' (p. 55), he explored Tao, the *I Ching*, the *Upanishads* and *Vedas*, the Tibetan and Egyptian *Book of the Dead*, the *Kabala*, Sufi poetry, Tantric and Hatha

Yoga, and pre-Socratic philosophers. Like Yeats, Crowley, Hitler and so many others influenced by the occult, he rejected 'the rot of Reason' and wrote a 'novel', *Héliogabale, ou l'anarchiste couronné*, positing a new fusion between the high and low, divine and earthly, good and evil, Yin and Yang, absolute and fragmented (as the political antipodes in the subtitle suggest). Heliogabalus's reign augurs

> Ordre, Desordre
> Unité, Anarchie
> Poésie, Dissonance
> Rhythme, Discordance
> Grandeur, Puérilité
> Générosité, Cruauté[33]

But here 'explosive oneness' does not produce harmony, as lauded by Simon Iff. Heliogabalus's 'monotheism' is a denial rather than embracing of 'plurality of experience'. His sun temple, built around a sacred 'living stone' of phallic shape, is surrounded by 'gutters of blood representing the blackness and death that are the pitfalls of a sun-cult' (p. 61). Division, particularly sexual, is irresolvable, except in the uroboric, self-consuming moment. 'Having reached the paroxysm of ritual, [Heliogabalus] cannot sustain the effort. ... The androgyne reverts to the "masculine" identity as the aggressor, then to a "feminine" action as the pursued.' The new–old god unravels, and his 'new order' with him, rather like the survivor–victim Hitler. As elsewhere, Artaud here provides an accurate metaphoric prediction of what was going to happen to the Europe of his day.

For a time, he worked on a scenario, *Satan* – 'the image of fire as rebellion which consumes itself and combines burning and death' (p. 63) – but, having taken Western myth to such extremes, he abandons it and the Old Hemisphere at last. In Mexican culture, he finds fire the dominant element, especially in the form of the sun; but here the flame is united with earth, water and air; and the ancient cult of Quetzalcoatl implies no troubled European division of body and spirit. Sacred rites and dances are still performed by the Indians. Artaud finds these 'true' theatrical manifestations, and is disappointed to discover many Mexicans are more interested in his culture than their own. He pursues ancient wisdom to poor, primitive, remote places. In the Ciguri peyote initiation, he experiences 'the conflict of wills' between Eros and Caritas, God as an external 'Master of All Things' and Tutuguri 'the (black) sun, an overwhelming unity' (p. 69). Like Leary and the hippies who would 'succeed' with LSD, he recognizes through the drug 'the image of God's infinite power within himself' and through 'a flaming crucifixion' his own new role as martyr, God, messiah. This hard-won delusion only comes after 'twenty-eight days of suffering', of misunderstanding the rites of 'the Magic Circle', and of 'hostility' from the mountain landscape. As with Castaneda, the white-world outsider is not let in on the new–old knowledge easily. Once he has been, however, he becomes a 'true believer'.

Returning to Europe as if a man on fire, Artaud preaches that the Humanism of the Renaissance was 'a step backwards' and that 'humanity must rise to the level of nature rather than reduce it to human scale' (p. 75). This darkly enlightened, Rousseauesque faith induces him to announce the 'superiority of consciousness over morality'. He becomes 'obsessed with gesture'. Declaring himself 'the Revealed One', the 'Tortured One', the 'Mad–Wise One', he asserts that his name must vanish. Brandishing a weird knotted stick which he claims is the staff St Patrick lost when fighting the serpents, he travels to Ireland. Celtic culture, he has realized belatedly, is the way the West may 'find its way back' to Atlantean–Tarahumaran lost knowledge. This in itself is not so surprising: Yeats, D. H. Lawrence and numerous others had made similar noises already. Artaud's simultaneous prediction of sex wars, erection of absolutisms and destruction of democracies is more lurid but no less credible (the year is 1937). Still, the man's behaviour is now worse than eccentric; and, when he begins to beat a man with his stick for refusing to recognize him as a prophet, he is arrested, incarcerated and shortly declared insane.

At this point, we might pause to note that in spite of his anti-sexual rhetoric and loathing for reproduction, Artaud became engaged to the daughter of a Brussels businessman shortly after returning from Mexico. Why? Had his occult quest led to an extreme which made him secretly wish to 'find his way back' to nothing more eccentric than the bourgeois comforts of his parents' life? This is a nagging antithetical note almost always in the siren song of the bohemian, one which can be heard in Hesse and which became dominant in Hitler. But, if Artaud wanted to 'drop out' from 'dropping out' like so many of his successors in the early 1970s, circumstances and character – Yeats's 'body of fate' – would not let him. The girl's father cut off the engagement after Artaud 'insulted an audience' in his home town (Brussels, as in Baudelaire's time, was still considered the philistine capital of the French-speaking world by *avant-garde* Parisians); and it is shortly after this that Artaud started 'speaking like St Jerome'. Was his confinable behaviour the result of some rage at rejection, like Sade appears to have experienced from the young lady of his own class with whom he shared VD? We shall never know in this case, any more than in that one. Suffice it to say that Artaud was locked up for most of the next decade in an asylum near where Gérard du Nerval had hanged himself (pp. 81–2) – rather near as well to where the Cathar 'pures' had made a 'last stand' against armies of the pope and king.

There he wrote studies on tortured *voyant* precursors in whose tradition he saw himself: Nerval, Poe and Lautréamont among poets; Uccello, Bosch and Van Gogh among painters. The essay on the last, subtitled 'Le suicide de la société', constitutes his most towering Laingian statement. 'Society is so corrupt that an authentic madman is a person of higher moral standing than his contemporaries';[34] a brotherhood of 'aliénés authentiques' must be formed to oppose the 'murderous society of psychiatrists, religious forces of all persuasions, and their accomplices'. The anti-establishment message at last finds direct, pure expression. 'We are all, like poor Van Gogh himself, suicides of society' – 'white niggers' to use Norman Mailer's latter-day phrase.[35] Against 'us', a dominant 'Turkish' culture 'creates a façade of honesty behind which forces manoeuvre until they can steal Van Gogh's essence by killing him'.

During the Cambodian invasion of 1970, protesting American students would watch television news of campus riots and tote up marks of victory for 'us' or 'them'. The division for Artaud between brash, bovine bourgeois masters and their persecuted victims became as irresolvable as the oppositions of sex. In his last years, after his release from Rodez and while existentialist café society was celebrating him, his rhetoric became yet more extreme. This did not help him live, but it enabled him to apotheosize almost immediately after his death (a state in which, ironically, he disbelieved) from drug-related malnutrition and an overdose of chloralhydrate (p. 22). Costich tells two vignettes from this period which underline Artaud's appeal to the post-war antinomian mentality. The first is of a lecture he gave at the Vieux-Colombier Theatre in 1947. Apparently this occasion, attended by the important Left Bank intellectuals of the day, 'rapidly turned into a manifestation of the Theatre of Cruelty'. Artaud had been reading from his most violent poetry; then, without warning, he suddenly broke off and stared into space. Stony silence. Susurrus of whispers among the collected. Embarrassment. 'Finally,' Costich writes,

> André Gide mounted the stage and embraced Artaud, bringing the evening to a nominally satisfactory conclusion. But in the midst of the performance, Artaud had suddenly realized the futility of such an event, and found the French public so corrupt that only military violence could have an effect on its deadened consciousness. From then on, he would become a human theatre in himself, aiming a verbal machine-gun at the world.   (p. 21)

One of the results of this was his last book-length work *Pour en finir avec le judgement de dieu*. This was scheduled for radio performance; but a few weeks before his death the performance was cancelled. The work might prove offensive to the Americans, the authorities felt. Artaud had accused them of 'war-mongering', an 'insipid rational positivism', and having 'refashioned God in microbes with which the atomic bomb is made' (pp. 103–4). Against this 'depravity', he had lauded the 'purifying rituals of the Tarahumaras', based on 'cruelty in the elimination of God' and 'le hasard bestial de l'animalité inconsciente humaine'. Wanting to see a New Aeon in which 'the rites of the black sun' would install 'the reign of unreason and fragmentation', he had thus finally offered up his 'insanity' as a road map to the future. The way remained blocked, however. Old bourgeois hegemony had been re-established by virtue of the 'arsenal of democracy'.

Radical descendents of the Paris Commune would soon be heard to cry: *'Dynamitons! Dynamitons!'*

10 Sixties' *Zeitgeist*, III: Jim Morrison

The lead singer of the Doors provides a unique dramatic focus for discussing antinomian impulses in the prime, mass 'artform' of the 1960s. Those familiar with rock-and-roll 'troubadours' will immediately recognize why. Morrison was the epitome of the ersatz-intellectual street-punk – more so even than John Lennon, Bob Dylan, Pete Townsend or Mick Jagger. Jerry Garcia of the Grateful Dead might also provide fruitful discussion: beginning his career among the Merry Pranksters, he remained the most loyally countercultural of rock gods. Neither he nor any of the others, however, seriously aspired to let 'dark forces' loose. From the Beatles' arrival in 1964 till the Punk reaction after 1976, rock ethos was committed to the vague ideal of 'Love'. The Rolling Stones occasionally mocked this; but 'Street Fightin' Man' is a commentary of pop revolutionism, not a testament of faith; and 'Sympathy for the Devil' proved a highly successful commercial pose, not a true dedication.

'The Beatles and Stones are for blowing your mind', the *Los Angeles Free Press* wrote; 'the Doors are for afterwards, when your mind is already gone.'[1] If the Beatles suggest Fellini and the Stones Antonioni, this article goes on, the Doors have more in common with 'the eyeball slashing of Buñuel'. Cinema allusions are appropriate to Morrison; and this commentator's analogies underline the extent to which in his early years the rock star was a symbol of reckless revolt. Biographer Danny Sugerman adds, 'Though Jim was not evil, his behavior often was. He did advocate negativity. He certainly did not worship hell. But he did want to dynamite it so he could storm its gates and reveal it, exposing the domain of evil, until not a shred of mystery was left.'[2] At one point, we are told, Morrison became bridegroom in a 'witches' wedding'.[3] He seems to have known as much as contemporary Topanga Canyon

152

occultists about supposed Druidical rites. He liked to 'make people feel uneasy'; and, when one young admirer approached him for a 'reading list', he recommended among other 'sacred books' Baudelaire's *Les Fleurs du mal* and *Paradis artificiels* and Rimbaud's *Saison en enfer*.[4]

Morrison was strictly anarchic in the sense of being 'against authority'. His father was a US Navy admiral, and he was brought up in the rigid and *macho* milieu of the 'military brat'. Adolescence was met in the Deep South – an area of Florida where fetid heat creates an atmosphere of sullen sexuality and defiance, such as one finds in Tennessee Williams's plays. In late teenage, Morrison 'hit the road' for Los Angeles, which became his home for the rest of his brief life. Matriculating in the University of California at Los Angeles (UCLA), he proposed to study film and – like so many dreamers of that part of the world – 'break into' the great art 'industry' of the twentieth century. His student work is said to have shown promise.[5] He admired *cinema verité*, the Surrealists, and Kenneth Anger's *Lucifer Rising*. Instead of persisting with his first artistic love, however, he went down from the academic 'mountain' to become a boardwalk bum in LA's 'underground' bohemia: Venice.

There he lived on foodstamps and girlfriends, writing druggy poetry. Ray Manzarek, a keyboard-player and fellow ex-student, recognized Morrison's words as possible lyrics for the outrageous new 'acid rock' just growing up. Morrison thus, though his voice had no more range than 'perhaps three-quarters of an octave' and his phrasing 'wasn't particularly good',[6] started to sing. By 1966, he, Manzarek, a guitarist and drummer had formed the Doors and were becoming a sensation in the clubs of Sunset Strip. The source of appeal was Morrison's explosive theatricality. This was not easily conveyed on record. Nevertheless, a first album, appearing in early 1967, became an immediate hit. A half-dozen others followed, marking the group's 'meteoric' rise. *Dénouement* commenced when Morrison was arrested in Miami for public obscenity and incitement. In 1971 he quit music and exiled himself to Paris to become a 'literary' writer. There he died under mysterious circumstances, perhaps drug-related, from a heart attack in his bath.

The press tagged Morrison 'the King of Orgasmic Rock'.[7]

His longest set piece, 'Celebration of the Lizard', was dismissed by one critic as 'low comedy' filled with 'typical Morrisonian Crypt Comix imagery'[8] yet lauded by another as 'possibly the most powerful piece of music and words ever performed by any rock group, anywhere'.[9] *Aficionados* of D. H. Lawrence might find in 'Celebration' echoes of the poem 'Snake'. 'The lizard and snake are identified with the unconscious', Morrison himself remarked, Lawrentianly;[10] and in his cult, the young performer seemed to be creating a version of the phallic 'religion' which precursors such as Lawrence and Crowley had undertaken to initiate more than four decades before.

The phallus, of course, was the great totem of rock-and-roll in this phase. Mick Jagger knew as much and exploited it for every drop of commercial worth. Morrison, however, took the whole business farther. In an article I quote in *California Writers*, Joan Didion makes much of his skin-tight black-leather trousers, worn without underwear.[11] Reviews of Doors' concerts are as rife with reference to his exhibitions as his lyrics are with sexual suggestions. The scandalous charge leading to Morrison's arrest in 1969 (his trial coincided with the Manson murders) was that he had exposed himself on stage, simulated masturbation and (reputedly) fellatio with his guitarist. Such behaviour, if it actually occurred,[12] was but an exaggerated version of what had become *de rigueur* in rock performances in general. Morrison, however, continues to stand out. With more seriousness than any other,[13] he understood himself as trying to provoke a Dionysian rite which might – indeed, *should* – lead to orgiastic excess, even violence, and thereby initiation of a 'new age'.

One of the first articles written about Morrison appeared in the UCLA *Daily Bruin* under the title 'Artaud Rock: Dark Logic of the Doors'. It suggests how in halcyon days the androgynous 'brat' posed his appeal:

[He is] a gaunt, hollow Ariel from hell. . . . You could have lit matches off the look he gave the audience. . . . The inhuman sound he made into the microphone turned the carping groupies to stone. And in the tombed silence he began to sing; alternately caressing, screaming, terraced

flights of poetry. ... The edge is where all artists produce
the best ... black miracle ... theatre-of-cruelty. ... Vaguely
(pleased, disappointed: choose one) at his survival, Western
man has begun to look inside to see what went wrong, what
went right. ... Order and chaos have new levels of meaning
so that today a flogging can have as much validity in art as
an act of amative love. ... The evil magic is out, and
Morrison holds the only match in the Stygian darkness.[14]

Intoxicated with his stage powers, Morrison Artaudianly
fancied himself for some time as the prophetic 'seer' an age
and audience hungry for messiahs were eager to project on
him. 'After the plague, [he] wrote, there would be an incredible
springtime, a celebration. First, though, must come the plague,
and there must be death, famine, darkness, and sickness.
Those then must be cured by the shaman seance. Cured by
ecstasy and celebration.'[15] 'Shaman rock' was another epithet
the music press liked to apply, and Morrison encouraged this.
He praised the Indians (specifically Mexican Indians) as a
counterforce against predominant white bourgeois culture. The
shaman, a mystic guru-figure, he described thus: 'He was a
man who would intoxicate himself. See, he was probably
already an ... uh ... unusual individual. And, he would put
himself into a trance by dancing, whirling around, drinking,
taking drugs – however. Then, he would go on a mental travel
and ... uh ... describe his journey to the rest of the tribe.'[16]
   His early lyrics reflect his own progress at self-intoxication
and promote the results as a road-map for disciples:

> You know the day destroys the night;
> Night divides the day.
> Try to run,
> Try to hide;
> Break on through to the other side.[17]

Division, as for Crowley's black magician, is the route to
'instant Zen'; fire, as for Artaud's Satan, the agency of
'enlightenment'. Thus, in his best-selling single Morrison sings,

> The time to hesitate is through.
> No time, to wallow in the mire.

> Try now; we can only lose,
> And our love become a funeral pyre.
> Come on, baby, light my fire . . .
> Try to set the night on *fire*![18]

The aspiration here, more nakedly than even in 'decadent' followers of Pater, is for the performer to burn before his audience 'like a hard, gem-like flame'. In his own ersatz-intellectual terms, Morrison relates it to the Greeks and their most notorious champion of the 'Decadent' period, author of *The Birth of Tragedy out of the Spirit of Music*:

> See, there's this theory about the nature of tragedy, that Aristotle didn't mean catharsis for the audience but a purgation of emotions for the actors themselves. The audience is just a witness to the event taking place on stage. . . . Read Nietzsche [on] the Apollonian-Dionysian struggle for control of the life-force. . . . We want our music to short-circuit the conscious mind and allow the subconscious to flow free.[19]

The 'short-circuiting' is undertaken by playing on Oedipal terror, as in the long theatrical performance song 'The End':

> The killer awoke before dawn
> He put his boots on
> He took a face from the ancient gallery
> And he walked down the hall . . .
> He came to a door
> And he looked inside.
> 'Father?'
> 'Yes, son'
> 'I want to kill you . . . Mother . . .
> 'I want to FUCK YOU!'[20]

It is also undertaken by railing against the establishment for what has been made out of once-magical nature, as in 'When the Music's Over':

> What have they done to the Earth?
> What have they done to our fair sister?

> Ravaged and plundered and ripped her and bit her;
> Stuck her with knives in the side of the dawn. . . .[21]

Finally, too, it is undertaken by identifying 'us' against 'them', as in the anti-Vietnam War song 'Five to One', which provided Danny Sugerman the title for his biography ('No one gets out of here alive') and demonstrators of the time with one of their better slogans against the 'pigs' ('They got the guns, but we've got the numbers').[22]

All the same, Morrison was not 'political' in any conventional sense of the term. Anarchy is the only doctrine his message might relate to; also, perhaps, its neighbour on the great wheel – natural phallic-cult fascism. 'Religion' is a more appropriate term to describe the condition imagined once 'break-through' has been achieved. But, as with Hitler and Crowley and Artaud, Morrison's 'religion' suggests the cult of the 'white Christ' less than that of the hippy's fifth 'ingredient' – the 'holy' outlaw:

> Cancel my subscription to the Resurrection
> Send my credentials to the house of detention
> I've got some friends inside. . . .[23]

Celtic in spirit, Morrison's 'medallion' reminds one of that of the author of 'The Crucifixion of the Outcast', a story Wilde read and admired as he was taken to trial;[24] and in the end, as with Yeats, Morrison's 'hero' atomizes into the gossamer of a mystical beyond:

> Before I sink into the big sleep
> I want to hear
> I want to hear
> The scream of the butterfly. . . .[25]

The scream which soon comes, preceded by an other-worldly moan ('I hear a very gentle sound'), is truly *primal* in contemporary LA psychiatrist Arthur Janov's sense. With it, this second great performance number ends by voicing the *cri de coeur* of the coming 'Me' generation: 'We want the world and we want it/NOW!!!!!'

The message struck responsive notes. 'His lyrics go far

beyond the acceptable psychological limits of pop music,'
Teenset magazine effused; 'He isn't afraid to expose his fears
and hangups.'[26] Expressionism is excitement. To be 'moral' is
dull; to be thrilled, all. He who can ignite the latter condition
for a moment at least blots out the sun:

Then a shadow came out of the wings.
A beautiful phantom in a sloppy pea jacket, floppy light
brown leather cowboy hat, hair down to here, and these
impossible tight leather pants. . . .
There was instant applause and cheering.
He stepped to the microphone, grabbed the top with his
right hand and the stand with his left fingertips, and looked
up so the light hit his face.
The world began at that moment.
I felt like it was all a dream before that. Nothing was real
except his incredible presence. . . .
There isn't another face like that in the world. It's so
beautiful and not even handsome in the ordinary way. I
think it's because you can tell by looking at him that he IS
God. When he offers to die on the cross for us it's OK
because he IS Christ. He's everything that ever was and all
that ever can be and he KNOWS it. He just wants to let us
know that and so are we.
That's why we love him. (His soul has been around for a
long time. It's seen things he only hints at but I remember
things from a million years ago when he sings. He has one
of those really old souls.)
He starts out shrieking, eating the microphone, pressing
his thin leather leg against the stand. (The teenyboppers are
coming all over the place. There are incredible sexual groans
from the girls down the aisle at his every whisper.)
. . . He scared me to death. He grabbed the mike in both
hands and screamed and shook until everyone was sure he
was being electrocuted.
. . . By putting him on a pedestal we can only elevate
ourselves because he is determined to pull us up with
him. . . .
He's really an artist. I kept feeling that he was creating
right in front of me. . . . He IS and CREATES at the same
time.[27]

And at the same time, by unleashing such responses, the black magician creates for himself danger, ultimate repulsion, even disaster. What happens, for instance, when the fired-up worshippers do not get the performance they want – when the Expressionist has moved on to express new personal feelings but they are still clamouring for the old? Then the Dionysian orgy, frenzied and fickle as it is, begins to turn on the god himself. Orpheus ends by being ripped apart by his algolagnic devotees:

> He is the ultimate Barbie doll, and Barbie speaks when we pull her string, that's what she's supposed to do, and she only says what we want her to say because you see on the other end of the string is a piece of tape and that's why he's our Jim Morrison and that's why we want him to sing 'Light My Fire' and stop Stop STOP all these other strange sentences that the doll didn't say when we bought her. . . . We own her/him/the ticket/the poster/the record/the idol. He, he is made of plastic. . . . Give him a lobotomy, tear off his toy clothes, let's see what's in there. . . . The black bull pants are strangling his balls, never mind, children don't need balls. . . . The child is dying up there. . . . Someone strapped into the baby carriage by the big dyke governess of musicbusinesspromomedia exploitation and his mother is gone away and left him and if the governess can keep him for just another year she's got a good thing going, and if we can see him die we can grow up, or die with him, or ignore the whole thing, or kill him ourselves, because we are all children there with our popcorn pockets full of matches and sparklers, com'on baby Light my Fire, com'on baby.[28]

The dandiacal English 'homo' is the 'arbiter of modern culture', Raymond Chandler has his writer-persona, Roger Wade, tell Philip Marlowe in his most self-revealing novel, *The Long Goodbye*.[29] Anthony Burgess has recently indicated something of the kind in *Earthly Powers*, whose narrator is inspired in part by Maugham.[30] A questionably masculine, highly-educated English teacher influences the development of the young Sunbelt sensualist in more than one of the novels of 'hip' sixties author Larry McMurtry.[31] Influence of the older, more cultivated, inactive but slightly sinister thinker over the beautiful, active young man is a theme we picked up in *Dorian Gray* and can see threading through the career of Crowley. Sugerman tells us that as a teenager in Florida Morrison came under the spell of an older man, who seems to have indicated to him the possibilities of exploiting his attractiveness to men as well as women.[32] Jagger in the mid sixties, with what John Lennon disparaged as 'all that fag dancing',[33] was influencing American youth culture, in rebellion against parental puritanism, towards a 'decadence' it imagined to typify the older, more sophisticated culture of Europe, specifically England. Los Angeles had identified for some decades a principal anti-type as the Hollywood 'slicker', who might be a 'fag' or just a particularly slippery 'dude' with 'the ladies', but in any case was entirely *other* than the good-lawman 'God' of Western male myth. As Morrison *père*, the admiral, was this, so Morrison *fils*, the 'drop-out', had to be the *other*: young dandy Mephisto or fallen Lucifer, whose motto – like that of contemporary draft-card burners – was *non serviam*.[34]

The extent of Morrison's recognition of Old World origins of his 'black magical' emanations is uncertain. We have noted his familiarity with Baudelaire and Rimbaud. It seems likely that he would have known of Crowley – certainly he dabbled in the occult – and undoubtedly he had read bits of Nietzsche and Hesse. Kerouac he knew both from *On the Road* and, like most of his kind, by countercultural osmosis; thus pop Buddhism was an element. How specifically he was familiar with Red Indian and Mexican mysticism is also uncertain; but, again, this is a thread a young counterculturalist would have picked up willy-nilly – as Leslie Fiedler argues in *The Return of the Vanishing American*, the whole 'movement' was identifying with the native 'noble savage' whom its white ancestors had massacred and uprooted.[35] If Morrison-as-Faust has no specific Old World Mephistopheles we know of, Artaud remains the great *influencer* behind the scenes. That Morrison had read *Le Théâtre et son double* or *Héliogabale* is doubtful – Artaud's work was not readily available in translation like, say, Baudelaire's. On the other hand, he could have heard a good deal about 'theatre of cruelty' from his professors at UCLA and rather more from his attention to the 'Living Theatre'. (As one of his chroniclers points out,

Morrison was ever the classic bohemian and went to fringe performances – *The James Joyce Memorial Liquid Theatre*, stagings of Mailer's *The Deer Park*, and so on – with an avidity untypical of a culture expected to be 'low-art' and philistine.[36]) Then, too, he may have been exposed to examples of Artaud's acting through his study of early French cinema.

Whatever the extent of conscious influence, the legacy of Artaud in Morrison is striking. Some similarities apply to rock culture at large, others to Morrison in specific. In either case, they demonstrate the intimate attachment of elements in the American 1960s with earlier twentieth-century European aesthetic amoralism.

– Artaud's renunciation of poetry as 'a function of literary tradition'/rock's view of itself as a (the) living literary art form.
– Artaud's 'invented language'/rock's cryptic flows of words.
– Artaud's metamorphic action, in which 'objects proliferate and are transformed with no logical source or agent'/rock's 'surrealism'.
– Artaud's return to formal poetic use of assonance, internal rhythm, scansion/rock's dependence on rhyme, regular stanzas and 'breaks', and 'three-chord progression'.
– Artaud's belief in 'somatic self-perception'/rock's physicality – 'How do you *feel?*' *versus* 'What do you think?'
– Artaud's preoccupation with castration/rock's phallic cult.
– Artaud's 'manipulation of eroticism to overcome repression'/ rock 'sexploitation'.
– Artaud's wish for theatre to 'implicate the mind, the senses, the flesh, even the destiny of the audience [in an] obscenity which resembles an ancient mystery religion'/rock's apocalyptic messianism.
– Artaud's cult of violent, startling action/Morrison's screams, silences, LSD terror and murder images.
– Artaud's view of theatre as 'a language of signs': lighting, music, costume, set architecture, and so on/rock's 'total experience'.
– Artaud's vision of 'a mass extravaganza in a warehouse or even in the street'/rock's 'free' concerts.
– Artaud's dream that 'like the coming of the Messiah, such a miraculous event would change the minds, if not the lives

[of all involved], revealing a new cosmic order ... a mobile unity which marks the end of the old, dead world and its population of cadavers'/Morrison's lyric 'Dead cats, dead rats, sucking on a young man's bones. ... Break on through to the other side. ...'

- Artaud's desire 'to create a race of one sex'/rock androgyny.
- Artaud's passage from Northern European rationalism to sun-cult passionalism/Morrison's advocacy of the 'Dark Sun' over old, grey Snowbelt American puritanism.
- Artaud's creed that suffering, illness, and torture are essential to a man's right to speak/rock seers' emphasis on drink, drug, and sex 'initiations'.
- Artaud's 'aristocracy of pain' ('all true artists suffer')/ Morrison's exposure of his own 'hangups', nightmares, and love-loneliness.
- Artaud's greater concern with personal suffering than that of the general population/Morrison's Byronic self-contemplation.
- Artaud's charge that doctors create illness and psychiatrists are the worst/Morrison's stage aside, 'Some shrink sez I'm crazy. ... Fuck him!'
- Artaud in *Lettres de Rodez* blaming his suffering on 'the sexual misdeeds of cabalistic cults which are excluded from public awareness by a conspiracy of silence'/Morrison in *The Lords and the New Creatures* suggesting that the world (and the arts) are ruled by unseen masters who can only be opposed by mutant human, sly reptilian 'beasts'.
- Artaud's contention that Nerval hanged himself as 'an act of revolt against the world' and his own overdose/Morrison's 'suicidal' lifestyle, self-exile and 'accidental' death.
- Artaud's belief that, like birth, death should be a matter of choice, not an inevitability/the Morrison cult's faith that their 'messiah' did not die but simply changed his identity and disappeared.[37]

This list shows the persistence over time and space of a type of personality. Indeed, the origins of the victim–screamer-as-genius go back much further than Artaud, as we have seen. Here, for instance, is a list of motifs from Sade which may be found in Morrison and/or the related strain in the sixties' *Zeitgeist*:

- evil destiny/'born under a bad sign'/'bad blood'
- pariah/outcast
- incest ('Mother, I want to FUCK YOU!')
- opposition to family
- hunger for love provoking perversity
- female disciples
- sexuality as social (power tool), not biological
- no loss of Self in the 'other'
- rigorous discipline
- enforced submission (Jagger's 'Under my Thumb'[38])
- humiliation
- absolutism
- genius/madman/shaman
- moralist/immoralist
- always risk damnation
- passivity/aggression
- reason equals unreason (Manson's 'No sense makes sense'[39])
- to shock, to justify, to fool (Morrison spitting at audiences)
- passion for theatre
- bad art/pornography/the occult
- preference for sense of hearing
- quantity over quality
- perpetual motion
- transcendental dissatisfaction

These motifs relate to personal associations and attitudes. As the reader will readily see, they indicate the short distance a Morrison-like 'code' has to travel to reach Mansonism. In addition, consider these Sadean motifs relating to the outer world:

- opposition to the *ancien régime*/establishment
- opposition to jailers/police/'pigs'
- opposition to everyday life's banality
- opposition to property, approval of theft (when to personal advantage)
- opposition to abstract cruelty of institutions
- vendetta better than conventional 'justice'
- opposition to hypocrisy, secrecy, prejudice
- rhetoric of socialism equals hypocrisy
- 'crime' is transcendental

- kill, don't judge
- God is evil
- destruction is 'good'
- invention equals a revolutionary act

As already argued, many of the same elements might be found in Blake, Nietzsche, and elsewhere. The impulse to 'transvalue' and oppose in general is the common basis for all such antinomian thinking. A final list brings in a variety of further elements gathered at random from Hitler, Yeats, Crowley and others discussed:

- reactiveness against being bullied
- superior evil lurks behind the apparent good of the bourgeois
- overcome alienation by accepting 'natural' bloodiness
- release sexual aggression (*versus* Freud)
- opposition to psychology (all understanding means all accepting)
- opposition to psychology (all-understanding means all-
- the artist ('liberated individual') needs chaos
- art and writing downrated in favour of 'Life'
- the *voyant* is greater than the mere artist
- fantasy and the Ideal over Reality
- a *Midsummer Night's Dream* congeries of personae, spirits
- vulgarity as beauty
- the animal in man
- courage/survival
- Christ/victim
- fear
- distancing/meditating mystic
- transmigration
- defeat of Time
- the *séance*
- repetition

One might add here, in comment on what may appear a confusion of elements, that the cult of personality, once it achieves complete unlicensed wildness, becomes a law unto itself. Thus, contradiction becomes a cardinal characteristic. No principle is more sacred than its usefulness in the moment.

'Freedom', even from self, becomes all; paradox, even to a point of nonsense, the ultimate form of expression.

Morrison's period in the limelight spans exactly that of Manson's. 1967 marks his début as a performer and Manson's release from a federal penitentiary to the streets of Haight-Ashbury. 1969 marks the end of the 'rise', during which both men drew their 'disciples' around them, and the critical watershed, in Morrison's case arrest and trial, in Manson's initiation of the murders. Finally, 1971 ends the period of 'fall', with the disappearance of both men, discipleships and powers in ebb, Morrison to his apparent death, Manson to solitary confinement in Folsom Prison.

The correspondence in time is remarkable. So too is a correspondence in space: both men reached notoriety in the steamy hip bohemia of LA, just at a moment when – as Didion recalls – 'the idea of sin' had taken on pervasive fascination.[40] It is also germane to point out that the moment marked too, almost exactly, America's most antipathetic acts in Vietnam (the build-up had begun in 1965, the pull-out came in 1973). Finally, as we are on the subject of coincidences, it might be pointed out that in style and demeanour Morrison and Manson actually resembled one another – particularly during the period of their trials. Both had dark hair, worn long. Both oscillated between a clean-shaven, sweet-Jesus persona and a heavily bearded redneck or desert-rat look. Such oscillation was apparent in their personalities as well: both were changers, chameleons – Manson, however, with far more radicalness than Morrison. The murderer had, between innocent and 'bad-ass' faces, a seemingly infinite range of others – including ones suggesting a used-car dealer, a pimp, a Buddhist monk, even a goateed French diabolist.[41]

Such superficial details should not be overlooked. In the predominantly visual, 'medium-is-the-message' culture of LA, only the sharply etched and dramatic create an effect. Pressure for recognition on any basis provokes self-exposure of a kind which can quite readily 'burn out' the exposed in a swift number of years. Morrison died months short of his twenty-eighth birthday. Like Byron is said to have been by his death, he was in many respects an old man. Raging young Satan had

disappeared entirely since *l'affaire Miami*. During his trial,
Morrison had grown notably subdued – not zombie-like so
much as inwardly retreating. The seriousness of the charges
against him apparently shocked him; likewise the pervasiveness
of the outcry. A 'campaign against public indecency',
specifically citing Morrison, drew as many to a rally at the
Orange Bowl as had ever attended one of his concerts. To this,
President Nixon, ingratiating himself with 'Middle America'
as he would later by declaring Manson guilty before the jury
had even recessed, sent a personal message of support.

The trial cost Morrison an enormous slice of his recording-
income. 'Gigs' were cancelled from Boston to Hawaii. The
Mexican government refused him permission to perform free
for the poor or at the National University. Further exclusions
followed, based on the suspicion that where Morrison went
there would inevitably be trouble. Some of this was justified –
personal (though not legal) testimony suggests that Morrison
did harass a stewardess on a flight to Phoenix to see the
Rolling Stones.[42] On the other hand, the overall impression of
Morrison's last two years is of a man fading into a type more
in line with his father's than with its former, apparent obverse.

Now he drank, instead of taking drugs. Perhaps late in the
evening he would 'eat' a few amphetamines or barbituates;
but this was in the style of the low-rent 'macho man', not the
glittering 'seer' of LSD days. Living unostentatiously in a
transient motel on Santa Monica Boulevard, he had few
possessions, in spite of his wealth. In many ways, he was
transforming into a character out of Kerouac: a shade of Neal
Cassady prowling skid-row saloons, aspiring simply to be 'a
good buddy'. His women (particularly his common-law wife
Pamela) began to nag at him in age-old 'trouble-and-strife'
fashion[43] – here was Adonis to the groupies no longer. The
pictures on the cover of one of the Door's later albums,
Morrison Hotel, shows the erstwhile androgyne fat in the jowls
and wearing jeans considerably less form-fitting than the
leathers a reputation had been made on.

His voice became gutsier, boozier, more bluesy – 'like an
old Negro singer', one commentator remarked.[44] His lyrics,
decidedly less apocalyptic, looked forward to the country
sound beginning to overlay acid-rock – Crosby, Stills and
Nash, the 'new' Byrds, and recent albums by the Grateful

Dead. Morrison's style now had more in common with the 'cowboy' Palomino Club of the San Fernando Valley than 'flash' trendy bars on Sunset Strip. He was reverting to something intrinsically American, of the Sunbelt, quiet and authoritative. Indeed, in time, it seemed as if the young outlaw was going to turn into a rock version of Judge Roy Bean in Huston's film: the eccentric 'lawman', living by guile and the Bible; a pirate who becomes defender of faith and country, as in the naval traditions of his father, stretching back to Sir Francis Drake.

'I am primarily an American, second, a Californian, third, a Los Angeles resident', Morrison had written for an early Elektra Records biographical sketch.[45] The order might also be reversed. Indeed, in the Doors' last studio album, *LA Woman*, Morrison staked a claim to be remembered as the most distinctive artistic voice his city had produced since Chandler.[46] The music press did not miss this. In reviewing the album, one Morrison-watcher described the band's mystique thus:

> The Doors might have been treated with disdain because they were from Los Angeles, which seems to hang like a pall of smoke over all the bands that start out there. . . . They were hurt in the minds of the intelligentsia for having the crass lack of taste to actually like ol' Rip-Off City. . . .
>
> Thousands of flower children, and their intellectual cohorts, who were trying to save the world through love, were put off by that punk in his black shirt and pants made of the leather of an unborn lamb, or whatever it was, singing about killing his father, raping his mother, throwing animals out of boats in the midst of horrible storms, walking in streets with blood up to his knees, and so on. . . .
>
> The Doors came on looking like a road gang and completely ruined the [hipper-than-thou flower child] effect. We used to hear strange rumours of the Doors forsaking acid for heroin. And this was at the time when Timothy Leary was still stomping the Ivy League circuit. . . .[47]

Morrison's antinomianism was typical of 'the city everybody loves to hate' – indeed, the Doors were called 'the band

everybody loves to hate'.[48] In quest always of the *avant-garde*,
he, like other bohemians of West Hollywood, would inevitably
swim against the prevailing tide – especially if that tide were
flowing out of the more 'intellectual' hip citadels of arch-rival
cities, San Francisco and New York. At the same time as the
Doors came out with *LA Woman*, San Francisco's premier
band released *American Beauty*; but, whereas there was now a
confluence in 'Western' styles, the old antinomy between
Morrison's punk blackness and Jerry Garcia's cult of hip
'Love' remained. 'Riders in the Storm' takes its title from the
same tradition of Zane Grey tales as 'New Riders of the
Purple Sage' (the name of a Grateful Dead offshoot band
Garcia played with at the time); still, Morrison's last great
composition betrays no Dead-like nostalgia for the carefree
spirit of a mythological, vanished Wild West:

> There's a killer on the road.
> His brain is squirmin' like a toad.
> Take a long holiday,
> Let your children play.
> If you give this man a ride,
> Sweet family will die . . .
> Killer on the road.[49]

So he sang in a song whose first stanza includes the lines:
'Into this world we're thrown/Like a dog without a bone.'
Morrison remained the unhappy child – a male version of the
'lost little girl' he had sung about in *Strange Days*, previewing
the type of female to be spellbound by Manson. The laments
in such songs come closer to the philosophizings of losers than
the rantings of militants. Kerouac eclipses Artaud. Morrison's
town remains the LA of 'human predators, illegal aliens,
rough trade, mistakenly freed madmen, apprentice pimps,
learner-permit whores, would-be Charles Mansons, teenage
dope fiends and all-sorts scuzz who prowl Hollywood
Boulevard';[50] at the same time, it has become the simple,
beyond-hope but before-despair living-place of part-time actors,
stunt men and props people who have seen far too much
disappointment and lunacy to be impressed by much other

than the next good witticism at the System's expense and the
origin of the next six-pack of beer. Before he finally left LA for
Paris, Morrison, reverting to his first artistic love, made a
movie. *Highway* is about a hitch-hiker out in the desert. It has
ominous potential – the man could be a Mansonite: the 'killer
on the road'. Instead, he is merely the representative of an
increasingly aimless, yet benign, American progress from wild
nature to stultifying city-life. 'There is no story really
[Morrison answered when asked to explain the film's meaning].
. . . No real narrative. . . . He drives into the city. . . . He
goes out . . . or something. . . . It just kind of ends like that
. . . and when the music's over, turn out the lights.'[51]

Philip Marlowe might have appreciated the laconic, laid-
back, curiously defeated *citoyen* of LA Morrison had turned
into by the end – indeed, he might have enjoyed having a
drink with him. Marlowe's creator, with his lifelong dream to
return to an Old World literary bohemia in London, might
have understood the impulse which drove Morrison to Paris,
there to sit in cafés where Artaud had once been celebrated
and watch ardent students and aspiring *artistes* pass by, slogans
of the latest *mouvements* on their lips. It may seem remarkable
that the successful rock star should have wanted to turn into a
kind of Hemingway; but something in it attached to the *macho*
code of both his father and his father's Wild Western outlaw
obverse. Literary writing seemed to promise space for the
'mature' fatalistic wisdom Morrison felt he was growing into.
Then, too, Old World culture satisfied more amorphous
yearnings just below the surface in American cultural and
academic life, even such as Morrison had known in West
Hollywood and at UCLA.

Paris itself, in its cafés and street scene, was also, in many
ways, what hip bohemian America – whether in Greenwich
Village, San Francisco's North Beach, or even zany Venice –
had in its urban aspect aspired to be. It remained the great
Western city of arts: primary mecca outside their homeland
for expatriates (a particular breed of antinomian in themselves)
of the two racial groupings Morrison could claim descent
from: the Americans and the Celts. Like James Joyce and
Kerouac, he felt himself a 'word man'. *The Lords and the New
Creatures*, collecting his early poems, was meant to augur a

new beginning. Back to the starting-point for *gnosis* the American paraclete sought to return: back from 'evil' to 'good' to re-embark. The epitome of the rock god had demoted himself to a status human, all-too-human: that of the artist-*manqué*.

11 The Manson Phenomenon

1969 was the watershed year for the cultural revolution of the 1960s. Lyndon Johnson had been evicted from the Presidency, but Richard Nixon had taken his place. Hippy moral hegemony seemed to have been established by the mass concert at Woodstock, but less than six months later it was summarily discredited by the debacle at Altamont. In the spring, as noted, Jim Morrison was arrested in Miami; and, in the heat of August, Roman Polanski's pregnant wife, Sharon Tate, and three of her Hollywood–Beverly Hills friends were ritually murdered for no immediately apparent reason. Along with the equally bizarre slaying of a wealthy middle-aged couple the next night, this sent a wave of terror around the swimming-pools of LA,[1] in both its swinging show-biz and its quieter middle-class precincts. 'Political piggy', 'Rise', and 'Helter Skelter' were found written in blood at the murder sites; and, when Charles Manson's hippy communal 'family' was later brought to trial, it emerged that these epithets had been inspired by the Beatles' latest, double or so-called 'white' album – indeed, that the Beatles, unwittingly, had helped to 'reveal' the way to acts which further drove nails into the coffin of an era of dreams.[2]

Of course, the Beatles were far from the only hammerers of discord among music-making 'gods' of the subculture. Also in 1969, rock cryptographer Bob Dylan, breaking three years' silence after a motorcycle crash, released an album, *John Wesley Harding*, which showed him to be a socially conscious protest-singer no longer, nor even a tapestry-of-images druggy surrealist, but a devotee of the cult of the outlaw, part Robin Hood, part conman. Meanwhile, the San Francisco Sound led by the Jefferson Airplane and the Grateful Dead, which had given voice to the values of Haight-Ashbury's 'summer of

171

Love', now had moved on to a new 'bad-ass', violent-toned, 'heavy metal' phase in such albums as *Volunteers* and *Live Dead*, and openly boasted its relations with the Hells' Angels. Country-rock idylls had not yet dispersed acid-rock dark nights of the soul. In LA, as said, the Doors were still on top, preaching their macabre *fin du globe*-ism[3] –

> The music is your special friend
> Dance on fire as it intends
> Music is your only friend
> Until the End . . . .[4]

– and the Buffalo Springfield, who had recently recorded an ominous 'hit' about the hippy riot on Sunset Strip which had climaxed with the burning of cult rock club Pandora's Box, had now broken up, in an event auguring the diaspora of many rock groups and peripatetic self-seekings of individual 'stars', including in this case the eventual migration of quaver-voiced Neil Young to Topanga Canyon and Zuma Beach, there to compose raw-nerved ballads about friends dying of heroin overdoses and Mexican Indian civilization rising up to revenge itself against the 'bad karma' of Cortez and his 'killer' white colonialists.

This is the atmosphere in which the Beatles album, awaited like a message from the flagship of a war-fleet, finally arrived in California. The most influential of all troubadours of the era were on the verge of breaking up too, following a contentious, ill-conceived 'pilgrimage' to the Maharishi Mahesh Yogi in Indià, in quest – like millions of would-be Siddharthas – for post-LSD *gnosis*; and the 'white' album, evidently a grab-bag of songs and scraps composed while in India and just before and after, is the first Beatles effort in which a preponderance of tracks were performed by individual members of the group, with supporting sounds 'laid down' after. John Lennon, the Beatles' original 'leader' and always its supposed 'seer', remains the dominant spirit behind the whole. But the album was to prove in many respects the last vigorous expression of his 'genius', such as it was. Subsequently, the more whimsical yet less charismatic Paul McCartney would take musical control of the group, thereby speeding its fragmentation.

A whiny Kerouacian *Angst* had been present in Lennon even in such early 'pop' numbers as 'I'm a Loser' and 'Help'; it would be taken to a primal-screaming zenith in the album he would cut when under the influence of LA therapist Arthur Janov. In the 'white' album this is mixed with the stagy stream-of-consciousness, suggesting for some higher intellectuality, which Lennon had deployed to happy effect in 'Strawberry Fields', 'I am a Walrus', and several of the tracks of *Sergeant Pepper's Lonely Hearts Club Band*. Now, however, Lennon's Lewis Carroll-like streak was showing signs of being played out. Festive sallies stop short and/or turn back, as in the disturbing 'Happiness is a Warm Gun'. There are sudden descents into raspy, jagged bouts of hard rock, perhaps semiconsciously imitative of the Rolling Stones, who had always played satanic second-fiddle to the Beatles' messianic lead but now were threatening to become the more popular of the ever-contrasted duo. The most overtly 'bad art' of these efforts is a cut entitled 'Yer Blues', which begins with the lines 'Yes I'm lonely / Wanna die' and repeats a death-wishing message in a series of permutations which culminate with this confession: 'Feel so suicidal / Even hate my rock-and-roll.'

Such tracks give a craven 'realism' to the 'white' album which is absent in the zany 'psychedelic' works which preceded it (*Sergeant Pepper* and *Magical Mystery Tour*) and the polished, studio efforts which would follow (*Abbey Road* and *Let It Be*). The idealism of the original flower-child vision was cracking; marijuana dreams were being chased by an LSD burn-out. The 'revolutionary' new lifestyle the Beatles were living and projecting simply *was* for the time being; and the album reflects stagnation. Without any of the irony the Stones would use in, say, 'Dead Flowers',[5] it presents some of the generation's least promising characteristics: preference for fantasy over morality; an overall mood of childishness; petulant kicking against authority, all 'closed doors' whether figurative or actual; defiant rather than glorious expressions of self. Lennon had in this period declared himself and the Beatles 'more popular than Jesus'. He wore his hair Galilee-long and allowed himself to be photographed beatifically naked or in all white. Soon he would sing an overtly autobiographical ditty proclaiming:

Christ, you know it ain't easy
You know how hard it can be
The way things are goin'
They're gonna crucify me.[6]

Given as much, it is hardly surprising that extreme devotees
should have interpreted the Beatles' most extensive creative
statement as a sort of Bible, complete with its own Revelation
and intimations of Final Judgement.

It might be added here that in their opus in general the
Beatles had suggested a range of personality and behaviour
which constituted for their listeners a kind of full circuit of the
'great wheel', from the Yeatsian 'holy fool' and the Christ to
the Crowleyan magician and the Leninist–Trotskyite.[7] In the
'white' album, however, this is far more apparent than in any
other effort – indeed, only neo-Nazi tendencies are absent: it
remained for post-Jagger punks to project these. Still, it was
possible for Charles Manson, with his exaggerated, jail-
intensified punk-hoodlum streak, to hear an admonition to
Aryan action in the Paul McCartney ditty 'Blackbird'.[8] That
an ardently criminal mind could find such justification in an
innocuous work of art is in part owing to the blatantly anti-
establishment and subtly violent message irrefutably contained
in George Harrison's 'Piggies' and Lennon's 'Bungalow Bill',
also the complacently antinomian gaming of Lennon's
'Revolution' and its anti-song in feedback 'Revolution Number
9'.[9] It is also, more importantly, owing to a pervasive tendency
to obscurity, 'underground' eye-winking, and pseudo-prophecy
throughout this great monument of bad art.

Manson wanted to be a rock star – specifically, a cult figure in
the style of Lennon, Dylan, Jim Morrison, and Garcia of the
Grateful Dead: a *voyant*, whose cryptic-apocalyptic 'poetry'
would be accompanied by ragged but 'real' guitar, sitar and
drum 'sounds' of a kind which might seem outrageous to slick
pop-music producers and their middle-of-the-road listeners but
would seem to be speaking directly to and for and even out of
the brains of millions of young followers, almost all artists-
manqué like himself, beating tom-toms and blaring harmonicas
in the newly liberated 'people's parks' and 'love streets' and

communes. This would be a factor of less moment were it not for the scores of people – and not all just drug-crazed 'freaks' – who at one time or another believed that Manson was just what he promoted himself to be: a 'genius' in the style of the age. Terry Melcher and Gregg Jakobson, film and record producers of some prominence in LA, encouraged him, gave him money and recording-facilities, discussed contracts and possibilities of stardom. Nor were their relations with Manson of a 'conning' variety typical of Hollywood 'hype'. This five-foot-four[10] 'shaman', aka (also known as) Jesus and the Devil, seemed special. The evidence suggests that these producers were genuinely impressed with his talent and not able to 'get together' any concrete promotion because, even in an era of commercial pursuit of the 'far out', he was simply too exceptional.

Nor were Melcher and Jakobson the only legitimate music-biz people to be struck by Manson. Dennis Wilson of the hugely successful Californian band the Beach Boys was so enthralled that for several months he let Manson and the 'family' live in his mansion off Sunset Boulevard, drive his cars, wear his clothes, and generally indulge in their hippy–revolutionary 'everything is everybody's' lifestyle. The Beach Boys were persuaded to record one of Manson's compositions (though they angered him by changing its title from the death-trippy 'Cease to Exist' to 'Cease to Resist' to, finally, the emasculated 'Never Learn Not to Love'[11]). In an interview with the music press on a London tour, Wilson referred to Manson as 'the Wizard' and stated that he would soon be recording on the Beach Boys' own 'Brothers' label. This failed to transpire, as did the breakthrough to the 'big time' held out by Melcher and Jakobson. Manson, like frustrated 'artists' since at least the days when Hitler was roaming the 'mean streets' of Vienna, was upset. Few, however, have taken revenge to such lengths: the Tate–Polanski house chosen to begin 'Helter Skelter' had previously been Melcher's residence.

The charisma in Manson which overwhelmed people such as Wilson was, of course, largely extra-artistic; and this may be a prime reason no one could discover an appropriate way to 'exploit' it. Manson's case in this respect constitutes a signal instance of the artist-*manqué* appearing as superior to the established artist. The Beach Boys in the late sixties were in a trough in their career. Their famous songs about surfing seemed insufferably 'plastic' against the druggy, pop-revolutionary new wave; and their following and staying-power were no longer secure. Manson, recently come down from the vortex of *avant-garde*-ism in Haight-Ashbury and with his remarkable mesmeric influence over a protean clan of disciples, seemed to display a knowledge from which they might profit. The age was in love with the idea of the guru, from Leary to rock 'heroes' to some undiscovered, 'noble savage' version of Siddhartha. Manson, a consummate embodiment of the 'drop-out cult' fifth ingredient, the outlaw and 'beautiful loser' who would inherit the Earth, sold himself as this last type. Some bought; others didn't. Frank Zappa, founder and leader of the ultra-weird San Fernando Valley group the Mothers of Invention, turned down invitations to visit the Manson commune at nearby Spahn Movie Ranch.[12] Nor could Paul Rothchild, producer of the Doors, be seduced into trying to make the ex-con into the next Jim Morrison.

There was in LA at this time – as in California in general and perhaps the entire counterculturalized West – a fascination not only with 'sin', as Joan Didion relates, but also, more significantly and lastingly, with 'power'. Carlos Castaneda's tetralogy about a Mexican Yaqui Indian shaman, Don Juan, was just starting to be published. *The Teachings of Don Juan, A Separate Reality, Journey to Ixtlan* and *Tales of Power* would sell hugely over the next several years to an occult-minded, countercultural audience. They would sum up in new Western form many principles of the old European heretical *gnosis*, adding to them the romantic appeal of a subterranean, older North American mysticism and aspects of a 'cool' style particularly sympathetic to the *macho* Angeleno concept of what it might mean to be a fully realized, New Age man.

Don Juan's teachings propose to reveal the secrets of 'sorcery'. Principal among these is an ability to '*see*'. *See*ing liberates a man to Nietzschean realms beyond good and evil, where 'not a single thing he used to know prevails'.[13] 'Once we *see*, nothing is known', Don Juan relates; '*see*ing makes one realize the unimportance of it all.' But achieving such cosmic nihilism brings danger as well as power; thus the development must proceed somewhat further:

> By opening himself to knowledge a sorcerer becomes more vulnerable than the average man. On the one hand his fellow men hate him and fear him and will strive to end his life; on the other hand the inexplicable and unbending forces that surround every one of us, by right of our being alive, are for a sorcerer a source of even greater danger. ... A sorcerer, by opening himself to knowledge, falls prey to such forces and has only one means of balancing himself, his will; thus he must feel and act like a warrior. I will repeat this once more: Only as a warrior can one survive the path of knowledge. (*Separate Reality*, p. 221)

The warrior, we are told, 'is geared only to struggle'. He approaches each event as if it were 'his last battle on earth'. In this way, he maintains a state where all outcomes 'matter very little to him'. Whereas he has *seen* that 'the world is an endless mystery', so too he realizes that 'what people do is endless folly' (p. 226); thus he can view his own existence simply as 'an exercise in strategy'. The warrior 'doesn't care about meanings' (p. 188). He 'cannot indulge, thus he cannot die of fright'. He only enters battle 'when he is good and ready'. He never continues battle after he has established sway. He always engulfs the enemy's spirit into himself. Thus he succeeds in being 'the master at all times' (p. 257).

In contrast to Don Juan, the adept Castaneda cannot become a warrior – he is dependent on his rational mind.[14] Furthermore, he has never been sufficiently 'humiliated' or 'defeated'. 'To be defeated,' he is told, 'is a condition of life which is unavoidable.' Depending on one's ability to accept this, one becomes either a 'persecutor or a victim'; but the man who can *see* can 'dispel the illusion of victory, or defeat, or suffering' and prevent himself from becoming locked into either Sadean antipode (p. 145). Free, natural oscillation between victory and defeat will destroy hate, replacing it with equanimous, alert pragmatism.[15] The warrior will learn that 'the countless paths one traverses in one's life are all equal', that 'oppressors and oppressed meet at the end, and the only thing that prevails is that life is altogether too short for both'.

This Yin–Yang oneness of oppressor and oppressed, Nietzschean master and slave, hinges on the all-consuming power of death; and, at one point in his revelations, Don Juan avers that 'every bit of knowledge that becomes power has death as its central force' (p. 157). This is a concept Manson understood intimately and employed to disarming effect. He had a trick which Ed Sanders mentions several times in his excellent study, *The Family*, of handing an antagonist a knife and inviting him to use it.[16] When, invariably, the antagonist would decline, Manson would take the knife back and declare that he had now been ceded the right to use it himself. This 'Kill Me–Kill You' stunt derives from the pop-Jungian creed of the time that 'We are all One'.[17] It also shows how effectively Manson, like Hitler, was able to wear the Janus-mask of victim–survivor. He had, as Sanders relates, feral cunning and meanness ('coyotenoia', the energizing fear of his favourite beast, the ragged desert scavenger[18]) as well as hippy 'Love'. He would be Christ being crucified or Satan presiding over *Walpurgisnacht* – both were one: 'everything was everything'. If he wanted something of someone, he might very well get down on his knees and kiss that person's dirty feet. If, on the other hand, he were displeased, he might sneak up from behind and brandish one of the family's favourite six-inch Buck knives under the same person's jugular vein.

These are instinctive, animalistic 'survival tactics' which Manson had learned in the only schools he had known, reformatory and prison; and certainly his knowledge of 'life on the inside' contributed to his aura as warrior–sorcerer among the sensation-seekers of LA, as it had done with *satori*-seekers in Haight-Ashbury. It qualified him as one of that antinomian 'elite' who, like his detested Black Panthers,[19] had fought and been beaten, buggered and been buggered, and knew violence as personally as footsoldiers in Vietnam – surely a 'red badge of courage' at the time. It must be remembered that, in the milieu Manson entered when he was (allegedly unwillingly[20]) 'sent down from the mountain' of penitentiary, every young 'dude' with 'balls' had either become or was aspiring to become a petty criminal through 'dope deals'. Hyped-up, Cassady-style existentialists 'cruised' the streets. Total experience was the ideal, the more 'far-out' the better. Music, sex, drugs, mysticism, outlawry – with the songs he had composed in prison, the pied-piper retinue he collected around him, the LSD he lavishly (and slyly[21]) dispensed, the patter of occult new-speak he 'rapped', and his 'record' as car thief and pimp, Manson, born a bastard, seemed to have passed every stage of 'initiation' sheltered middle-class souls could only fantasize about in their urge to throw off conditioning and 'break on through to the other side'. He had been there already and returned, his 'wooden ship' laden with the unholy weapons angry young creatures of a media culture imagined they needed to command attention.

Diminutive in stature, Manson appears to have always been preoccupied with attention, as well as getting control. His song-writing and apocalyptic prognostications are part of this, as of course are the murders. From an early age, he was on the look-out for any technique or idea which might confer personal advantage. More stands behind his 'powers' than Don Juan's relatively clean warrior 'will', or the Hitlerian trick of the stare-down. In jail, we are told, he studied 'magic, warlockry, hypnotism, astral projection, Masonic lore, scientology, ego games, subliminal motivation, music and perhaps Rosicrucianism'.[22] He read *Transactional Analysis* by Eric Berne and 'may have developed his perverse doctrine of Child Mind' from it. He also rated among favourite books *Stranger in a Strange Land*, which Sanders described as 'the story of a power-hungry telepathic Martian roaming the earth with a harem and a quenchless sexual thirst while proselytizing for a new religious movement'. From this, as well as works of Nietzsche and Hesse, he took ideas and phrases. All the same, it did not prevent him from later commanding it to be burnt along with the rest of the Family's reading-matter.[23]

Scientology seems to have provided the fundamental element of his 'education'. 'Power' is a central term in L. Ron Hubbard's 'Science of Knowing How to Know'; and the 'auditing' process by which a novitiate in the Scientology 'church' is made 'clear' may be adapted to less noble manipulative ends. Manson was 'audited', made 'clear', and given 'power' in prison.[24] It is not known whether he ascended to the level of 'OT [Operating Thetan] 8', whence the Scientology initiate may theoretically begin to time-travel,

astral-project and metempsychose. However, he knew something about the higher powers Scientology is supposed to
confer: shortly before the murders, when the Family was
beginning to unravel and he was having trouble getting the
hard core back to Death Valley from LA, he postulated on
more than one occasion that a desert-rat gold-prospector who
had formerly been a Scientologist was sending out 'vibes' to
thwart him.[25]

According to its founder and guru figure,[26] Scientology
derives from the *Vedas* via the *Tao Te Ching*, Buddhism and the
'civilizing' part of Judaism (Christianity), which incorporates
elements from the Egyptian *Book of the Dead* and pre-Socratic
Greek philosophers. The tradition of 'wisdom' begins in the
East, not the West, because the East is where Time was
allowed to stand still and man to contemplate and listen. It
moved toward the West, according to Hubbard, in the
seventeenth century – that is, about the time of the
burgeoning of Freemasonry – and revivified moribund
Gnostic undercurrents. To 'wisdom', the Occident added its
characteristic dynamism, which is equally essential to effective
operation of the complete personality. In the latest, American
phase of the tradition, the 'Science of Knowing' must naturally
incorporate the great discoveries of the twentieth century, from
psychoanalysis to methods of brainwashing used in the Second
World War to the larger conceptual truths underpinning
nuclear physics.

Hubbard has stated that the American government,
recognizing his genius, approached him in 1947 to help them
find ways to 'make people more suggestible'.[27] Hubbard refused
(and claims that thirty years' harassment followed); but the
US Government was by no means the last organization to try
to 'rip off' (in a phrase of the era) his 'white magic'. Sanders
tells of a 'black-caped, black-garbed, death-worshipping'
English sect called 'The Process', whose leaders first met at the
Hubbard Institute in London around 1964.[28] They diabolized
Scientological ideas by adding worship of Jehovah, Lucifer,
Hecate and War and preaching the 'unification of Christ and
Satan' into one personality, described in this 'Kill Me–Kill
You' way:

Christ said: Love thine enemy. Christ's Enemy was Satan

and Satan's Enemy was Christ. Through love, enmity is destroyed. Through love, saint and sinner destroy the enmity between them. Through love, Christ and Satan have destroyed their enmity and come together for the End. Christ to judge, Satan to execute the punishment.[29]

Sanders speculates that Manson had contacts with members of The Process when they came to America in the later sixties, hoping, like Crowley fifty years before, 'to make converts and plant the seeds of their cult'. In any case, whether or not Manson knew members of this sect personally, he was likely to have seen issues four and five of the magazine they distributed on the street in Hollywood in 1968 and 1969. These were devoted, respectively, to the subjects of 'SEX' and 'DEATH'.

Such elements of the *Zeitgeist* are important when discussing a man who aspired to adulation for being more outrageously diabolical than anything else in a peculiarly 'black magical' period. Sanders cites among other 'sleazo imputs' Jean Brayton's Solar Lodge of the Order of Oriental Templars, the Crowleyan sect, located near the University of Southern California and out in the desert near Manson's hideaway, which specialized in 'sex-magick' rites using inundations of animal blood.[30] Like Francis King, Sanders suggests that Manson attended OTO meetings. He also cites Family associates who claim that Manson and others conducted their own sex-and-sacrifice rites, and perhaps on occasion used humans rather than dogs or chickens for blood. Video 'nasties' proving as much are alleged to be in existence.[31] We are back in the realm of Sade as well as Crowley; only in the wide open spaces of the Land of the Brave and the Free where – as the Jefferson Airplane sang – 'You can *live* and leave all the stories behind!',[32] prison-playlet fantasies could become flesh.

There are other elements. Bobby Beausoleil, the most charismatic of Manson's followers and first known to commit a murder, had previously been the star of English occultist Kenneth Anger's *Lucifer Rising*;[33] and Manson may have felt compelled to try to out-devil the powerful previous guru of the one member of his Family who could conceivably become a rival. Then too there may have been association with the mysterious cult of Kirké, or Circe, another black-magical group around LA at this time, which worshipped evil in the form of a red-headed, black-clothed, silver-nailed high priestess, also reputed (as so many witches and warlocks post-Crowley were) to be English.[34] According to Sanders, the Kirké cult attracted members of two motor-cycle clubs familiar to Manson, the Straight Satans and Satans' Slaves, whom he hoped would ride with the Family like SS shock-troops when he finally unleashed 'Helter Skelter' against the 'pigs' and the blacks.

Racism was endemic to Manson's poor-white background and had been intensified by prison. Prosecutor Vincent Bugliosi contends that Manson was afraid that his unknown father may have been part black;[35] but then Bugliosi is much less dependable in psychology than in recording details of the investigation and trial of the murders. He tells us also that Manson was a devotee of Hitler, citing an old copy of *Time* magazine found with Family materials in Death Valley which contains an article about Rommel's Afrika Korps, and an alleged comment of Manson's that Hitler 'took care of the karma of the Jews'.[36] That Manson did imagine himself tearing around the California desert at the head of a Rommel-like 'attack battalion' of dune buggies is confirmed by Sanders in the later chapters of his book and lampooned in its mordant subtitle.[37] Beyond this, such 'Nazism' as Manson exhibited was confined to sporting a swastika as a 'third eye' on the forehead during his trials – in short, the sort of Punk touch which would become familiar on the streets of London in the 1970s and had long been affected by Hell's Angels and other Californian 'biker' organizations.

Manson entirely lacked what one might describe as the bourgeois, civic, 'responsible' qualities which advanced Germany's *Führer* to a pinnacle of power and maintained him there. The two personalities are as different in this respect as one of Manson's carping, 'witchy' head-girls might be from Margaret Thatcher. On the other hand, similarities are obvious. We might merely indicate them by recalling phrases from Joachim Fest:

– Fear, the overwhelming experience of his formative years.
– Great liars are also great wizards.
– Craving for revenge, wild fantasies of destruction.

- Neurasthenic craving for sheer movement.
- Energy multiplied by disaster.
- Somnambulistic calm, seemingly divorced from reality.[38]

Both Hitler and Manson focused hatred on popular lower-middle class 'enemies', Jews, blacks and establishment 'pigs'. Both played on a spirit of 'revolution' in the air. Both believed their group's destiny to be foretold in music – Wagner and the Beatles. Both put into practice a peculiarly manipulable sort of anarchic authoritarianism. Both, after 'liberating' their 'people' and restoring a perverted version of 'psychic wholeness', invoked war as the ultimate 'game'. Both ended by being destroyers of the worldview which had brought them to public attention – indeed, in the case of Manson, whose contempt for hippies was more vocal than Hitler's for the Germans,[39] some believe that this was intentional and see the invisible hand of the FBI or some other establishment 'occult' force behind it.

Manson came from West Virginia, then one of the poorest and most backward states in the Union, home of coal-miners, the unemployed, hillbillies and 'white trash'. His mother, Kathleen, may have been a prostitute and small-time hold-up girl; in any case, she was a tramp and wandered out of her boy's life with as much regularity as he as a teenager would wander out of hers. In 1957, when he was in federal prison for the first time, his mother informed Manson that his pregnant new wife, Rosalie, had run off with another man. This appears to have upset the twenty-one year old greatly, as deficiency in mother-love and rejection by a fiancée seems to have maddened young Sade. Manson's subsequent brutality to his hippy harem no doubt stems from such experiences as much as from the fact that his basic training in how to 'relate' came from the school of hard knocks 'on the inside'.

The Family was comprised for the most part of low-down, unhappy sons and daughters of what Scientology might call 'low-tone' middle-American parents: types who supported the Vietnam War, decried student riots and unrest in the ghettoes, voted for Nixon, and put 'AMERICA: LOVE IT OR LEAVE IT' stickers on the bumpers of their late-model Buicks paid for on time. They came from the dominant white American *mélange* of Scottish, Irish, English and Germanic blood. Whatever idealisms may have been being preached by Mario Savio at Berkeley or Allen Ginsberg in New York, these kids were instinctively racist and xenophobic. They also had lower-middle class feelings of envy and inferiority towards the upper middle class, and rural–suburban feelings of awkwardness and exclusion *vis-à-vis* 'sophisticated' big-city life.

Generalizations are dangerous, and exceptions can be pointed out. Still, an overall identity is discernible here and deserves to be mentioned to illustrate how the Manson phenomenon reveals greater social tensions. These might be expressed in terms of class, or as town *versus* city, failure *versus* success, drop-out *versus* committed. Taking the cue from Manson himself, another label to apply might be 'racial'. I am not speaking of the white-*versus*-black race war 'Helter Skelter' was supposed to initiate. That was and is a theoretical projection and does little to explain why the prime victims should have been the wife of a famous Polish–Jewish director, his Polish *émigré* friend who was a dope-dealer, his heiress girlfriend who was a liberal activist, and a mutual friend to all who was hairdresser to Hollywood stars.

These people were 'internationalist' types, while the Manson Family was indigenous, Celtic–Germanic American. They were stylish 'swingers' who liked to 'experiment' with drugs, sexual perversion, the occult, and 'soft' sin, while the Family – free of all façades of manners or taste – got 'down and dirty' and dug into hard drugs, hard sex and perversion and porn, serious black occultism, and outright cruelty instead of trendy 'bitchiness'. The Tate murders may have had several immediate inspirations: a drug 'burn' involving the *émigré* dealer; the connection to Melcher and Manson's artistic rejection; Polanski's reputation for 'satanism' (*Rosemary's Baby* was his most recent film) and general 'decadence'.[40] But behind them lurks a force too often overlooked: the angry resentment of the native hipster for jet-set 'beautiful people'. Anyone familiar with greater Hollywood should recognize this: it continues to fester today.

This is the point at which the events of August 1969 link to brown-shirt violence in Berlin and Vienna in the 1930s. Over both hovers an age-old metaphysical conflict between cults of 'heroism' based on the 'dare' (in these cases perverse) and the necessary 'superficiality' and 'hypocrisy' of civilization. Manson's final falling-out with Melcher, according to Sanders, occurred when the latter suggested making a film about the Family which would gloss over rough edges and be a documentary paean to communal love and flowers.[41] Manson insisted on 'telling it like it is'. He envisioned a kind of *cinema verité* production which would 'zap' the consciousness of those who saw it by glorifying the Family's wildness: a modified 'biker' film which would attract more disaffected kids and *épater* the 'pigs' set in their media-world of pastel toilet-paper commercials.

In his belligerent, destructive unwillingness (indeed, inability) to compromise, Manson shows a lumpen-prole version of the brute, aristocratic contempt for bourgeois nicety we first encountered in Sade. Nor is it impossible to romanticize this. At safe remove, the man's raw, self-damning, cowardly acts of manipulation and crime suggest paradoxical courage. Pure, instinctive hatred of everything the majority deems 'good' – even what his hip brethren deemed 'beautiful' – takes us once again 'beyond the rim' and allows us to glimpse how fragile, indeed vain and perhaps finally arbitrary, the rules we construct really are. Why not evil? What *is* evil? How can 'evil' exist when, as the *Time* magazine cover flashed in *Rosemary's Baby* proclaimed, there is no God? Or, indeed, when God, as Governor Reagan liked to imply, was on the side of the 'pigs' truncheoning the 'street people' of Berkeley who wanted to turn some unused industrial land into a park.

Manson languishes to this day in solitary confinement in one of California's most secure prisons. He deserves to be there: in the words of one of the songs on the 'white' album, he 'broke the rules' and 'got his'.[42] So he has returned to what he has called both 'the only home [he has] known' and his 'only father'.[43] Parole has been denied more than once, as is just: the murders were unspeakable, nor is it likely that such an ardent 'transvaluer' could ever be 'rehabilitated' into a 'decent' citizen. At the same time, it seems weirdly 'tragic' that a human being of such powers and imagination (who, after all, would think of making a judge withdraw from a trial by 'zapping' him with Masonic signs? or, more recently, breaking out of prison via a mail-order, assemble-yourself hot-air balloon?) must remain in permanent exile from all social activity.

His 'worth', in terms the most materialistic 'pig' might swiftly grasp, stands at countless millions, spent on investigations, arrests, trials and incarcerations. In this too, he has achieved the perverse 'godly' mission of revealing the ironies inherent in any order mere mortals imagine they can secure over their mysterious universe – or for that matter themselves.

12 Concluding: The 'Soul of Man'

The impact of two bodies of *mores*, the 'old' European and 'new' American, has had its part to play in the development discussed here – the latter upon the former in the cases of Wilde with his frequent reference to *aperçus* picked up while on lecture tour in America, Hitler with his fantasies of cowboys *versus* Indians as read in Karl May novels, Crowley with his frustration in attempts to 'convert' America to his cause, Artaud with his 'pilgrimage' to Mexico and subsequent railery against American 'imperialism'; the European upon the American in the myriad ways indicated by the influence, direct and otherwise, particularly on one generation, of Old World mysticism, occultism and amoralism in general, from sources as disparate as Nietzsche, Crowley, Hesse and the Beatles. Division between these apparent antipodes of Western culture, making the culture sometimes seem two opposed parts rather than one unity, has contributed, as Simon Iff might have predicted, to outbreaks of the Manichaean, the 'black magical', things 'evil', based perhaps in simple misunderstanding, native cultural arrogance or xenophobia. Now, however, the era of 'bringing it all back home' from Europe to America has largely ended; and the Nietzschean spasms Europe went through in the early decades of this century seem to have been passed through by America in her adventures of Vietnam, the 1960s and beyond.

A growing Western, if not world, consensus has created – at least short of what used to be called 'the iron curtain' – a oneness, like that of the Roman Empire perhaps, in which a largely secure establishment rules, 'evil' is pretty clearly defined by law, and 'good' has become comfortably synonymous with adherence to what recent *Times* leaders like to describe as 'the accepted norm'. Pressure for a unifying 'world order' bears down upon our heterogeneous, increasingly multiracial societies. A dynamic socialist alternative seems to be fading in the West, and perhaps everywhere. Thus the prime arena for the antinomian spirit (at this point we might call it an eternal 'spirit of opposition') to express itself is in individual acts of defiance and subversion, or the machinations of increasingly secretive, 'underground' groups. America, which from the first has been a collection of antinomian principles protesting and competing against one another, remains a locale where pressures for imposed unity can be seen most evidently. Los Angeles, the new 'melting-pot' with its alleged 4 million immigrants in the last dozen years alone, is where in America these may be seen in their sharpest relief.

This explains the geographical, as well as temporal and metaphysical, destination of this study. To a real extent, Los Angeles-style culture is perpetually fragmented against itself. This is its strength: its superior 'sanity' in terms of the great wheel of human variety. At the same time, it is a major source of its continuing undercurrent of 'evil', its police-cult authoritarianism, its fascination with 'sin' and 'death' and 'power' – in short, its peculiar 'madness'. To help illustrate this, I should like to return for a moment to a cultural artefact which thrust its way into this study by accident – happy accident as it turns out. It is a product of greater LA culture and reflects its worldview, as interpreted by a director who stands as father figure to many of the Hollywood types most fascinated and threatened by the Tate–Polanski murders. I mean John Huston and his *The Life and Times of Judge Roy Bean*.

The plot of this film is as follows: a thirty-year-old outlaw in the Wild West of a century ago comes into a remote saloon after having pulled off a successful hold-up. The saloon is in effect a poor-white-trash commune of the Manson variety, and its seedy retinue of con men and whores jump the newcomer as soon as they discover he has money. Whimsically, they hang him from the back of his horse. Bean (that is the outlaw's name) survives, by some miracle. A Mexican girl from a nearby village which has been terrorized by the communal vandals in the past brings him a gun. In the night he returns to the saloon, surprises its drunk, fornicating occupants, and shoots them to death one and all.

He takes over the saloon and restyles it a courthouse: 'the only law this side of the Pecos'. Declaring himself judge, he supports his pretension with a book of statutes and an old Bible an itinerant preacher has left behind. The nearby Mexican village is more content to live under his 'justice' than that of his barbaric predecessors; the girl who gave him a gun becomes his sweetheart in spite of his religious adoration of the far-away, civilized European lady, the English actress Lily Langtry, a poster of whom he hangs on the saloon wall. To this, he makes his deputies swear fealty, as to his two 'sacred' books. The deputies are recruited from other itinerant outlaws. The 'new order' they create rests upon booty absconded from less co-operative types who have wandered into 'Judge' Bean's domain.

All is well. Life becomes an easy succession of poker games, beer-guzzlings, and rough *macho* justice. Then a city slicker, an educated Easterner, appears on the scene bearing a piece of paper which declares his inherited claim to the land. Bean rips up the paper. The slicker, however, is not intimidated. Setting up shop as a lawyer, he gains influence over the wives of Bean's deputies, ex-whores who now want to be seen as 'ladies'. Eventually, while Bean is off chasing 'Miss Lily's' performance-tour of the States, the slicker manages to have himself elected 'mayor'. He demotes Bean's deputies and denounces the judge as an arbitrary, uncouth autocrat. Bean on return is disgusted but helpless, and rides off to the wilderness.

The slicker discovers oil and transforms Bean's dusty hamlet into a bustle of twentieth-century industry. Huge profits enable him to buy and sell justice and maintain a ruthless police force. In the end, his hegemony is opposed only by Bean's daughter (whose Mexican mother died, romantically and pathetically, in childbirth while Bean was off chasing Langtry). The girl refuses to sell the courthouse to the slicker. When her opposition finally comes down to gunpoint, Bean himself – now an old man – magically reappears. Like the 'sleeping warrior' of ancient Norse legend, he rouses his old deputies out of their despair and leads an apocalyptic 'last battle', in which all the slicker's wells and police go up in flames.

The hero, of course, goes up in flames too. Thus the 'town' is returned to its original condition. One rickety saloon and a few out-buildings stand in the middle of nowhere. They are preserved by a single remaining, white-haired Bean deputy as a museum in honour of 'Miss Lily'.

The point of rehearsing this tale here is that it turns on a theme lurking behind all the 'cases' and stories presented in this book: what, in fact, is true justice? Huston rejects not only the animalistic barbarism of Manson-like vandals (and by implication all Sadean anarchy and regimes of terror) but also the bureaucratic police-statism of exploitative capital. In glorifying Bean as the least of all evils, he proposes a system of leadership centred on an individual who is fully tested in an amoral school and toughened, like Castaneda's 'warrior'; who has a reasonable degree of instinctive fairness, yet prejudiced mistrust of 'manipulative' Reason and a deep, ungovernable antinomian streak which may resurface at any time; who is close to the earth yet not so enmired in it as to prefer dirt to decency – in short, a figure who in many respects stands but a step or two removed from Old Testament, Protestant and Masonic traditions of manliness.

There is some hope in such an embodiment. At the same time, I must confess that – attractive as it is – it seems inadequate. Bean's order, as the end of Huston's film (perhaps unintentionally) suggests, is only sufficient in a vanishing era of the pastoral. 'Justice' in the modern world, if it can be approached at all, requires the widest possible vision and imagination. Fascination with death, opposition to the norm, pursuit of power and expression by any means (even those a substantially philistine majority may brand 'evil') are eternal impulses, unkillable and never to be satisfied. One man's 'justice' – indeed, one majority's or world's imposed body of 'unified' beliefs – will inevitably create another's Luciferian, equally human, and very possible 'liberating' rebellion. This simple truth societies cannot afford to forget. Nor is it out of place in this context to suggest that the Western world's drift back towards a kind of *ancien régime* disparity of wealth and status cannot be healthy, ultimately for rich and privileged masters any more than for what amount to (use Sade's term or Nietzsche's) their 'victims' or 'slaves'.

The 'sanity' of our world, as of individual personality, depends on recognition and acceptance of as many phases as possible on the great wheel. We shall have 'sinners' and 'doers of evil' and shall be better for our serious attention to them; for, in every case, they are reminding us of things we may not wish to credit about the larger mystery of existence. Meanwhile, in terms of social morality (which remains essential to civilization if eternally absurd from a cosmic point of view), the guideposts to *goodness* should be clear enough. They may be found in Wilde most readily of those discussed in this study and *The Soul of Man* best among his works. The finest exemplar we have for human behaviour remains, in spite of His 'wetness', Christ; the finest programme for human organization a benevolent socialism which keeps material anxiety at bay and provides everyman with the maximum potential for individual self-realization.

This may seem a facile conclusion: one more 'instance of tacking, for form's sake, a moral ending onto an immoral tale' (see Ch. 4, end of first paragraph). But there is point to the finale of *Don Giovanni*, as to the coda to Virtue at the end of *Justine* or the 'turning' in *Dorian Gray*. Hitler must be discredited, Manson confined. Continuance of human life in the aggregate demands as much; antinomianism taken to logical extremes invites it. Of course, the picture may look different to countless prisoners (real and figurative), broken dreamers, and hopeless have-nots. Inasmuch, it seems appropriate to add that a future of destruction and creativity belongs to them no less than to the artist, the artist-*manqué*, the cloistered thinker or the smug grandee.

Notes

CHAPTER ONE   INTRODUCTORY: THE ARTIST-MANQUÉ

1. Stoddard Martin, *Wagner to 'The Waste Land'* (London: Macmillan, 1982). See 'Conclusion'.

2. Stoddard Martin, *California Writers* (London: Macmillan, 1983). See 'The Sixties and After'.

3. Valuable background here might be Mario Praz's *The Romantic Agony* (London: Oxford University Press, 1933).

4. Enid Starkie suggests this in her *Baudelaire* (London: Faber, 1957).

5. In conversation, University College London, Dec 1983.

6. An idea of Henry Woodhouse's. In the same conversation, Dec 1983.

7. Oscar Wilde, *The Picture of Dorian Gray*, ed. Isobel Murray (London: Oxford University Press, 1974) p. 56. FURTHER PAGE REFERENCES IN TEXT.

8. In conversation, British Library, Dec 1983.

9. In conversation, Gloucester Crescent, Dec 1983.

10. See *Encyclopaedia Britannica*, 1910–11 edn, I, 130–1.

11. See Ch. 5. Also George Woodcock's chapter on Winstanley in *Anarchism* (Harmondsworth: Penguin, 1963). PAGE REFERENCES TO THIS WORK IN TEXT.

CHAPTER TWO   MARCUSE'S 'EROTIC REALITY'

1. Herbert Marcuse, *Eros and Civilization: A Philosophical Inquiry into Freud* (1955) (London: Sphere, 1970). PAGE REFERENCES IN TEXT.

2. In this type and the new reality he initiates, Marcuse also foresees a triumph of the 'polymorphous perverse' over the performance-oriented sexual mores of bourgeois society: 'The classical tradition associates Orpheus with the introduction of homosexuality. Like Narcissus, he rejects the normal Eros, not for an ascetic ideal, but for a fuller Eros. Like Narcissus, he protests against the repressive order of procreative reality' (ibid., p. 155).

3. Friedrich Schiller, *The Aesthetic Letters, Essays, and the Philosophical Letters*, trs. J. Weiss (Boston, Mass.: Little, Brown, 1845).

4. Harry Stack Sullivan, *Conceptions in Modern Psychiatry* (Washington, DC: William Alanson White Psychiatric Foundation, 1947) p. 96.

5. Charles Odier, 'Vom Ueber-Ich', *Internationale Zeitschrift für Psychoanalyse*, XII (1926) 280–1.

CHAPTER THREE   SADE'S CULT OF EVIL

1. Marquis de Sade, *Justine, or Good Conduct Well-Chastised*, trs. Richard Seaver and Austryn Wainhouse (New York: Grove Press, 1965) p. 611. FURTHER PAGE REFERENCES IN TEXT.

2. See Ronald Hayman's *Sade: A Critical Biography* (London: Constable, 1978) p. xxv.

3. Oscar Wilde, *De Profundis*, ed. Vyvyan Holland (London: Methuen, 1929) p. 24. FURTHER PAGE REFERENCES IN TEXT.

4. Simone de Beauvoir's essay is included in Marquis de Sade, *The 120 Days of Sodom and Other Writings*, trs. Richard Seaver and Austryn Wainhouse (New York: Grove Press, 1966). See p. 20.

5. Geoffrey Gorer, in his *Life and Ideas of the Marquis de Sade* (London: Peter Owen, 1953). See p. 212.

6. See Hayman, *Sade*, p. 116 and elsewhere.

7. Roland Barthes, *Sade, Loyola, Fourier*, trs. Richard Miller (London: Jonathan Cape, 1977). See p. 171. FURTHER PAGE REFERENCES IN TEXT.

8. See Hayman, *Sade*, p. 16.

9. See ibid., p. 23; also Beauvoir, in Sade, *120 Days*.

10. See Sade, *Justine*, p. 657, for instance.

11. See Barthes, *Sade, Loyola, Fourier*, p. 17.

12. Hayman, *Sade*, pp. 29–30.

13. See ibid., p. 236.

14. In Sade, *120 Days*, p. 9.

15. See the argument of Pierre Klowosski, 'Nature as Destructive Principle', trs. Joseph H. McMahon, ibid., pp. 69–80.

16. Gorer makes this connection (*Ideas of Sade*, p. 108).

17. In reference to D. H. Lawrence, as quoted by Harry T. Moore in *The Novels of John Steinbeck* (New York: Kennikat Press, 1968) p. 27.

CHAPTER FOUR   WILDE'S ANTINOMIAN AESTHETIC

1. Hayman, *Sade*, p. 236.

2. See Sade, *Justine*, pp. 554–7, for instance.

3. This matter is explored in depth by Rodney Shewan in *Oscar Wilde: Art and Egotism* (London: Macmillan, 1977), esp. in the two chapters entitled 'Crime and Egotism'.

4. In 'The Critic as Artist' Wilde admiringly quotes the opening lines of Baudelaire's 'Madrigal Triste':

Que m'importe que tu sois sage?
Sois belle! et sois triste!

And Shewan links Wilde with Marcuse's type (*Art and Egotism*, p. 144).

5. See Isobel Murray's Introduction to the Oxford edition of *Dorian Gray*.

6. Hayman, *Sade*, p. 230.

7. For discussion see Gorer, *Ideas of Sade*, pp. 90–5.

8. See Wilde, *Dorian Gray*, pp. 21, 36 and elsewhere.

9. Wilde, *De Profundis*, pp. 68, 74, 88–92, 114–16, etc., on Sorrow; p. 144, on mysticism.

10. See Wilde, *De Profundis*, p. 101, on 'the cry of Marsyas'.

11. A favourite term of Nietzsche's. See *La Gaya Scienza*, section 382.

12. See Shewan's chapter 'The Dandy's Progress' (*Art and Egotism*).

13. Last lines of Goethe's *Faust*.

14. As Wilde relates: *De Profundis*, p. 66.

15. See Hayman, *Sade*, p. 69.

16. Ibid., p. 108.

17. Wilde, *De Profundis*, pp. 46, 64, etc.

18. W. B. Yeats, *Autobiographies* (London: Macmillan, 1955) pp. 327–8.

19. In Joseph Campbell, *The Masks of God: Creative Mythologies* (London: Souvenir Press, 1974) pp. 262–7.

20. 'Back Door Man' was one of Jim Morrison's early songs. See Ch. 10.

21. Walter Pater, *The Renaissance*, quoted by Murray in an appendix to his *Dorian Gray*.

22. Gorer indicates extensive connection between the ideas of Blake and of Sade. See *Ideas of Sade*, pp. 89, 171, etc.

23. In *The Little Lady of the Big House*. See Martin, *California Writers*, pp. 60–1.

24. Also a Nietzschean term. See Friedrich Nietzsche, *The Will to Power*, trs. Walter Kaufmann and R. J. Hollingdale (London: Weidenfeld and Nicolson, 1968) pp. 49, 50, 703, etc.

CHAPTER FIVE   POLITICAL INTERLUDE: ANARCHISM

1. See Martin, *Wagner to the Waste Land*, p. 94.

2. See Martin, *California Writers*, p. 25.

3. Oscar Wilde, *The Soul of Man under Socialism* (London: Arthur L. Humphreys, 1912) p. 1. FURTHER PAGE REFERENCES IN TEXT.

4. In a famous letter to his brothers George and Tom, 22 Dec 1818.

5. Winstanley, Godwin and the English origins of anarchism are subjects of Woodcock's early chapters.

6. See Leo Tolstoy, *Lettres à Botkine* (Paris: Fayard, 1926) p. 10 and elsewhere.

7. Marie Constant, 'La Dynamite'.

8. 'Play on Love' on *Red Octopus* (RCA Victor, 1975).

9. Title track on *Crown of Creation* (RCA Victor, 1968).

10. As reported by Tom Wolfe in *The Electric Kool-Aid Acid Test* (London: Weidenfeld and Nicolson, 1969). See Ch. 16, 'The Frozen Jug Band'.

11. See Barthes, *Sade, Loyola, Fourier*, p. 118.

CHAPTER SIX   'POWER' AND THE OCCULT

1. See occultist and Wagnerian Édouard Schuré's description of this in *The Great Initiates*, trs. Fred Rothwell (London: Rider, 1912) pp. 347–62. This famous book, along with others such as Houston Stewart Chamberlain's *Foundations of the Nineteenth Century*, is central to the creation of the *Zeitgeist* of the early twentieth century which we shall be talking about in this and the following chapter.

2. Undine of de la Motte Fouqué's tale is a rare instance of a spirit who gains a human soul. But this brings Undine sorrow and is relinquished eventually.

3. In a 'lordly conversation' with Hugh Kingsmill. See *The Best of Hugh Kingsmill* (London: Gollancz, 1970) pp. 273–6.

4. This version is close to the one which Janko Lavrin tells in his *Nietzsche* (London: Studio Vista, 1971).

5. *The Birth of Tragedy*, in *The Complete Works of Friedrich Nietzsche*, ed. Oscar Levy (London: T. N. Foulis, 1909–13) III, Preface to later edn subtitled 'Hellenism and Pessimism'.

6. Nietzsche uses this line again in *Ecce Homo*, ibid., XIII, 26.

7. See *Human, All-too-Human*, ibid., VI, 349, and VII, 191.

8. *The Antichrist*, ibid., XVI, various places. Also Lavrin, *Nietzsche*, p. 41.

9. Nietzsche, *Ecce Homo*, various places. Also Lavrin, *Nietzsche*, p. 44.

10. Nietzsche, *Beyond Good and Evil*, in *Complete Works*, XII. See 'Dionysian Dithyrambs' (added 1888).

11. Lavrin, *Nietzsche*, p. 74.

12. Nietzsche, *Thus Spake Zarathustra*, in *Complete Works*, XIV–XV; *The Will to Power*, trs. Kaufmann and Hollingdale, 858.

13. Ibid., 1019.

14. Nietzsche, *The Joyful Wisdom*, in *Complete Works*, X, 19.

15. Nietzsche, *Beyond Good and Evil*, 296 (last words).

16. Lavrin, *Nietzsche*, p. 125.

17. In a letter to Baron von Seydlitz, 12 Feb 1888. See *Selected Letters*, trs. Antony M. Ludovici (London: Heinemann, 1921) p. 218.

18. This is the way James Joyce characterizes a contemporary Nietzschean, probably his brother Stanislaus, in his story of that title in *Dubliners*.

19. Lavrin, *Nietzsche*, p. 110.

20. See Denis Donoghue, *Yeats* (London: Fontana, 1971) p. 31. FURTHER REFERENCES IN TEXT.

21. See Martin, *Wagner to the Waste Land*, p. 208.

22. *The Will to Power*, 884.

23. Speech of Owen Aherne in the playlet 'The Phases of the Moon', included in the introductory material to *A Vision* (Dublin: Cuala, 1925).

24. Nietzsche, *The Will to Power*, 656, 696.

25. *The Collected Plays of W. B. Yeats* (London: Macmillan, 1953) p. 135.

26. Ibid., p. 702.

27. From *Michael Robartes and the Dancer* (1921) in *Selected Poems and Two Plays of William Butler Yeats*, ed. M. L. Rosenthal (New York: Macmillan, 1962) p. 91.

28. See W. B. Yeats, *Letters*, ed. Allan Wade (London: Rupert Hart-Davis, 1954) pp. 339–46.

29. See Francis King, *The Magical World of Aleister Crowley* (London: Weidenfeld, 1977) pp. 19–32. FURTHER PAGE REFERENCES IN TEXT.

30. For instance, Captain J. F. C. Fuller, who wrote *The Star in the West* (1907) adulating Crowley's prose and poetry. According to King (*Magical World*, p. 42), Fuller later became a friend of Hitler's.

31. See King (ibid., p. 112) on how Crowley advised the German Zeppelin force, which had been missing its targets, to bomb the house of a tiresome aunt.

32. 'Body of fate' is one of the four principle forces governing personality, according to Yeats in *A Vision*. *Amor fati* joins 'eternal recurrence' to form the fundamental anti-Christian faith of Nietzsche, according to Janko Lavrin. The 'left-hand way' is a phrase used by Joseph Campbell to designate a range of antinomian manifestations in Western tradition (see Ch. 4, n. 29).

33. Reputedly it was to make contact with the Duke of Hamilton and other high-ranking latter-day members of the Order that Rudolf Hess made his bizarre flight to Britain in 1941. See Jean-Michel Angebert's *The Occult and the Third Reich*, discussed in the following chapter.

34. Wilde's personal dabbling in the occult seems to have been confined to his friendship with the chieromancer Edward Heron-Alleyn, who inspired 'Lord Arthur Savile's Crime' and possibly *Dorian Gray* (see Isobel Murray's Introduction to the Oxford edn), and to what he may have gleaned from contemporary French Symbolists such as Catulle

Mendès (cf. Catulle Sarrazin, author of the book Lord Henry gives Dorian Gray), who was intimate with the mysterious Marquis de Guiata whom King (*Magical World*, p. 10) numbers among the French nineteenth-century precursors of the Order of the Golden Dawn, and Count Villers de l'Isle-Adam, whose 'Rosicrucian' play *Axël* so inspired young, hashish-smoking Yeats on a trip to Paris in 1894. However, Crowley contended that Wilde, like Mathers and other 'decadents' of the 1880s and 1890s, had been a conscious practitioner of 'vampirism': a form of fellatio whereby 'the soul or spirit of a subject is imprisoned by ingesting his semen, which symbolizes the life force and is not to be lost'. See King, *Magical World*, p. 107.

35. In John Symonds, *The Great Beast* (London: Macdonald, 1971). See pp. 19, 20, 147, etc.

36. Yeats's vision may have even more to do with the occult fascination for creating an homunculus. This Crowley in particular had resurrected out of the teachings of Simon Magus, Paracelsus and the alchemists. (It is the central theme of Somerset Maugham's fictional portrait of Crowley in his early novella *The Magician*, which we shall discuss in Ch. 8.) King tells us that Crowley believed that 'the birth of a non-human foetus of the desired nature' could be obtained by having a pregnant woman go to the desert and concentrate on the required spirit (see King, *Magical World*, p. 109), and something like this forms the theme of Crowley's novel *Moonchild*, which we shall also discuss in Ch. 8. It would be intriguing to know how much Yeats may have known through the occult 'grapevine' of Crowley's experiments in this regard when, at the same time as his ex-rival was settling down in semi-desert-like Sicily with a new pregnant 'Scarlet Woman', he sat down to compose 'The Second Coming'. Crowley himself had no doubt that Yeats and other ex-associates were obsessively tracking his movements, as a reading of *Moonchild* will show.

37. Berlioz makes reference to Swedenborg's formulation in his libretto, which adapts Goethe's poetry from occultist Gérard du Nerval's translation. (Swedenborg, it might be remembered, was a principal influence on Blake, among other mystics, and, via him, Yeats.) See King, *Magical World*, p. 52, for discussion of Crowley's 'Enochian language'.

38. This description of Crowley's rite was given by Harry Kemp in *World Magazine*, Aug 1914. See also King, *Magical World*, p. 76.

39. Trevor Ravenscroft, *The Spear of Destiny: The Occult Power behind the Spear which Pierced the Side of Christ* (London: Neville Spearman, 1972). See p. 167, on Crowley.

40. See King, *Magical World*, pp. 130–5. These practices were prescribed by Crowley in his earlier tract *Of Eroto-Comatose Lucidity*, which preached 'constant sexual aggravation' and contended that 'the most favourable death is that through orgasm'. See King, *Magical World*, p. 106.

41. By the *Sunday Express*. See King, *Magical World*, pp. 138–9.

42. Symonds makes this identification (*The Great Beast*, pp. 392–4). Hubbard claims he became a Crowleyan 'only to break up black magic in America'.

43. See Praz, *The Romantic Agony*, pp. 395–6.

44. A description of the filth at the Abbey of Thelema was given by one female 'pilgrim' whom Crowley took all possessions from, gave a coarse shawl, and made stay alone in a lean-to for a month in order to 'find her inner reserves and force'. See King, *Magical World*, p. 133.

CHAPTER SEVEN   HITLER

1. Of the biographies available, I have found Joachim Fest's *Hitler*, trs. Richard and Clara Winston (New York: Harcourt Brace Jovanovich, 1974), the most useful. Fest understands the Hitler phenomenon from a European – specifically German – point of view and provides more credible context and analysis than, say, John Toland in his *Adolf Hitler* (New York: Doubleday, 1975). On the other hand, Fest's tone suffers sometimes from the smugness and glibness of journalism, while Toland, an historian, is more satisfyingly and properly mythic.

2. Other than, of course, Third World fascist and Islamic fundamentalist movements, which have sometimes even been consciously imitative of Hitler's example (cf. Nasser's and Sadat's early readings of *Mein Kampf*).

3. Toland repeats a rather touching vignette about how Hitler's wind problems (perhaps related to his vegetarian diet) earned him the mockery of one of the ex-Kaiser's daughters. Never at ease with persons of established class, he also felt mocked by the King and Queen of Italy (*Adolf Hitler*, pp. 460–2).

4. I am using the term made famous by Hannah Arendt in her study *The Origins of Totalitarianism* (New York: Meridian, 1971).

5. Michael Angebert, *The Occult and the Third Reich: The Mystical Origins of Nazism and the Search for the Holy Grail*, trs. Lewis A. M. Sumberg (New York: Macmillan, 1974). PAGE REFERENCES IN TEXT.

6. See Gibbon, *Decline and Fall of the Roman Empire*, chs 54–5.

7. See, for example, Ravenscroft, *The Spear of Destiny*, pp. 307–13 and elsewhere. Himmler was deeply involved with the Ahnenerbe, the 'Nazi occult bureau'.

8. Adolf Hitler, *Mein Kampf*, trs. Ralph Mannheim (London: Hutchinson, 1969) p. 24. FURTHER PAGE REFERENCES IN TEXT.

9. Fest, *Hitler*, p. 37, for instance, where he quotes the headline from Lanz von Liebenfels's *Ostara*: 'Read the library for blonds and advocates of Male Rights.'

10. T. S. Eliot, 'Burbank with a Baedecker, Bleistein with a Cigar', in

Poems 1920. Eliot's anti-Semitism is discussed in the last chapter of Martin, *Wagner to the Waste Land*.

11. Hitler refers frequently to the 'feminine' character of the *Volk*, as when discussing propaganda on p. 167 of *Mein Kampf*: 'The people in their overwhelming majority are so feminine by nature and attitude that sober reasoning determines their thoughts and actions far less than emotion and feelings.'

12. See August Kubizek, *Young Hitler*, trs. E. V. Anderson (London: Allen Wingate, 1954) pp. 63–6. Young Hitler also tried to write his own opera.

13. Fest, *Hitler*, p. 541.

14. In Hermann Rauschning, *Hitler Speaks* (London: Thornton Butterworth, 1939). As trs. Angebert in *The Occult and the Third Reich*, pp. 258–9.

15. Walter Benjamin, *Illuminations*, trs. Harry Zohn, ed. Hannah Arendt (New York: Schocken Books, 1969) p. 241.

16. Fest, *Hitler*, p. 541.

17. See Rauschning, *Hitler Speaks*, p. 233; Angebert, *The Occult and the Third Reich*, pp. 258–9.

18. In the *Daily Telegraph*. Cited by D. C. Watt in his Introduction to *Mein Kampf*, p. xv.

19. Reproductions of one of his water-colour postcards and some of his architectural drawings done in Landsberg Prison can be found in Fest's book between pp. 132 and 133. In his Introduction to *Mein Kampf*, Watt tells us that for a time in Vienna Hitler sold his work through a Jewish agent and that later in Munich he was earning 100 marks a month in this way – 30 marks a month more than a contemporary bank clerk, i.e. not much for an aspirant Great Painter but considerably better than many a garret artist (for instance, Hamsun's writer-*manqué* anti-hero in *Hunger*).

20. Fest describes Hitler's artistic taste and preferences in *Hitler*, pp. 552–4.

21. See Louis Lochner, Introduction to his translation of *The Goebbels Diaries* (New York: Eagle Books, 1948).

22. This poem was written by the mysterious Marquis de Guiata, friend of Éliphas Lévi and later Wagnerite Catulle Mendès, whom (as mentioned in Ch. 7, n. 34) Francis King cites as one of the figures behind the late nineteenth-century pan-European occult revival which led among other things to the Order of the Golden Dawn.

23. From Marshal von Blomberg's testimony at Nuremberg. Quoted by Angebert in *The Occult and the Third Reich*, p. 233.

24. Ibid.

25. Quoted ibid.

26. See Albert Speer, *Inside the Third Reich* (London: Weidenfeld and Nicholson, 1970) p. 100.

27. Fest, *Hitler*, p. 598. That the Devil is associated with movement is an old idea – see, for instance, Berlioz's treatment of the last scene between Faust and Mephisto in his *Damnation of Faust*, in which they gallop across the plains of Hungary towards the abyss. The association has an interesting resonance in Kerouac, whom we shall discuss in Ch. 8. Mephisto to his Faust was Neal Cassady, whom the 'Merry Pranksters' later nicknamed 'Speed limit' and who took the American obsession with movement to a new automobile-age high.

28. Fest, *Hitler*, p. 62.

29. One of the *Führer*'s more memorable epigrams (ibid., p. 458).

CHAPTER EIGHT   SIXTIES' ZEITGEIST, I: MYSTICISM

1. Aleister Crowley, *Moonchild* (1929; London: Sphere, 1972) p. 270. FURTHER PAGE REFERENCES IN TEXT.

2. See Rauschning, *Hitler Speaks*, pp. 250–1.

3. According to Dennis Wheatley, in his annotation of the Sphere edn.

4. An idea of Dr Richard Wiseman's, among others. In conversation, California State University, San Francisco, Spring 1974.

5. The formulation is Dennis Wheatley's, who, among a variety of occult activities (including the editing of Crowley), anticipated Angebert's study of the occult and the Third Reich in *They Used Dark Forces* (1964).

6. The phrase is Warren French's. He uses it to describe Frank Norris's resistance to the new economic order of 'symbol-handlers' at the turn of the century. See Martin, *California Writers*, p. 9.

7. Somerset Maugham, *The Razor's Edge* (London: Pan, 1976) p. 108. FURTHER PAGE REFERENCES IN TEXT.

8. See Yeats, *A Vision* (London: Macmillan, 1937), esp. 'The Soul's Judgment'.

9. See Martin, *California Writers*, 104.

10. More than one of Zaehner's studies is applicable here, but the one I found most to the point is *Drugs, Mysticism and Make-Believe* (London: Collins, 1972). PAGE REFERENCES IN TEXT.

11. *Chandoyga Upanishad*, VII.25; as quoted by Zaehner in *Drugs, Mysticism*, p. 65.

12. Which also takes its title from Blake: *Heaven and Hell* (1956).

13. Timothy Leary, *The Politics of Ecstasy* (London: MacGibbon and Kee, 1970) pp. 106–7. FURTHER PAGE REFERENCES IN TEXT.

14. Zenkei Shibayama, *A Flower Does Not Talk* (Tokyo: Tuttle, 1970) p. 106.

15. See Wilde, *De Profundis*, p. 98.

16. Lao Tzu, *Tao Te Ching*, 19; as quoted by Zaehner, in *Drugs, Mysticism*, p. 130.

17. *Kaushītakī Upanishad*, III.1–2; as quoted in Zaehner, *Drugs, Mysticism*, p. 162.

18. *Bhagavad-Gita*, XVIII.17; as quoted by Zaehner in *Drugs, Mysticism*, p. 163.

19. 'Piggies' by George Harrison on the 'white' album (Apple, 1969).

20. It is provocative in this connection to reflect that, for some years, Zaehner has been under suspicion of having been a Communist agent – this in part because of connections with various members of the greater Philby-Burgess group. See recent articles on Peter Wright's revelations about MI5 in *The Observer*.

21. See Dietrich Bonhoeffer, *Letters and Papers from Prison* (1953; London: Fontana, 1963) p. 50.

22. Carl Jung, *Memoirs, Dreams, Reflections* (London: Collins, 1963) p. 50.

23. See Bonhoeffer, *Letters and Papers from Prison*, pp. 161–2.

24. See Martin, *California Writers*, pp. 188–9.

25. Jack Kerouac, *Desolation Angels* (1960; London: Mayflower, 1969). PAGE REFERENCES IN TEXT.

26. See Dennis McNally's *Desolate Angel* (New York: Random House, 1979) p. 90.

27. The first line of 'Howl' (1957).

28. Jack Kerouac, *Lonesome Traveller* (1962; London: Panther, 1972) pp. 164, 173.

CHAPTER NINE   SIXTIES' ZEITGEIST, II: CRUELTY

1. Thomas Mann, 'The Sufferings and Greatness of Richard Wagner', in *Freud, Goethe, Wagner* (New York: Knopf, 1943) p. 176.

2. See Mann's afterword to *The Magic Mountain*, in edns since 1930.

3. In Joyce's *Portrait of the Artist as a Young Man*. The 'nets' are family, nation and bourgeois expectations.

4. In Wolfe, *The Electric Kool-Aid Acid Test*, p. 144.

5. Hermann Hesse, *Steppenwolf* (Harmondsworth: Penguin, 1973). PAGE REFERENCES IN TEXT.

6. In the title song of *Hotel California* (Asylum, 1976).

7. On their first album, *The Grateful Dead* (Warner Bros, 1967).

8. One of the finest, most rugged 'counterculture' novels of the 1970s, it shows nihilistic ruthlessness as more heroic than hypocritically idealistic trendyism. Robert Stone, *Dog Soldiers* (London: Secker and Warburg, 1974). See pp. 186–204.

9. An opera in which somewhat hippy-like youths undergo initiation into Masonic secrets. The connection may be significant. There is evidence that secret societies – the Masons and certainly San Francisco's

Bohemian Club – looked on without disapproval while the Western cultural revolution raged in the 1960s (just as the Masons are reputed to have done during the events in France, 1789–93, the elimination of the Bourbon king and his régime being interpreted by some as a 'revenge' for the destruction of the Cathars and later their champions the Knights Templar, whose last leader, Jacques De Molay, gave his name to a Masonic sect still active today, and whose practices and ideas are said to be direct antecedents of Freemasonry, by Angebert in *The Occult and the Third Reich* and the authors of *The Holy Blood and the Holy Grail* among others). Forces with unitary–antinomian moral bases may prosper in chaos as much as order. A connection between Masonic and hippy metaphysics may be seen in (for example) the Egyptological interests of the Grateful Dead. See in this connection Hank Harrison, *The Dead* (Millbrae, Calif.: Celestial Arts, 1980). This book is dedicated to 'the Boys at the Bohemian Club' and begins with a chapter on 'Uncle Adolf' – Sutro that is, not Hitler – one of the founders of the anarchic cultural tradition of San Francisco.

    10. Hermann Hesse, *Siddhartha* (London: Picador, 1973) p. 16.

    11. Ibid., p. 110.

    12. On the *Beggar's Banquet* album (Decca [London in America], 1969).

    13. By Joni Mitchell, but made famous in a version by Crosby, Stills, Nash and Young. On *Déja Vu* (Atlantic, 1970).

    14. Homesickness–*nostalgie* is a transcendental emotion with origins in earliest myth: the lost Atlantis, etc. It is a strong motif in the hippy world view, as it has been in all eras of romanticism. Hermine's comment evokes Nietzsche's lines about the 'homesick ships' waiting on the shore wondering when the winds are going to let them 'set sail toward happiness'; also Baudelaire's lines in 'L'Invitation du voyage' about the ships 'avec l'air vagabonde' which wait to take him and his beloved away to enchanted isles ('La, tout n'est qu'ordre et beauté / Luxe, calme et volupté', a line we have already seen Marcuse quoting). Often this motif is related to ships, sailing, etc., as in 'Wooden Ships' by Crosby, Stills and Nash (first album) and Jefferson Airplane (*Volunteers*); but in later days of the hip–punk period it appears in a song by David Bowie about an astronaut lost somewhere in space, marked by plaintive echoing refrain 'Can you hear me, Master Tom?' (*Space Odyssey*, RCA Victor, 1974).

    15. See Vincent Bugliosi with Curt Gentry, *Helter Skelter* (1974; Harmondsworth: Penguin, 1977) p. 527. 'Susan went on to explain that she knew what she was doing "was right when I was doing it". She knew this because, when you do the right thing, "it feels good". Q. "How could it be right to kill somebody?" A. "How could it not be right when it is done with love?"' See also p. 366, where Leslie Van Houten admits to a fellow female prisoner that 'at first she had been reluctant to [stab

someone], but then she'd discovered the more you stabbed, the more fun it was'.

16. The confluence of seriousness and whimsy in the Magic Theatre's offerings suggests among other things the mix of 'hi-jinks' and 'low-jinks' in the Bohemian Club's theatrical get-togethers. See n. 9.

17. 'Man is not capable of thought in any high degree, so he describes the breakdown of unity of the soul in terms of two parts, not many' (Hesse, *Steppenwolf*, p. 71). 'Harry consists of a hundred or thousand selves, not of two' (ibid., p. 70). Cf. the finale of *Siddhartha* (pp. 117–19), in which the Buddha-to-be tells Govinda to kiss him on the forehead; then: 'He no longer saw the face of his friend Siddhartha. Instead he saw other faces, many faces, a long series. . . . He saw the face of a murderer, saw him plunge a knife into the body of a man; at the same moment he saw this criminal leaning down, bound, and his head cut off by an executioner. . . . Yet none of the [multiple Siddharthas] died, they only changed, were always reborn. [Siddhartha's] countenance was unchanged after the mirror of the thousandfold forms had disappeared from the surface. He smiled peacefully and gently, perhaps very mockingly, exactly as the Illustrious One [Gotama Buddha] had smiled.'

18. In hippy-era values this was not necessarily considered a bad thing. See the Rolling Stones' 'Monkey Man' on *Let It Bleed* (Decca/London, 1969); the Beatles' 'Everybody's Got Something to Hide 'Cept for me and my Monkey' on the 'white' album; also Randy Newman's 'Sail Away' ('Be as happy as a monkey in a monkey tree') on the album of the same name (RCA Victor, 1972).

19. I am making a play here on Arthur Symons's comparison of the youthful Romanticism of Beethoven to the 'Decadence' of Wagner: 'He lived in an age in which joy had not yet become a subtle form of pain' (see Martin, *Wagner to 'The Waste Land'*, p. 74). Hesse makes a similar comparison, only between Mozart of *Don Giovanni* and the 'men in black' (Brahms, Wagner, etc.) who were 'striving for redemption' (*Steppenwolf*, p. 239).

20. The phrase comes from the title of T. S. Eliot's 1932 study on the futility of contemporary heresies, *After Strange Gods*. Hesse could easily have been included with D. H. Lawrence and the others criticized.

21. See G. E. White's *The Eastern Establishment and the Western Experience: The West of Frederic Remington, Theodore Roosevelt, and Owen Wister* (New Haven, Conn.: Yale University Press, 1968).

22. Texts written over a period of eight years are collected under the title *Les Tarahumaras* and appear in Antonin Artaud, *Oeuvres complètes*, IX (Paris: Gallimard, 1956).

23. See Philip Norman's *The Stones* (London: Elm Tree, 1984), Prologue. My use of the French trendy term *auteur* is not meant to confuse

the songwriter with the director (*auteur*) of the film *Sympathy for the Devil* (Jean-Luc Godard), merely to point up the Francophile tendency of Jagger in his 'high' pop-art vein.

24. *Artaud le Mômo* is one of his last works. 'Mômo' also has the sense of *mots-mots* (words-words). The holy 'OM' (he spelled it 'aum') is a concept Artaud ridiculed. See Julia Costich, *Antonin Artaud* (Boston, Mass.: Twayne, 1978) p. 93. FURTHER PAGE REFERENCE TO THIS WORK IN TEXT.

25. See Artaud, *Oeuvres complètes*, XII, 97–8.

26. Actually, the psychiatrist declared this of him.

27. The statement comes from Artaud's last work, *Pour en finir avec le jugement de dieu*.

28. In the opening chapters of *The Female Eunuch* and the play *The Immortalist*, respectively.

29. Artaud, *Le Théâtre Alfred Jarry et l'hostilité publique*, in *Oeuvres complètes*, II, 51.

30. See Antonin Artaud, *Le Théâtre et son double* (Paris: Gallimard, 1938).

31. Letter to Louis Jouvet, in Artaud, *Oeuvres complètes*, III, 256.

32. Ibid., IV, 271.

33. Ibid., VII, 127–8.

34. Ibid., XIII, 17. As paraphrased by Costich in *Artaud*, p. 86.

35. In his essay of that name.

CHAPTER TEN   SIXTIES' ZEITGEIST, III: JIM MORRISON

1. Gene Youngblood, review of *Strange Days*, in *Los Angeles Free Press*, 1 Dec 1967.

2. See Danny Sugerman, Introduction to *The Doors: The Illustrated History* (London: Vermilion, 1983) p. xii. This book, with its collection of the important reviews and articles about the Doors, is of invaluable assistance.

3. Danny Sugerman, *No One Gets out of Here Alive* (London: Plexus, 1982) pp. 295–6.

4. Sugerman, Introduction to *Illustrated History*, p. ix.

5. But he was not able to make his own films until years later (ibid., p. 188).

6. Comments of Jim Pagiasotti reviewing a Doors concert for the *Denver Post*, 13 Apr 1970.

7. For Morrison's reaction to this title see Morrison–Sugerman interview in *Illustrated History*, p. 61.

8. Lester Bangs, review of *Absolutely Live*, in *Fusion*, Nov 1970.

9. Patricia Kennealy, review of *Absolutely Live*, in *Jazz and Pop*, Nov 1970.

10. In an interview with Bob Chorush entitled 'The Lizard King Reforms', in the *Los Angeles Free Press*, Apr 1970.

11. See Martin, *California Writers*, pp. 14–15. Didion's article is in *The White Album*.

12. There is still great dispute about what occurred. As Stephanie Harrington wrote in the *Village Voice* at the time: 'It must have been rather like the *Titanic*. Unless you were there you couldn't know exactly what happened, and the survivors were so dazed that all reports didn't fully jibe.'

13. Except perhaps Grace Slick of the Jefferson Airplane, who, it might be noted, came – like Morrison and unlike so many other rock stars – from a comfortable upper-middle-class background.

14. By Bill Kerby, in *Daily Bruin*, 24 May 1967.

15. See Jerry Hopkins's Foreword to *Illustrated History*, p. vii.

16. To Richard Goldstein in 'The Shaman as Superstar', *New York Magazine*, 5 Sep 1968.

17. 'Break on Through' from *The Doors* (first album).

18. 'Light my Fire' from the same album.

19. See Goldstein, 'The Shaman as Superstar', *New York Magazine*.

20. On the first album.

21. On *Strange Days* (second album: Elektra, 1967).

22. On *Waiting for the Sun* (third album: Elektra, 1968).

23. 'When the Music's Over' (*Strange Days*).

24. See Yeats, *Autobiographies*, p. 287.

25. 'When the Music's Over'.

26. Judith Sims, 'Who's Afraid of Jim Morrison', in *Teenset*, Feb 1968.

27. Kris Weintraub, 'Oh Caroline: The Doors at Fillmore East', in *Crawdaddy*, no. 16 (1968).

28. Liza Williams, 'The Doors at the Forum: Morrison, the Ultimate Barbie Doll', in *Los Angeles Free Press*, 1969.

29. In *The Second Raymond Chandler Omnibus* (London: Hamish Hamilton, 1962) pp. 354–5.

30. The narrator is an English playwright and non-experimental novelist who has lived in London, Paris and the south of France. He is homosexual, and his exceptionally long life has allowed him to view from a cool distance most of the literary, spiritual and political events of the twentieth century.

31. *All My Friends are Going to be Strangers* and *Somebody's Darling*, at least. McMurtry, interestingly, once wrote a thesis on the Earl of Rochester.

32. See Sugerman, *No One Gets out of Here Alive*, pp. 30–1. Owner of the 'Renaissance' bar.

33. See *Lennon Remembers: The Rolling Stone Interviews*, ed. Jann Wenner (San Francisco: Straight Arrow Books, 1971).

34. This is the model also of Stephen Dedalus in Joyce's *Portrait of a*

Young Man, another young wordsmith who experienced his Icarian 'fall'
in Paris.

35. Leslie Fiedler, *The Return of the Vanishing American* (London:
Paladin, 1972).

36. Harvey Perr, 'Stage Doors', in *Los Angeles Free Press*, 8 Aug 1969.

37. Again, I am indebted to Julia Costich's *Artaud* in compiling this
list.

38. On *Aftermath* (Decca/London, 1965).

39. See Bugliosi, *Helter Skelter*, p. 141.

40. See n. 11.

41. See photos captioned 'the faces of Charles Manson' between
pp. 312 and 313 of *Helter Skelter*.

42. From Tom Baker, the out-of-work actor who was Morrison's
drinking-buddy and companion on this flight.

43. See Sugerman, *No One Gets out of Here Alive*, pp. 223, 261–6, etc.,
'Trouble-n-strife' (or simply 'Trouble') is Cockney rhyming-slang for
'wife'.

44. Edd Jeffords, reviewing a later Doors concert, in *Poppin*, Summer
1970.

45. For the Doors' first album. Repr. in *The Illustrated History*, p. 9.

46. There is an argument for this. Apart from film makers, the other
candidates might be, in literature, James M. Cain and Joan Didion, and,
in rock music, Jackson Browne and the Eagles.

47. Rob Houghton in *Creem*, Apr 1971.

48. Ibid.

49. On *L A Woman* (Elektra, 1971).

50. Quoted from Clancy Sigal, 'Los Angeles: A Profile of the 1984
Olympic City', *Observer Magazine*, 17 June 1984, p. 30.

51. To Chorush in 'The Lizard King Reforms', *Los Angeles Free Press*.

CHAPTER ELEVEN   THE MANSON PHENOMENON

1. This is described by Ed Sanders in *The Family* (London: Rupert
Hart-Davis, 1972). See Ch. 18, 'Fear Swept the Poolsides', pp. 297–307.

2. Therefore the title of Prosecutor Vincent Bugliosi's memoir, *Helter
Skelter*, subtitled 'An Investigation into Motive'. Part IV, 'The Search For
the Motive', deals with the Beatles factor extensively. This is convincing,
as is Sanders's discussion of the 'white'-album influence. What jars in
both accounts is the assumption that the door found at Spahn Ranch on
which was scrawled '1 2 3 4 5 6 7 ALL GOOD CHILDREN (Go To
Heaven?) . . . HELTER SCELTER [*sic*]' confirms that the 'white'
album was long-brooded upon prior to the murders. It no doubt was;
still, the inscription on the door could not have been painted until well
after. The lines 'One two three four five six seven / All good children go

to Heaven' come from the *Abbey Road* album, which did not come out until the late autumn of 1969, when Manson and company had already left Spahn and were enjoying their last days of freedom in Death Valley.

3. The phrase is Dorian Gray's, near the end of his progress. See Martin, *Wagner to the Waste Land*, p. 38, where I discuss it at some length.

4. 'When the Music's Over' on *Strange Days*.

5. On *Sticky Fingers* (Rolling Stones Records, 1971).

6. 'The Ballad of John and Yoko', a single (Apple, 1969).

7. 'The Fool on the Hill' is the second song on the *Magical Mystery Tour* album. Crowley is one of the many 'precursors' depicted with the Beatles in Peter Blake's collage on the cover of *Sergeant Pepper*. Lennon's trendy association with Lenin and Marx was lampooned by Don McLean in his historical rock-ballad 'American Pie' (United Artists, 1971).

8. Bugliosi discusses this. See *Helter Skelter*, p. 292. The song is thought to be the origin of the murder-scrawl, 'Rise'.

9. In the original single of 'Revolution', Lennon sang the lines 'But when you talk about destruction / Don't you know that you can count me out'; however, in the more 'laid back' version on the album, he follows the word 'out' with the word 'in', leaving his position provocatively ambiguous. 'Revolution Number 9' follows a brief McCartney ditty asking the question 'Can you take me back where I've been to / Brother, can you take me back?'; it suggests the answer 'no' by mixing sounds of the 'old' culture – church hymns, football-game cheers, BBC-commentator voices – in an anarchy of young-girl babble, screams ('rise' reappears), and gunfire. Penultimate track on the album (preceding the ironically innocuous 'Good Night'), this reinforces the overall apocalyptic mood.

10. Bugliosi says he is five foot two, but Sanders refers to him repeatedly as five foot six. It is possible that the 'man with a thousand faces' could also alter in height? Or is it merely that arrest 'cut him down to size'?

11. See Sanders, *The Family*, pp. 97, 121 and 130. Both Sanders and Bugliosi recognize Manson's original title as Scientology jargon. See ibid., p. 29, and *Helter Skelter*, p. 178.

12. See Sanders, *The Family*, pp. 186–7.

13. See Carlos Castaneda, *A Separate Reality* (1971; Harmondsworth: Penguin, 1973) p. 201. FURTHER PAGE REFERENCES IN TEXT.

14. To his regret. The last lines of *A Separate Reality* (p. 268) are: 'I began to weep. . . . For the first time in my life I felt the encumbering weight of my reason.'

15. Don Juan's parents were murdered by assassins and, before his death, his father made him promise vengeance. 'I carried that promise with me for years', the sorcerer tells Castaneda; '[but] now the promise is changed.' Because he can '*see*', Don Juan no longer has time for vendettas. Anyone who does, he implies, is a false 'warrior'.

16. See Sanders, *The Family*, p. 197, and Bugliosi, *Helter Skelter*, p. 112, on Manson as a 'knife freak'. The first attempted murder Manson is known to have been involved in (of a black Hollywood dope-dealer) may have been preceded by the 'Kill me–Kill You' routine with a gun (see Sanders, *The Family*, p. 208).

17. Manson liked to use this phrase (see ibid., p. 195). So did Mick Jagger; but, when he tried to invoke it in a moment of panic at Altamont, it failed to keep the Hell's Angels from beating up people with sawn-off pool cues and actually killing one black man.

18. See ibid., p. 129, for Manson's glorification of this animal, which had such appeal to his time and place that a member of the San Francisco Mime Troupe (who later became head of the California Arts' Council under Governor Jerry Brown) changed his name to Peter Coyote.

19. Sanders tell us that 'Manson seems to have considered any self-assertive black man a Black Panther' (ibid., p. 210) and that, particularly in the period preceding the murders, he was paranoid of the Panthers 'invading' the Spahn Ranch. Bugliosi speculates that Manson may have had ties with the Aryan Brotherhood, 'a cult of white prison inmates, dedicated largely to racism but also involved in hoodlum activities, including murder contracts' (*Helter Skelter*, p. 592).

20. Bugliosi claims that Manson 'begged' not to be let out of prison (ibid., p. 180). Sanders repeats this story but refers to it as a 'legend' (*The Family*, p. 33).

21. Bugliosi suggests that Manson administered the drug to others far more than he took it himself (*Helter Skelter*, p. 291).

22. See Sanders, *The Family*, pp. 28–30.

23. Ibid., 108.

24. In 150 sessions of 'processing' by one Lanier Raymer (see ibid., p. 29). Bugliosi claims that Manson 'reached the highest stage, "beta clear"' and thus had 'no more need for Scientology' (*Helter Skelter*, p. 579).

25. See Sanders, *The Family*, pp. 146, 197. This ex-Scientologist convinced at least two of Manson's followers to leave the Family. At least two others who left on their own subsequently joined the LA 'church'.

26. In L. Ron Hubbard, *The Phoenix Lectures* (Scientology Publications, 1968) Chs 1–3.

27. See *Have you Lived this Life before?* (Scientology Publications, 1978) p. 303.

28. See Sanders, *The Family*, Ch. 5: 'The Process', pp. 80–96.

29. The opening 'plexus' of *As It Is* by Process leader Robert De Grimston.

30. See Sanders, *The Family*, Ch. 10, pp. 161–7.

31. See ibid., pp. 201 and 228–34.

32. In 'Play on Love'. See Ch. 5, n. 13.

33. See Sanders, *The Family*, p. 47. Anger introduced Beausoliel to the works of Crowley.

34. See ibid., p. 157.

35. See Bugliosi, *Helter Skelter*, p. 506.

36. See ibid., pp. 152, 158 and 583–5.

37. Sanders, 'The Story of Charles Manson's Dune Buggy Attack Battalion', in *The Family*.

38. See the last paragraph of Ch. 7.

39. See Sanders, *The Family*, p. 194, on how Manson 'hated hippies'. Bugliosi quotes defence attorney Paul Fitzgerald (to whom, incidentally, Sanders dedicates his book) as calling Manson a 'right-wing hippy' (*Helter Skelter*, p. 496).

40. See Sanders, *The Family*, pp. 330–7. Sanders quotes Manson associate and ex-Straight Satan Danny De Carlo as saying 'the true motive has not been told'.

41. See ibid., pp. 187–93.

42. 'Sexy Sadie', which reputedly vents the Beatles' anger at the Maharishi and was a favourite of the Manson family because of its correlation to 'Sadie Mae Glutz', the alias given head-girl Susan Atkins.

43. See Bugliosi, *Helter Skelter*, p. 181 and elsewhere.

Index